Stealth Lobbying

Politicians and lobbyists have incentives to conceal any quid pro quo relationships between them, leaving scholars largely unable to link campaign money to legislative votes. Using behind-the-scenes information gained from novel data sources, such as legislators' schedules, fundraising events, legislative amendments, and the campaign contributions of individual lobbyists and the political action committees these lobbyists control, Amy McKay investigates how lobbyists influence the content of congressional legislation. The data reveal hidden associations between lobbyists' campaign assistance and legislators' action on behalf of those lobbyists. Relative to constituents and even other lobbyists, the lobbyists who provide campaign money to Members of Congress are more likely to secure meetings with those members, to see their requests introduced as legislation, and to achieve a larger portion of their legislative goals adopted into law. These findings raise important normative concerns about the ability of some to use money to co-opt the democratic process.

Amy Melissa McKay is Associate Professor of Political Science at the University of Exeter.

Stealth Lobbying

Interest Group Influence and Health Care Reform

AMY MELISSA MCKAY

CAMBRIDGE
UNIVERSITY PRESS

CAMBRIDGE
UNIVERSITY PRESS

Shaftesbury Road, Cambridge CB2 8EA, United Kingdom

One Liberty Plaza, 20th Floor, New York, NY 10006, USA

477 Williamstown Road, Port Melbourne, VIC 3207, Australia

314–321, 3rd Floor, Plot 3, Splendor Forum, Jasola District Centre, New Delhi – 110025, India

103 Penang Road, #05–06/07, Visioncrest Commercial, Singapore 238467

Cambridge University Press is part of Cambridge University Press & Assessment, a department of the University of Cambridge.

We share the University's mission to contribute to society through the pursuit of education, learning and research at the highest international levels of excellence.

www.cambridge.org
Information on this title: www.cambridge.org/9781009188920

DOI: 10.1017/9781009188937

First published 2022
First paperback edition 2024

A catalogue record for this publication is available from the British Library

Library of Congress Cataloging-in-Publication data
NAMES: McKay, Amy Melissa, 1975– author.
TITLE: Stealth lobbying : interest groups and influence in health care
reform / Amy Melissa McKay.
OTHER TITLES: Interest groups and influence in health care reform
DESCRIPTION: Cambridge, United Kingdom ; New York, NY : Cambridge
University Press, 2022. | Includes bibliographical references and index.
IDENTIFIERS: LCCN 2021061791 (print) | LCCN 2021061792 (ebook) | ISBN
9781009188944 (hardback) | ISBN 9781009188920 (paperback) | ISBN
9781009188937 (ebook)
SUBJECTS: MESH: United States. Patient Protection and Affordable Care Act | United
States. Congress | Health Care Reform | Lobbying | Legislation as Topic | Interest
Groups | United States
CLASSIFICATION: LCC RA399.A3 (print) | LCC RA399.A3 (ebook) | NLM WA 540 AA1 |
DDC 362.1/0425–dc23/eng/20220120
LC record available at https://lccn.loc.gov/2021061791
LC ebook record available at https://lccn.loc.gov/2021061792

ISBN   978-1-009-18894-4   Hardback
ISBN   978-1-009-18892-0   Paperback

Contents

Figures

Tables

Acknowledgments

This project would not have been possible without the American Political Science Association Congressional Fellowship Program and those who supported me in it, especially Jeff Biggs, Tom Mahr, Lindsay Toohey, Toni P. Miles, Jennifer Nicoll Victor, and Senator Kent Conrad. It was also aided by a Georgia State University research initiation grant (2010) and the faculty there who deemed my project worth funding. Very helpful comments have been made by Scott Ainsworth, Tim LaPira, Jeff Lazarus, Jennifer Madsen, and especially Beth Leech. Mike Munger made important contributions to Chapter 2 and more broadly as my mentor and PhD advisor at Duke University. Special thanks to Toni P. Miles for her important contributions to this research including co-authoring an early conference paper with me (McKay and Miles 2010). I also benefitted from the feedback of the Cake for Comments group run by Nicole Bolleyer and Katya Kolpinskaya. Brian Webb provided excellent research assistance, and Erin Reardon provided superb editing. I especially appreciate the personal and professional support of my friends Catarina Thomson, Katharine Tyler, Dreolin Fleischer, Travis Coan, Sarah Lucas, Lorien Jasny, Nigel Pleasants, Krista Wiegand, Amy Feistel, Christine Roch, Jeff Lazarus, and Amy Steigerwalt. A big thank you to my parents, David S. McKay and Mary Fae McKay, my sisters, Susannah McKay and Jill McKay-Fleisch, and my children, Eleanor Reifler and Lila Reifler, for always encouraging me. And most of all, thanks to Jason Reifler, my partner in life and in political science, for his invaluable contributions to my professional and personal contentment.

Identifying the Hidden Influence of Lobbyists in Public Policymaking

The Patient Protection and Affordable Care Act of 2010 changed the provision of health care in the United States forever. Despite being challenged countless times in courts and in Congress, the law remains President Obama's proudest achievement. He campaigned on health reform and oversaw its creation. But President Obama did not write the law. The law known as Obamacare was in fact designed by Democratic members of the United States Senate Finance Committee.

The Congress in which these Members and their staff work is more open to outsider lobbying than any other legislature in the world. The first amendment to the Constitution guarantees the freedom to petition government for redress of grievances, and this right gives businesses and other organizations essentially unlimited access to congressional representatives' offices. The purpose of lobbyists' visits, ultimately, is to persuade legislators to create and adopt laws that are, by definition, in organizations' interests (and not to adopt laws that are not in their interests).

Putting these two facts together, health care lobby groups in 2008–10 had an immense opportunity to influence the content of the Affordable Care Act as it was being written by the Senate Finance Committee. In those three years, nearly 5,000 unique registered lobbyists representing 2,500 health care organizations – not to mention 500 health-related political action committees (PACs) – were registered to lobby on Capitol Hill. This means that for every single Member of Congress, there were nine individuals and six organizations lobbying about health reform. More to the point, for every member of the Senate Finance Committee, there were nearly 200 lobbyists who pressured, incentivized, and coaxed members to shape the law into exactly what the lobbyists' clients, employers, and supporters wanted. Lobbyists paired their requests with campaign contributions, fundraising activities, and strategically packaged policy information that together provided remarkable incentives for politicians to entertain lobbyists' requests.

Yet Members of Congress are not subservient to lobbyists. The large number of lobbying messages and campaign dollars Members receive may liberate them to pursue their own agendas, rather than constrain them to follow others' agendas. Members care first and foremost about reelection (Mayhew 1974) and therefore have little interest in fulfilling lobbyists' requests if they conflict with their constituents' preferences on issues that are salient to constituents (Denzau and Munger 1986). Some representatives and senators have sizable legislative responsibilities, such as committee and party obligations, that limit the level of time and attention they afford to lobbyists. Members representing ideologically homogeneous areas have a much easier time convincing people to donate or vote for them, relative to members from heterogeneous states and districts. Similarly, for two-thirds of senators, one or two elections will intervene before their own voters evaluate them at the polls, thus dampening their need to attract votes and contributions.

Even if members are highly influenced by lobbying attempts, this influence is nearly impossible to observe. Especially when lobbyists are working on low-salience legislative requests, when lobby groups oppose rather than support proposed laws, and when lobbying on one side of an issue is counterbalanced by lobbying on the other side, it prevents scholars, journalists, and the public from observing the effects of this lobbying. Moreover, since lobbyists and Members of Congress both have every incentive to camouflage their deal making, outsiders can seldom identify it.

Lobbying is neither bad nor good; it is both. This book considers the two facets of lobbying: The lighter facet displays the appropriate transmission of information and preferences from individuals and groups to their elected representatives. The darker facet reveals the tremendous pressure politicians feel to secure the campaign assistance and public support of organized, biased interests. Yet one side – the lighter side – is far easier to see.

For years I focused on the lighter facet, believing lobbyists to be largely ineffectual in their efforts to influence powerful federal officials. Today, having witnessed in person and in writing the many efforts of lobbyists to co-opt the policymaking process – and the conditioned willingness of Members of Congress to accommodate lobbyists' requests – I am not so sanguine. I present in this book the darker facet of lobbying, which I call *stealth lobbying* – the quiet efforts of lobbyists to access politicians, shape the content of laws, and secure microlegislation in exchange for lobbying support and campaign assistance. Over the past twelve years, I have gathered, coded, and analyzed data from sources that have never been analyzed in a large-scale, systematic way before. These data include the daily schedules of Members of Congress, amendments raised in committee, written communication between lobbyists and Members, personal campaign contributions from individual lobbyists and the PACs they run, details of fundraising events, and more. The serendipitous confluence of transformative legislation, unprecedented transparency, and my own position in the middle of it have allowed for unique and important discoveries. Analysis of these in conjunction allows me to demonstrate, rather than just to infer, the influence of lobbyists' financial and substantive pressure over Members of Congress.

1.1 THE CASE OF BECTON DICKINSON AND SENATOR MENENDEZ

Today, most Americans know what the Affordable Care Act does: It makes more comprehensive health insurance available to more people, by mandating that individuals and families are covered, by subsidizing insurance for lower-income brackets, by expanding eligibility for the Medicaid program, and by regulating what insurance companies must provide and what they are allowed to charge. Less well known is the considerable fine-tuning the law has made to Medicare, the program for the elderly and disabled, which provides for the health needs of 60 million Americans and pays 600,000 providers. Insurance companies typically follow the lead of Medicare, making decisions about Medicare even more consequential.

Among the tweaks to Medicare was creation of value-based purchasing (VBP) – an effort to link Medicare hospital reimbursements to the quality, rather than the quantity, of patient care. The VBP program had been proposed by the committee in 2008 and was absorbed into health reform legislation in 2009. It would require hospitals to report data on the health outcomes of their patients in five areas: four common conditions – heart failure, heart attacks, pneumonia, and surgical care – plus patients' perceptions of their care. Hospitals in the worst-performing quartile would risk overall payment cuts of up to 5 percent. The law gave the federal Department of Health and Human Services the power to expand the areas in which VBP was assessed. But before this, the committee needed to finalize the bill. That is where the lobbyists come in.

In May 2009, the New Jersey company Becton Dickinson (BD), makers of clinical tests for infections, submitted a letter to the Senate Finance Committee as it was working on health reform legislation. The company requested that senators insert, in the section on VBP, a short phrase – twenty-nine words, not even a full sentence – about hospital-acquired infections. These infections – including methicillin-resistant *Staphylococcus aureus* (MRSA); antibiotic-associated *Clostridium difficile*; and others linked to the use of catheters, central lines, and surgical incisions – are pervasive but invisible threats to the health and even the lives of patients who are in the hospital for other reasons. Becton Dickinson wanted the committee to include hospital-acquired infections as a sixth area in which health quality was measured for payment adjustment. The company had recently developed two products that, its lobbyists hoped, would become more popular if their proposed change was made. These products were BD Max^{TM}, an automated system that tested multiple specimens for multiple infections simultaneously, and a new two-hour MRSA test that improved markedly over previous tests that took several days.

During the process of marking up the bill in committee, in September 2009, New Jersey Democratic Senator Bob Menendez introduced an amendment that fully endorsed BD's suggestion. The amendment would include in the VBP program "healthcare-associated infection[s, as measured by the] prevention metrics and targets[, as] established in the Department of Health and Human Services' HHS Action Plan to Prevent Healthcare-Associated Infections or any successor plan." This is a near-verbatim reproduction of what BD asked for (except for what is in brackets; see Figures 1.1 and 1.2). For anyone who asked, the intention of the added language was to incentivize sterile procedures, not to encourage testing patients for hospital-acquired infections.

The amendment was submitted in writing as required by committee rules. It was not discussed at all during the markup of the bill. Then it appeared in the chairman's final version of the bill. Undoubtedly, it was discussed off the record, and Senator Menendez was able to persuade committee chairman Max Baucus to include the language. The committee voted favorably on the bill, which went on to pass the full Senate on December 24, 2009. A week after the Affordable Care Act – better known as Obamacare – was adopted by Congress in March 2010, BD's PAC gave a $5,000 contribution to Senator Menendez's campaign. In addition, three lobbyists and one family member of a lobbyist representing BD collectively gave the Menendez campaign $4,700, and BD employees

---

Proposed Amendment to 2008 Senate Finance VBP Discussion Draft
Include Healthcare-Associated Infections in Value-Based Purchasing Authorization

The Senate Finance Committee released a discussion draft of a value-based purchasing proposal in 2008. We recommend the following changes (in **bold**) to section 2 of the proposal to include prevention of healthcare-associated infections as a quality measure under the value-based purchasing authority.

SEC. 2. HOSPITAL VALUE-BASED PURCHASING PROGRAM.

   (a) PROGRAM.—
      (1) IN GENERAL.—Section 1886 of the Social Security Act (42 U.S.C. 1395ww) is amended by adding at the end the following new subsection:

"(n) HOSPITAL VALUE-BASED PURCHASING PROGRAM.—
     "(1) ESTABLISHMENT.— ….

     "(2) MEASURES.—
        "(A) IN GENERAL.—The Secretary shall select measures for purposes of the Program. Such measures shall be selected from the measures specified under subsection (b)(3)(B)(viii).
        "(B) REQUIREMENT FOR FISCAL YEAR 2012.—For value-based incentive payments made with respect to discharges occurring during fiscal year 2012, the Secretary shall ensure the following:
           "(i) CONDITIONS OR CLINICAL PERFORMANCE AREAS.—Measures are selected under subparagraph (A) that cover at least the following ~~four~~ **five** specific conditions or procedures:
               "(I) Acute myocardial infarction (AMI).
               "(II) Heart failure.
               "(III) Pneumonia.
               "(IV) Surgeries, as measured by the Surgical Care Improvement Project (formerly referred to as 'Surgical Infection Prevention' for discharges occurring before July 2006).
               "(V) Healthcare-associated infection prevention metrics and targets, as established in the Department of Health and Human Services' *HHS Action Plan to Prevent Healthcare-Associated Infections* **or any successor plan.**
           "(ii) HCAHPS.—Measures selected under subparagraph (A) shall be related to the Hospital Consumer Assessment of Healthcare Providers and Systems Survey (HCAHPS)."

FIGURE 1.1 Becton Dickinson's suggested legislative language, included in a letter submitted to the Senate Finance Committee

gave another $19,138 to Menendez. Menendez was in fact the number-one recipient of contributions from BD in the 2012 election cycle.[1]

On the surface, this seems to be a clear case of corrupt, quid pro quo politics. Menendez did exactly what a private business lobby wanted him to

---

[1] Data on top recipients, lobbyists' family members, employees, and more are provided by the Center for Responsive Politics and are available on its website, OpenSecrets.org.

Menendez Amendment D# 3 to Chairman's Mark of America's Healthy Future Act

Title III, Subtitle A

Short Title: Including Healthcare-Associated Infections in Value-Based Purchasing Authorization

Description of Amendment:

Measures for the hospital VBP program would be selected from the measures used in the RHQDAPU program. The measures would focus on the same areas that are the focus of the RHQDAPU program: heart attack (AMI); heart failure; pneumonia; surgical care activities; and patient perception of care; and in addition would include healthcare-associated infections, as measured by the prevention metrics and targets established in the Department of Health and Human Services' HHS Action Plan to Prevent Healthcare-Associated Infections or any successor plan.

Offset: No cost anticipated

FIGURE   1.2 Amendment   introduced   by   Senator   Bob   Menendez   in September 2009

do, and he was rewarded with money for his campaign. In fact, Menendez has been accused of corruption and bribery in other cases. In 2018 he was tried for eighteen counts of corruption and bribery (along with his friend Salomón Melgen, who was subsequently convicted of Medicare fraud and is serving a life sentence). The case resulted in a mistrial, and later, seven of the eighteen charges were dismissed. Depending on which count of the indictment the judge was addressing, the judge wrote, a rational juror could conclude there was an "implicit agreement to exchange things of value for official acts" – but on a different count, "no rational juror could infer an explicit quid pro quo." The difficulty here lies in the legal standard for proving bribery at the federal level: The Third Circuit claimed that to constitute bribery, it must be the case that "the payor provided a benefit to a public official intending that he will thereby take favorable official acts that he would not otherwise take" (*United States* v. *Wright*, 2012). But proving that an official would not have acted in the way he did in the absence of a contribution is literally impossible. It is a perfect example of what social scientists call the fundamental problem of causal inference: We cannot observe the outcome both with and without the hypothesized cause, and therefore we cannot determine that the event caused the outcome.

Furthermore, several factors point away from a quid pro quo in this case. First, it cost Menendez's campaign $16,226,545 to win reelection in 2012. Even combining contributions from the PAC, the lobbyists, and the employees, BD contributed less than 2 percent of the campaign's total expenditure. Of the eighteen lobbyists representing BD in 2009–10, just three of them gave any money to the Menendez campaign. Second, the BD letter was received in May, the amendment was offered in September, and the contribution was given the following March. The contribution, therefore, might have been given as a token of appreciation or support rather than payment for services. Third, it is not even clear that the Affordable Care Act works to the advantage of BD. In annual reports, the company does not tout the health care–associated infection change as a victory. Rather, the company describes the effects of the law as uncertain and laments the law's 2.3 percent excise tax on sales of certain medical devices, which the company estimated would cost $40 million per year.[2] Menendez voted for the version of the bill that assessed this excise tax on BD, as did the other Democrats on the committee, and still BD supplied $42,138 in combined contributions to committee members in 2012.

Thus, we are left with our dual-faceted dilemma. On the lighter side, lobbyists are expected to doggedly pursue biased interests, and legislators are adept at spinning their decisions to coincide with their constituents' and their own ideological preferences. On the darker side of lobbying, it is clear that lobbyists use money to try to influence Members of Congress, who require votes and campaign contributions to keep their jobs. The two facets of lobbying are difficult to distinguish. And yet, there is something inherently objectionable when lobbyists use money to bias public policy in ways that advantage certain groups while disadvantaging citizens and other groups that are not as well-organized or well-funded. Legislators alter their behavior just slightly enough to benefit lobby groups while also escaping public notice, and lobbyists use donations and fundraising to incentivize and reward this behavior.

These exchanges of money for favors are exceedingly difficult to observe. Too often, social scientists are governed by the data that are most readily available. Like searching for lost keys in the light of the streetlamp, identifying influence using well-established, downloadable datasets of PAC contributions or congressional votes ignores two

---

[2] United States Securities and Exchange Commission Form 10-K, Annual Report for Fiscal Year 2012. www.sec.gov/Archives/edgar/data/10795/000119312512478705/d402053 d10k.htm.

important facts: first, that lobbyists and legislators in reciprocal relationships have every incentive to conceal them, and second, that the influence of political money is subtle and rare, like needles in a haystack of constituent-focused, ideologically driven legislative decision-making. And yet, I argue, Members' willingness to engage in stealthy exchanges of policy manipulation for campaign rewards is rampant in the US Congress. These quiet efforts of lobbyists and legislators to benefit each other in ways that are typically invisible to outsiders are examples of stealth lobbying.

The BD story, and others like it that will be presented in this chapter, is made possible through a rare confluence of events that have enabled me to see relationships that have not been systematically demonstrated before. As a result of intentional transparency on the part of certain Members of Congress regarding legislation and Members' daily personal schedules, along with recent regulations requiring the disclosure of lobbyists' personal campaign contributions, crowd-sourced data about fundraising events, and successive drafts of legislation and amendments as they were proposed, modified, dropped, or adopted, I am able to identify positive links between legislative acts and campaign money that have historically been almost impossible to find.

This study varies from previous attempts to identify lobbying influence in Congress in important ways. I examine what goes on in committee, not on the floor. I look at patterns of access, not patterns of votes. I evaluate lobbyists' personal campaign contributions, rather than their oft-studied PAC contributions. I examine what I call microlegislation, not full-length bills. I analyze legislative development, not legislative outcomes. I focus on the elite halls of the Senate, rather than the more porous offices of the House. I use never-before-analyzed sources of data, such as interest groups' responses to draft legislation and the daily schedules of Members of Congress. These departures enable me to identify relationships between money and power that cannot be dismissed as endogenous or merely coincidental.

This book peers into the black box of legislative decision-making. It illuminates, for the first time, details about the integral role of lobby groups in shaping legislation at every stage of the process. By focusing on the highly salient health reform effort of 2008–10, I have stacked the deck somewhat against positive findings, and yet I do find numerous kinds of influence and dozens of examples of lobbyists' money being used to increase the attention, access, and legislative responsiveness of Members of Congress.

The book considers three themes in particular.

1.2 THEME 1: LOBBYISTS ARE MORE INFLUENTIAL WHEN THE SALIENCE OF THE LEGISLATION IS LOW

Stealth lobbying occurs when lobby groups make hidden requests for low-salience legislation. The politician has an interest in doing the things that will help secure reelection while avoiding things that might generate negative attention. Stealth lobbying achieves this by facilitating microlegislation – very short pieces of legislation requested by lobby groups and added to amendments, bills, and committee reports. Microlegislation helps lobbyists obtain benefits that can easily mean millions of dollars for the client, especially if the client is a business. For BD, encouraging hospitals to check for infections before discharge (or even before admission) would, the company must have hoped, result in a significant increase in sales of its BD Max testing devices. The individual lobbyist that secured the micro-legislation can use this written evidence in the future to demonstrate that they were professionally successful. Meanwhile, the change in wording would likely lead hospitals to test more patients more often, causing potential delays in admissions and discharge, and adding to the consider-able costs of Medicare and private insurance.

For Senator Menendez, there was little reason to expect that anyone would notice any of the following events, all of which had to occur together for people to suspect a quid pro quo: (1) BD requested micro-legislation that (2) was offered by Senator Menendez as an amendment to the Chairman's Mark, and (3) was associated with campaign contribu-tions from BD executives or lobbyists for BD to the Menendez campaign.

The dense legalese of microlegislation conceals – probably intentionally – the benefits the change brings to the requester, and this helps the advocates avoid attention. Though not labeled as microlegislation, there are numer-ous examples in the literature of legislators' providing private policy bene-fits outside of public view: Distributive earmarks appear in committee reports without ever having been voted on (Lazarus 2010); directives to agencies from Congress accompany legislation instead of being written into the text of the law (Evans 2004); tax breaks for specific firms are obscured in details about the year and location in which the firm was chartered (Bartlett and Steele 1988, cited in Richter et al. 2009); and tax rates are adjusted legislatively in ways that favor campaign contributors (Alexander et al. 2009). The common theme is that legislative favors given to special interests are deliberately hidden in low-visibility microlegislation.

When lobby groups seek particularistic benefits that legislators can provide without attracting public attention, campaign contributions often *are* associated with particular actions by legislators, as we will see. Other scholars have also pointed to the importance of salience, and the direction is always the same. When salience is high and groups and the public want different things, the public wins (Smith 2000; Witko 2006; McKay 2012a; Rasmussen et al. 2018). When salience is lower, however, and the public has no opinion, groups are more likely to be influential (Schattschneider 1960; Smith 2000; Fellowes and Wolf 2004; Witko 2006; Lowery 2007; Klüver 2011; Hojnacki et al. 2012; De Bruycker 2017; Rasmussen et al. 2018, 2021).

Importantly, by salience, I mean two closely related concepts. First is the more traditional way of using the term salience, defined as the level of public interest in a policy issue. I also use the term salience to describe the level of attention the public pays to a policy *debate*. Both describe the degree of interest the public has in what the government is doing, or might do, regarding a policy issue.

⇒ **The salience hypothesis:** Legislators are more inclined to accommodate lobbyists' preferences on issues of lower public salience, relative to other issues.

1.3 THEME 2: LOBBYISTS ARE MORE INFLUENTIAL WHEN THEY MAKE THEMSELVES USEFUL TO POLITICIANS

Assuming that reelection is the first and most important goal of Members of Congress (Mayhew 1974; Fenno 1978; Arnold 1990), and given the enormous quantities of money needed to secure reelection, providing financial assistance to a Member's campaign is an important way that lobbyists can make themselves useful to legislators. In Chapter 2, we discuss in detail how lobbyists make themselves substantively useful to Members of Congress by meeting with Members who introduce the bills lobbyists are interested in and knowledgeable about. Lobbyists also make themselves useful by providing to Members the campaign assistance they need in order to keep their jobs.

⇒ **The usefulness hypothesis:** Lobbyists who make themselves electorally and substantively useful to Members of Congress are likely to be granted greater access, and achieve more of their policy objectives, than other lobbyists.

There are two key forms of electoral financial assistance we consider in this book: campaign contributions and fundraising assistance.

1.3.1 Campaign Contributions

Campaign contributions help Members with their overriding goal of reelection. Members therefore want to encourage contributions. The literature identifies three ways in which legislators' behavior may be influenced by campaign money: buying votes, buying access, and buying favors.

First, despite a plethora of studies of PACs, the common refrain in the literature has been that there is little evidence that campaign contributions buy congressional *votes* (for examples of this refrain, see Mahoney 2007; Lewis 2013; Kalla and Broockman 2016; Powell and Grimmer 2016). The reason for the persistence of this myth is that the votes of Members of Congress are overdetermined. In particular, Members' votes are a function of party (Kingdon 1989), ideology (Poole and Rosenthal 2007), and the constituency (Arnold 1990). Interest groups can therefore usually anticipate Members' vote decisions, and PACs naturally tend to contribute to those who vote in the interest group's preferred way.

In fact, the preponderance of evidence shows that campaign contributions do influence congressional votes (and vice versa), even when controlling for a wide range of confounding variables. Since 2000, there have been more than a dozen peer-reviewed empirical studies that demonstrate a significant link between campaign contributions and the roll-call votes of Members of Congress. By contrast, just a handful of articles try but fail to find a significant connection (Wawro 2001; Wright 2004; Callahan 2019). Granted, journal editors are more likely to publish pieces that find an effect than pieces that find no effect (Gerber et al. 2001), so the numbers of articles alone are not definitive. However, it is the case that an increasing variety of studies provide empirical evidence that under specific, identified conditions, contributions do affect votes in Congress. Moving through time, the following studies find significant evidence that campaign donations are associated with congressional votes even while controlling for other relevant factors.

- Baldwin and Magee (2000): Contributions from labor were linked to votes against freer trade, and contributions from business were linked to votes for freer trade, while accounting for economic conditions in each Member's district and the Member's predispositions.
- McGarrity and Sutter (2000): Contributions from the National Rifle Association over the three previous congressional cycles appeared to influence congressional votes.

- Stratmann (2002): Changes in contributions from the financial industry were associated with concomitant changes in Members' votes.
- Cohen and Hamman (2003): Votes on identical legislation at two different points in time indicated that House Members' votes were influenced by PAC contributions.
- Fellowes and Wolf (2004): Contributions from business PACs and individuals working for business interests had an influence over congressional votes regarding tax policy but had notably less influence over direct spending, where legislators wanted to avoid "the appearance of an embarrassing quid pro quo."
- Roscoe and Jenkins (2005): A meta-analysis that pooled results from thirty studies estimated that one-third of roll-call votes were influenced by campaign contributions.
- Stratmann (2005): A meta-analysis of 40 studies of contributions and roll-call votes indicated that contributions have a significant effect on votes across studies.
- Witko (2006): PACs influenced eight out of ten congressional votes on low-salience issues (but only one out of ten ideological votes).
- Mian et al. (2010): Campaign contributions from financial services interests increased Members' odds of voting in favor of the Emergency Economic Stabilization Act, a bill that benefitted the financial services industry, while controlling for the number of mortgage defaults in the district and the proportion of constituents working in the industry. (And, as evidence that contributions were altering behavior, members in their last terms were not influenced by campaign contributions.)
- Dorsch (2013): Financial services' contributions exerted significant influence over votes on the Wall Street bailout.
- Mian et al. (2013): Contributions from the mortgage industry between 2002 and 2007 were related to housing-related roll-call votes by Members whose districts were disproportionately targeted in subprime lending.
- Igan and Mishra (2014): Campaign contributions by the financial industry from 1999 to 2006 were associated with the probability that a legislator changed positions to vote in favor of deregulating the industry.
- Choi (2015): Campaign contributions from pro-free-trade PACs increased the probability that legislators voted for the US–South Korea free trade agreement.

- Zhang and Tanger (2017): Contributions from the forest industry were associated with Members' decisions to vote for bills the forest industry was lobbying for.

Further support for a connection between lobby groups' campaign contributions and legislative votes is found in numerous articles from the 1990s (Hall and Wayman 1990; Langbein and Lotwis 1990; Neustadtl 1990; Stratmann 1991; Quinn and Shapiro 1991; Fleisher 1993; Nollen and Quinn 1994; Stratmann 1995; Brooks, Cameron, and Carter 1998; Calcagno and Jackson 1998) and in more recent articles studying the US states (Powell 2012; Lewis 2013; Fouirnaies and Fowler 2022). Given all this evidence, even in the face of failure to link particular contributions to particular votes, it is difficult to deny that some votes some of the time are influenced by money.

Second, in addition to buying votes, campaign contributions likely buy greater *access* to politicians. Langbein (1986) showed that as the amount of time a Member of Congress spent with lobbyists increased, so too did their fundraising income – and at an exponentially increasing rate. Kalla and Broockman (2016), in a randomized field experiment, found that when lobbyists were described to congressional offices as "local donors," they were three to four times more likely than when those same lobbyists were described as "constituents" to secure meetings with senior-level congressional staff, including the Member of Congress. And in Chapter 2 of this book, I show that while most Members will accept meetings with lobbyists once per year, campaign finance assistance will secure more than one meeting in a year.

Third, contributions may buy legislative *favors* – those other things Members can do that are greatly beneficial for specific lobbyists and their organizations. The favors that Members provide to lobby groups include earmarks (de Figueiredo and Silverman 2006; Rocca and Gordon 2013), federal contracts (Leech 2006; Witko 2011; Dusso et al. 2019), and tax breaks (Alexander et al. 2009; Richter et al. 2009). Yet only a few scholars (Witko 2011; Rocca and Gordon 2013) have positively identified a link between campaign contributions and legislative favors.

⇒ **Usefulness subhypothesis 1.** Campaign contributions help lobbyists make themselves useful to Members.

1.3.2 Fundraising Assistance

In addition to direct contributions, lobbyists can and do host fundraising events for Members of Congress. Fundraising is a way for lobbyists to "give" far more to a congressional candidate than they may legally give directly. By hosting an event, inviting potential donors, soliciting the contributions, and bundling them together to give to the candidate, lobbyist-fundraisers can deliver to Members contributions of tens of thousands of dollars – amounts many times greater than the maximum individual contribution amount of $2,900 (in 2022).

Indeed, we will see in Chapter 2 that lobbyists who fundraise for Members are more likely to get multiple meetings with Members, and in Chapter 4 we will see that, in addition to greater access, lobbyists who fundraise for Members are also more likely than other lobbyists to get requested microlegislation into bills.

⇒ **Usefulness subhypothesis 2.** Campaign fundraising helps lobbyists make themselves useful to Members.

The following story illustrates how fundraising assistance is used to influence Members of Congress. On November 18, 2009, at Bistro Bis on E Street, a fundraiser was held for the *Stabenow for Senate* reelection committee. This restaurant, whose slogan is "Where Capitol Hill Dines," is on the Senate side of the Capitol building, steps away from the Senate office buildings. The hosts listed on the invitation were four individuals few Americans have ever heard of. But these hosts were actually long-time Washington insiders interested in health care who targeted Stabenow and other members of the Finance committee just as they were writing what would become known as the Affordable Care Act, the most important health care bill in a generation.

It is interesting to note the strong ties that these fundraiser hosts had to the Finance committee on which Senator Stabenow (D-MI) served:

- Shannon Finley had been the political director for Committee Chairman Max Baucus (D-MT) for the six years immediately before she went to work for the lobbying firm Capitol Counsel. Finley represented fifty-six clients at Capitol Counsel in 2009, and in that year she also made contributions to nine of the twenty-three members of the Finance committee.
- John Raffaelli had been legal counsel for the committee for four years in the 1980s, but had been a lobbyist since the 1990s. He did not report making any contributions to federal candidates in 2009.

- David Jones had worked for Finance member Orrin Hatch (R-UT) as Counsel to the Senate Judiciary Committee's Intellectual Property Subcommittee, which Senator Hatch then chaired. In 2009 Jones represented forty clients, including AstraZeneca, the Healthcare Leadership Council, Fresenius, and the Pew Charitable Trusts. He donated to five Senate Finance Committee members in 2009.
- James Gould had been the staff director for the Finance committee itself before becoming a lobbyist in 1989. He represented large and wealthy clients including Golden Living, the Healthcare Leadership Council, and the Pharmaceutical Research and Manufacturing Association, better known as PhRMA. In addition to co-hosting a fundraising event for Stabenow, James Gould made a contribution to her on December 14, 2009, which was before the Senate passed the bill but after the committee had amended and voted on it. In addition to Stabenow, Gould donated to eight other members of the committee.

Senator Stabenow was not unique in receiving a contribution from these four lobbyists, who were all nurturing connections to their former congressional offices. Yet, Stabenow was the only senator for whom the group's lobbyists hosted a fundraiser in 2009 as the bill was being drafted by the committee. And she was the only senator to offer an amendment in committee that was requested by the group.

The four fundraiser hosts all worked for a client that had an interest in health reform – the Joint Commission on the Accreditation of Healthcare Organizations. In May 2009, the Joint Commission submitted to the committee an eleven-page letter stating its preferences regarding health reform legislation. I use italics now to indicate phrases that appear exactly or in essence in both the group's letter and the senator's amendment to what became the Affordable Care Act. The Commission described itself as having "a long history of promoting improvements in healthcare quality and safety" and said that it "has been instrumental in raising the bar of quality standards *for both governmental and non-governmental providers* since its inception in 1951." The letter recommends creation of a "center or institute" that

be a *not-for-profit* entity in the private sector; have demonstrated competencies in understanding the factors that contribute to successful quality improvement and patient safety initiatives; possess the resident knowledge and expertise to fulfill the above five objectives; have a demonstrated track record of broadly engaging relevant stakeholder groups; and have the capacity to leverage *quality improvement and patient safety* change *across the care continuum.*

In September, Senator Stabenow offered an amendment proposing that the Secretary of Health and Human Services

contract with a *non-profit organization* or organizations that have at least five years of experience in developing and implementing the [five] new strategies; have operated such programs *for both governmental and non-governmental providers* to *improve patient safety and the quality of health care* ... working with a *variety of institutional health care providers, physicians and other health care practitioners.*

The group requested that $35 million be allocated to this center; the Stabenow amendment contains "a mandatory appropriation of $25 million per year for FY10, FY11, and FY12." While we cannot conclude that there was a causal relationship between the group's fundraising event and the senator's amendment-offering based on this evidence, we do see a clear association.

The fundraiser occurred one month later. The four lobbyists who hosted it do not host any other known fundraising events for committee members until the following March (2010), after which no known fundraisers were held by any lobby group for committee members until 2012. The Joint Commission had spent $260,000 on lobbying in 2009–10 and was set to receive a proposed $75 million back. The lobbyists who pressed for this amendment had proof in writing of their progress, which they could show off to their client and future potential clients. Indeed, the Commission hired all four of them again the following year. But it would be Chairman Baucus, not Senator Stabenow, who decided which amendments became part of the bill and which went into the recycling bin. Though the commission and the four lobbyists had showered attention on Stabenow, they did not host any fundraisers for Senator Baucus, and they did not even contribute to him in 2008 or 2009. The amendment was not adopted.

Thus, while stealth lobbyists can be partially successful in using campaign assistance to influence well-placed Members of Congress, this story demonstrates that such influence may still not be enough to turn micro-legislation into law.

1.4 THEME 3: COLLECTIVELY, LOBBYISTS' MONEY HAS LITTLE NET EFFECT ON PUBLIC POLICIES

Positively identifying the influence of interest groups over public policy-making – let alone the influence of groups' campaign contributions – is notoriously challenging. We now speak directly about why it is so hard to find something that so many people believe is there, that is, the influence of lobbying and money over public policy decisions. This difficulty has two key explanations: methodological difficulty and intentional concealment.

1.4.1 Methodological Challenges

A significant portion of the literature has tried and failed to find evidence that campaign money or related resources significantly influence legislative decision-making (see reviews in Smith 1995; Baumgartner and Leech 1998; Burstein and Linton 2002). There are several reasons for this.

First, donors give their voluntary contributions to those politicians whose policy stances they prefer. It follows that legislators act in a way that most of their donors prefer. Granted, this does not mean that the legislator is induced by the contribution to do something he or she otherwise would not do. Such endogeneity is often used as a response against findings of influence (see, e.g., Ansolabehere et al. 2003). When politicians take an action consistent with the wishes of a donor, it may look as if the contribution induced the behavior, but it is more likely that the legislator's general or anticipated behavior is what induced the contribution.

Second, resources and lobbying occur on both sides of the issue. In their landmark study of lobbying influence in Washington, Baumgartner et al. (2009) showed that resources tend to cancel each other out. That is, the two sides of a piece of pending legislation usually have approximately equal resources and, thus, it is a coin flip which side wins. While Baumgartner et al. (2009) found this to be true for ninety of their ninety-eight cases, in the eight cases in which the two sides were not equally wealthy (as measured through PAC contributions, lobbying expenditures, and organizational revenue), the side with greater resources won five times and the side with fewer resources won three times – a win for greater resources, albeit not a statistically significant one. Similarly, I found (McKay 2012b) that the side of a policy debate that had greater resources was not significantly more likely to win – but group resources were associated with greater lobbying intensity by the group – that is, more lobbyists and lobbying in more venues – and this greater intensity was associated with higher levels of success for that side of the debate.

Third, lobby groups often want to prevent a policy change, rather than to create one. Baumgartner et al. (2009) emphasized the profound effect that the status quo policy has on policy outcomes. In general, political parties and other institutions are biased against change, especially given the record levels of bitter partisanship occurring even before the election of Donald Trump (Poole and Rosenthal 2007). As such, anyone lobbying to leave things as they are has an institutional advantage that increases their odds of winning. Of the ninety-eight issues that Baumgartner et al. (2009) examined in depth, sixty-eight had not changed after two years, and fifty-eight had not changed after four years (Baumgartner et al. 2009, 219). We should therefore expect policy change in Congress to be the exception, not the norm, and lobbyists seeking to change the status quo are generally unlikely to do so. In fact, LaPira and Thomas (2017) and others have argued that the key reason many organizations hire lobbyists is to serve as insurance against unexpected and unwanted legislative change.

1.4.2 Intentional Concealment

In addition to the vexing challenge of identifying causal influence, there are incentives for legislators and lobby groups to conceal anything that might look like a link. This concealment increases the opportunities for lobbyists to stealthily secure particularistic policy benefits for the groups they represent. Washington lobbyists today are highly sophisticated and aware of the consequences of their actions. Washington politicians, too, would rather forego a donation than risk it being tied to a seemingly bought action by the legislator. Political opponents, journalists, government officials, and voters all have reasons to notice corruption or the appearance of corruption. As a result, in most cases, interest groups avoid making contributions that could be construed as buying anything. Contributions are given because politicians need them and ask for them. Like a clever criminal, as Powell puts it, "many of the influence pathways do not leave an observable data trail" (Powell 2012, 18).

As examples of seemingly intentional concealment of lobbyist–legislator links: Members of Congress exert more effort in committee on behalf of contributors than non-contributors (Hall and Wayman 1990). Business firms funnel campaign contributions through the individuals that work for them so that contributions are not linked to specific firms (Goldstein 1999). Lobbyists who formerly worked as congressional staff members or other government officials frequently do not report this previous employment as required (LaPira and Thomas 2017). And in a field experiment, Grose et al. (2019) found that legislators randomly assigned to be lobbied in a restaurant were two-and-a-half times more likely to say yes to the lobbyist's request than when they were lobbied in their own offices, where they were more easily observed.

More evidence that legislators try to obscure their links to lobbyists is found when legislators no longer feel the need to conceal them. Egerod and Lassen (2019) showed that senators in their final terms were more likely to introduce bills that benefit the firm that employs them upon their departure. Dabros (2015) showed that Members who are in their final terms before moving to the private sector take more international trips, presumably in an effort to enhance their worth to prospective employers. In short, when researchers succeed in getting past the intentional conceal-ment of relationships between lobbyists and legislators, the research is more likely to find that these relationships affect policymaking.

1.4.3 Negative Lobbying

A third explanation for why lobbying influence is so difficult to identify is what I call *negative lobbying*. Similar to lobbying to defend the status quo (Baumgartner et al. 2009), negative lobbying – lobbying against a measure – is a powerful phenomenon that tends to be more successful than lobbying in favor of a measure. Negative lobbying is effective because policymakers are risk-averse: Legislators and bureaucrats have a rational and asymmetric preference for avoiding blame over seeking praise, just as individuals routinely exhibit a steeper decline in satisfaction for losses relative to the more modest increase in satisfac-tion they derive from gains (Kahneman and Tversky 1979). Lobbying pressure in opposition to a proposal alerts policymakers to the potential of considerable public disapproval of the government action, which may bring electoral risks, infringed autonomy, public embarrassment, and similar consequences. Positive lobbying merely indicates that some interests would benefit from a measure – which is always the case. Indeed, Baumgartner et al. (2009) found that status quo defenders were more likely than status quo challengers to use negative arguments (p. 140) and to point out potential consequences such as electoral or partisan effects (p. 132). Thus, when policymakers observe high num-bers of opposition groups, their support for the proposal is likely to dwindle – even given high numbers of supporters. In a previous project examining seventy-seven federal policy proposals, I found that it takes an estimated three-and-a-half lobbyists in favor of a measure to coun-teract the effects of just one lobbyist against it (McKay 2012a).

Despite its power, the effects of negative lobbying are difficult to observe because they are often implicit. Negative lobbying implies a threat that *if* legislators do something, the response will be negative and overwhelming. The groups threatening to launch negative lobbying campaigns do not actually have to do it for negative lobbying to be effective. The effectiveness of implicit threats can be observed in the presidential veto, which modern presidents seldom need to use because the *threat* of the veto is sufficient for the president to influence the substance of congressional legislation. A quintessential example of negative lobbying is found in Democrats' last major attempt to enact substantial health reform, under Bill and Hillary Clinton 1993–94 – and again under Obama in 2009–10, as the next story illustrates.

1.4.3.1 Negative Lobbying on Health Reform

Prior to the efforts of President Barack Obama and Senate Finance Chairman Max Baucus, there were the efforts of President Bill Clinton and First Lady Hillary Rodham Clinton. In 1993–94, they and their colleagues crafted an extensive health reform proposal that was ultimately defeated by skillful negative lobbying. When the bill was first proposed, major health interest groups, including the American Medical Association, the Health Insurance Association of America, the US Chamber of Commerce, and many large corporations, generally supported the key elements of the Clinton plan, which were universal coverage and an employer mandate to provide insurance. But as cost concerns grew, the doctors and insurers began to back away from the bill. There was no clear alternative they could get behind, though numerous Democrats offered competing proposals. Health care groups galvanized on a general "no" to health reform.

The insurance industry, which would be aggressively regulated under the Clinton plan and other proposals, launched a massive ad campaign to try to raise citizens' doubts. This campaign featured Harry and Louise, a likable middle-class couple who spoke in nervous terms about the Clinton plan in their kitchen and driveway. They discussed qualms such as the possibility that health insurance costs would rise (as indeed they do every year). The direct effect of the ads was less on the relatively small numbers of viewers who saw them on television but on the news media coverage of the ads, which itself drew the attention of Members of Congress. (Recall that national television news coverage was at its zenith in the early 1990s.) As described by Hillary Clinton as it was happening, supporters "cannot possibly have the intensity that the negative forces have" (quoted in Clymer et al. 1994). Indeed, risk-aversion on the part of Members of Congress, in large part reacting to the Harry and Louise ad campaign, led to the utter rejection of the plan by Congress.

```
July 7 --

PhRMA DEAL
Commitment of up to $80 billion, but not more than $80 billion.
1. Agree to increase of Medicaid rebate from 15.1 - 23.1% ($34
billion)
2. Agree to get FOBs done (but no agreement on details -- express
disagreement on data exclusivity which both sides say does not
affect the score of the legislation.) ($9 billion)
3. Sell drugs to patients in the donut hole at 50% discount ($25
billion)
This totals $68 billion
4. Companies will be assessed a tax or fee that will score at $12
billion. There was no agreement as to how or on what this tax/fee
will be based.
Total: $80 billion

In exchange for these items, the White House agreed to:
1. Oppose importation
2. Oppose rebates in Medicare Part D
3. Oppose repeal of non-interference
4. Oppose opening Medicare Part B
```

FIGURE 1.3 A memo summarizing a deal with the pharmaceutical industry that was agreed to at a meeting between industry lobbyists and the White House in July 2009

In 2009, the experience of the failure of health reform in 1994 and the built-in risk-aversion of Members of Congress motivated Senate Finance Committee Chairman Max Baucus and others to secure the support of the key groups familiar with the 1993 effort, including the national hospital, doctor, insurance, pharmaceutical, and device-maker groups. As Democrats in 2009 considered how to get health reform legislation over the finish line, they were openly mindful of possibly fatal "Harry and Louise"–style negative lobbying. To that end, Baucus, with the approval of President Obama, ultimately decided to negotiate with these groups to ensure their support of the legislation. We will return to this part of the story in Chapter 6, but for now, observe the leaked notes of someone participating in the negotiations in Figure 1.3.

⇒ **Null effects subhypothesis 1.** Negative lobbying is powerful, pervasive, and difficult to observe.

1.4.4 The Inverse Pull of Access and Influence

A fourth and final reason for the prevalence of null effects in lobbying research is what I call the *inverse pull* of access and influence. Legislators in lower-visibility, less powerful roles may be more susceptible to the influence of lobbying because they are more electorally vulnerable and more legislatively inexperienced. As one example of this tendency, Stratmann (2002) found that junior Members of Congress are more responsive to campaign contributions than are senior Members. This finding is consistent with Fenno's (1978) assertion that Members are most focused on reelection in their first term in Congress. Even into their second and third terms, newer Members of Congress have less committee responsibility and lower power and prestige in the Congress relative to more senior Members. Thus, greater power in the legislature is associated with *lower* likelihood of being influenced by lobbyists, and lower power in the legislature is associated with more opportunities to meet with lobbyists.

⇒ **Null effects subhypothesis 2**. There is an inverse relationship between legislators' willingness to be lobbied and the influence they have over major legislation.

The following story provides a vivid example of the null effects that lobbying can have when it is aimed at legislators with little power to enact legislation. In 2008, Senators Max Baucus and Finance committee member Kent Conrad of North Dakota cosponsored a bill that would create a federal institute to evaluate the comparative effectiveness of treatments and drugs across a range of diseases. This decision was inspired by a popular (on Capitol Hill, at least) article in *Health Affairs* in which Gail Wilensky, who formerly ran the federal Medicare program, argued that the United States should create an entity similar to the United Kingdom's National Institute for Health and Care Excellence (NICE) (Wilensky 2006). NICE evaluates and conducts research on the effectiveness of medical treatments and makes recommendations, which the United Kingdom's National Health Service uses to decide how to allocate the scarce resource of health care.

As chairman of the country's most powerful revenue tool, Max Baucus, along with chairman of the Budget committee Kent Conrad, had a particular interest in restraining fast-growing Medicare costs. So Baucus included the comparative effectiveness bill in the broader health reform legislation he was working on. But, encouraged by numerous drug and device groups, four Republican senators objected to the Baucus–Conrad proposal. They introduced, in markup, an amendment to the legislation stating that the Secretary of Health and Human Services "shall not use data obtained from the conduct of comparative effectiveness research ... to deny coverage of an item or service under a federal health care program" (Kyl-Roberts-Crapo-Cornyn Amendment #D8, America's Healthy Future Act of 2009). This microlegislation would have had the effect of rendering the comparative effectiveness research institute moot by preventing the Centers for Medicare and Medicaid Services from using any of the institute's recommendations in deciding how to allocate federal dollars.

The amendment was jointly requested, as the data used in this book reveal, by AdvaMed, the Medical Device Manufacturers Association, the Biotechnology Industry Organization, drug companies Eli Lilly and Johnson & Johnson, and groups representing pathologists, rheumatologists, and Alzheimer's disease. Also requesting the amendment was a group calling itself the Alliance for Comparative Effectiveness Stakeholders, an apparently ad hoc coalition whose only purpose seems to have been to limit the scope of any comparative effectiveness research institute. The letter from the coalition, written by an employee of Patton Boggs, was signed by several of the previously listed groups in addition to Millennium Pharmaceuticals, Amgen, Sepracor, the American Medical Rehabilitation Providers Association, the National Hispanic Medical Association, and a few 501(c)3s for good measure (the National Council for Community Behavioral Healthcare, National Minority Quality Forum, the Treatment Effectiveness Now Project, the Men's Health Network, the National Alliance for Caregiving). Collectively, these groups gave the four senators at least $41,000 in contributions in 2009 and 2010. A group calling itself the National Health Council, whose 101 members include many of the companies and organizations just named and lobbyists working on its behalf, gave the four senators at least $387,000 and hosted fourteen fundraisers for them between 2009 and 2010, as reported by the Sunlight Foundation.

Despite this pressure, the drug and device makers and others opposing a powerful comparative effectiveness research institute were not successful in eliminating or neutering it, because Baucus was in control of the legislation. He and Conrad had already written a version of the proposal that would allow Medicare to take advantage of the institute's data and recommendations. Despite contributions from the amendment's requesters, which totaled $1,438,250 to Senator Baucus in 2009–10, it was the four Republicans who offered the amendment the groups wanted. The inverse pull of legislator power and legislators' willingness to cooperate with lobbyists kept the opponents of comparative effectiveness research from getting their way. As this example makes clear, since higher-powered members have the most influence over legislation – especially major legislation, rather than microlegislation – the influence of the groups over government policy is inherently, at least somewhat, limited.

1.5 A LOOK AHEAD

Stealth lobbying occurs when elite lobbyists, working under the radar, take advantage of money and connections to try to bypass the deliberative democratic process and win private goods for a privileged few. While most lobbying most of the time is sufficiently constrained and counteracted, some lobbying efforts have disproportionate influence driven by money and connections. This stealth lobbying is difficult or even impossible for most people to observe. The introductory chapter of this book has explained this central argument and offered stories that illustrate the three themes of the book – the importance of salience, the value of usefulness, and the dominance of null effects. In the coming chapters, I detail patterns of interactions in which campaign assistance by lobby groups coincides with specific actions by legislators. I will suggest that campaign contributions and fundraising assistance are frequently associated with the ability of lobbyists to secure mostly unobservable benefits for their organizations – even if the association is very difficult to recognize.

1.5.1 Chapter 2: Scheduling Influence and Buying Access

Chapter 2 examines, for the first time in the literature, the daily schedules of Members of Congress. I offer a theory of access that specifies the conditions under which Members of Congress are more likely to meet with a lobby group. The conditions include the Member's seniority, committee assignments, and legislative agenda, as well as campaign assistance provided for the Member by the lobby group. I show that campaign contributions are significantly associated with the probability that the Member meets more than once with a lobbyist in a given year.

1.5.2 Chapter 3: The Strategic Behavior of Individual Lobbyists and Their PACs

While most studies of campaign contributions rely on groups' limited PAC contributions, this chapter uses data that did not exist before 2008 regarding the personal campaign contributions of lobbyists to Members of Congress.

I show that as health reform legislation was being written, lobbyists working on health care issues gave more money to senators than did all other lobbyists combined, and that these donations flowed specifically to senators working on the bill at the most opportune times in the legislative process. We will see that while lobbyists' PAC contributions tend to be less sensitive than individuals' contributions to legislators' political position and timing, individual lobbyists give to key legislators at key times, consistent with attempts to influence the content and outcome of health reform legislation.

1.5.3 Chapter 4: Stealth Fundraising and Legislative Favors

Chapter 4 focuses on a largely unstudied phenomenon – the many fundraising events hosted by lobbyists on behalf of Members of Congress. I analyze data cataloging fundraising events, their beneficiaries, hosts, and dates. I use plagiarism detection software and other methods to identify written evidence of legislative favors performed by specific senators for lobby groups that hosted fundraisers for those senators. The analysis shows that when a group, or any of its hired lobbyists, hosts a fundraiser for a senator, the odds that the senator offers legislation requested by the group are at least three-and-a-half times greater than when the group does not host a fundraiser for the senator.

1.5.4 Chapter 5: Stealth Lobbying, Stealth Contributions, and the Affordable Care Act

This chapter provides the most direct examination of the relationship between campaign contributions and legislative decision-making. Using an original, highly granular dataset I built describing the preferences of hundreds of health care lobbyists and the outcomes of these requests at successive stages of bill development, I show that lobbyists who make campaign contributions to a senator tend to secure a greater portion of their interest group's preferences in legislative committee. Moreover, when stealth lobbying is accompanied by campaign contributions to specific senators, those senators are significantly more likely to introduce amendments requested by the group, relative to other interest groups that lobbied the same people at the same time but did not contribute to them.

1.5.5 Chapter 6: Conclusions about Money in Policymaking

The final chapter summarizes and reiterates the three themes and main arguments of the book. I show how the findings of the five empirical chapters are mutually consistent even as they highlight different aspects of lobbying behavior and government response. I present a list of ways in which previous studies have looked for influence in the wrong places, along with suggestions of where the influence is more likely to be observed. And I tell the end of the tale of the adoption of health reform legislation under President Obama.

We will see in the book evidence that lobby groups – in general – are limited in their ability to enact major public policies, including health reform. Yet stealth lobbying does occur, and with its low visibility and the fundraising and contributions that often accompany it, private interests are able to achieve outcomes that provide valuable benefits to narrow interests.

2

Scheduling Influence and Buying Access

Time is a House Member's scarcest and most precious political resource.
Fenno (1973, 34)

How Members of Congress spend their time on a daily basis is a consequential decision for American public policies. It is also, interestingly, the decision over which Members have the most control (Fenno 1978; Hall and Wayman 1990). Members decide, whether consciously or unconsciously, how much of their time to grant to lobbyists – and which lobbyists.

In this chapter, I specify the conditions that make it more or less likely that Members will meet with lobbyists. I use the daily schedules of a diverse array of Members of Congress to explain how Members allocate their time across the many demands placed on them. I test all three of the book's hypotheses as introduced in Chapter 1 – regarding usefulness, salience, and null effects – in a single model to show that while legislative interests are an important predictor of meetings between lobbyists and legislators, the two forms of campaign assistance – contributions and fundraising – also significantly increase lobbyists' access to Members of Congress.

2.1 A THEORY OF ACCESS

The benefits lobbyists provide to legislators are significant. Lobbyists provide to Members a legislative subsidy (Hall and Deardorff 2006) that helps Members to realize their goals in several ways. First, as we will discuss, lobbyists offer to legislators and their staff *policy information* and expertise about current policy and future hypothetical laws. Members of Congress must be generalists, with a little knowledge about a very broad range of public policies. Lobbyists, meanwhile, are specialists, having deep knowledge about a very narrow range of public policies. Thus, lobbyists normally possess more policy information than the Members and staff they lobby.

Second, lobbyists offer *political information* about how changes will be received by the legislator's constituents and by others on Capitol Hill. While Members have a high level of understanding of their state or district, lobbyists can afford to additionally provide details such as that an industry "employs 100,000 people in your district" or a state "ranks seventh in the nation in the use of telemedicine" – information that Members may not have easy access to.

Third, lobbyists can provide support for – or opposition to – a bill, as illustrated in Chapter 1's story of the failed Clinton health reform effort. And fourth, and not trivially, lobbyists provide direct monetary support that legislators need for their perpetual reelection campaigns.

In exchange for the benefits that lobbyists provide to legislators, Members provide to lobbyists two key benefits: requested public policies, especially microlegislation; and access, which is the potential to influence public policy. Later chapters will discuss microlegislation and influence. This chapter focuses squarely on the necessary precursor to policy influence: access to legislators in the first place – in the form of face-to-face contact with legislators or, to a lesser extent, with their trusted staff members. We study the important notion of access in the most direct way possible: by examining which lobbyists get more or fewer meetings with Members and their offices.

Members' daily schedules are an ideal source of information by which to gauge access. From 2008 to 2010, as health reform legislation was being written, many Members of Congress did not use email or even have Blackberrys or iPhones, the two government-issued devices that congressional staff had to choose from. (Their staff all used email, of course, but many Members did not; Parker 2015.) Thus, if a lobbyist had hopes of influencing a Member, the only access was through face-to-face contact – not by phone, email, Twitter, Facebook, or any other platform. Thus, real-time, in-person conversation was used, nearly exclusively, by lobbyists to communicate with Members. This meant that a Member's schedule was a reliable list of who was lobbying them on a given day.

All Members employ schedulers – staff members who collate requests for meetings and build them into a Member's daily schedule, factoring in the Member's travel schedule; the Member's committee, party, and chamber obligations; the availability of staff members who might substitute for the Member in the meeting; the identity of the requester as a constituent (Chin et al. 2000), campaign donor (Kalla and Broockman 2016), or neither; and other largely unobservable office priorities. These schedules are internally circulated so that staff members can accommodate the Member's activities, which may also include Members' committee business, political and party events (such as fundraisers), media interviews, travel plans, and personal time. Some Members opt to publish these schedules, usually weekly, on their congressional webpages, to show constituents what they are up to. For a time, all known published schedules were very helpfully collected by the Sunlight Foundation, and they serve as our key data source in this chapter.

Not all visitors to Members' offices are lobbyists – but nearly all are. Constituents count as lobbyists, given that they generally want the Member to do something for them in their capacity as elected representatives. Moreover, on Members' schedules, lobbyists frequently are described as individuals with a constituent connection, such as "Joe Smith from Bozeman." Much if not most of the time, Joe Smith is a lobbyist who spent some time in Bozeman at some point in his life, and was especially selected by his employer to visit the senator from Montana, in contrast to someone like "Mary King from Bismarck," who is sent by the same employer to the North Dakota offices. After examining many examples of Members' schedules, I decided that the only two categories of visitors I should not classify as lobbyists are school groups, such as visiting high school students in for a photo op (which happens surprisingly often), and officials from any level of government, who actually may be there to lobby the Member, but who do not represent private interests and do not have to register as lobbyists.

The theory of access I present here connects the three theses of the book. The theory holds that lobbyists are more likely to be granted meetings with Members of Congress when (1) lobbyists make themselves *useful* to Members, (2) Members have *less* power and prestige in Congress, and (3) the *salience* of what the lobbyist is asking for is low. As a result, the combined net effect of lobbying over policy outcomes tends to be low.

The stories in Chapter 1 provide some evidence for the three hypotheses that together constitute the theory. Recall the Michigan senator who offered an amendment requested by a group that hosted a fundraiser for her (usefulness), the Member from New Jersey who offered an amendment designed not to attract attention (salience), and the medical device makers that successfully persuaded several minority-party senators to offer an amendment that had no chance of becoming law (the inverse pull). What we have not yet discussed is the *relative* importance of these three explanations in predicting or explaining behavior. I now address this empirical question using data describing how Members of Congress actually spend their time and, moreover, the conditions that allow some lobbyists greater access to Members than others. After describing the variables, we will assess the data in a single model that tests all three hypotheses.

2.2 LOBBYISTS' USEFULNESS

The first component of the theory of access argues that lobbyists who are useful to Members are likely to get more meetings with those Members relative to other lobbyist-visitors. By providing political information about the constituency and about other parts of government, as well as technical information about exactly what the legislation should say and do, lobbyists can serve as needed assistants to Members of Congress, whose own staff are limited in number and time. I expect that two factors in particular increase lobbyists' usefulness to Members: when the lobbyist provides to the Member needed campaign assistance, and when the lobbyist and Member are working on the same legislation.

2.2.1 Campaign Assistance

As discussed in Chapter 1, financial contributions to the campaigns of legislators have been the subject of a large number of political science studies. Despite dozens of studies showing that campaign contributions have an effect on the decisions of Members of Congress, the prevailing rhetoric seems to be that we cannot prove that they matter.

To gauge the effect of contributions on the behavior of Members of Congress, I use the Federal Election Committee's data containing every contribution by an individual or political action committee (PAC) to the Members whose schedules I have between 2007 and 2010. This involved stripping names down to their basic components, eliminating titles, suffixes, initials, and using necessary disambiguation for those contributions coming from commonly or same-named individuals. Contributions were identified by merging a list of all PACs and individuals that donated to the

Member with a full list of the groups and individuals named on Members' schedules.

In addition to the many contributions Members receive every election cycle, there are, virtually every day in Washington, fundraising events, which we will pry into in Chapter 4. A large number of these fundraising events are hosted by individuals or groups that have business before Congress. This fact raises ethical concerns that the hosts of fundraising events may secure unfair advantages from the politicians benefitting from those fundraisers. Yet, it is perfectly legal.

Data regarding fundraising events were solicited from the public by the nonprofit group the Sunlight Foundation, which compiled them into a database that was made publicly available on the web. Since these data are crowd-sourced, we cannot be sure what portion of all fundraisers they represent. Yet the database contains more than 10,000 fundraising events across a ten-year period. These data are discussed in detail in Chapter 4 and include the date of each fundraiser, the names of hosts and beneficiaries, an address to send checks to, and suggested donation amounts, among other details. The host can be one or more individuals or a group, such as a PAC. The beneficiary can be the campaign committees or leadership PACs of one or more congressional candidates. From this database, I identified relevant fundraisers between 2007 and 2010 by merging a list of hosts with a list of visitors to the eleven Members captured in my sample of daily congressional schedules. I also identified in the fundraiser data all mentions of the eleven Members whose schedules I have. Fundraisers benefitting multiple Members were counted as fundraisers in all possible combinations between host and Member.

Because fundraising events are crowd-sourced, while contributions are disclosed as required by law, the number of captured fundraising events is lower and is likely to be an undercount. To compensate for this, I combine the two into one variable. I expect the number of contributions or fundraisers, which together I label *campaign assistance*, in a Member-group dyad to be positively related to the number of meetings that occur in the dyad.

2.2.2 Bill Overlap

A lobbyist who can provide technical and political information that helps a Member craft a bill that will please their audience is useful to that Member. Therefore, when a Member introduces a piece of legislation on which the lobbyist is also working, the number of meetings between the two should be greater as they work to draft a mutually beneficial bill or amendment.

Registered lobbyists disclose quarterly a description of the issues on which they work for particular clients in reports known as LDA-2 disclosures. Filers are asked to include bill numbers if they exist. The Center for Responsive Politics (CRP) uses these filings to generate cleaned data containing the bill numbers on which lobbyists report working. I create a variable to capture the extent of the overlap between bills the Member introduces and bills being worked on by the lobbyist. Specifically, I count the number of bills that were both (1) listed on lobbying disclosure forms and (2) introduced by the Member in the same congress (regardless of which client the lobbyist represents on the issue). Similarly, in case the number of bills is less important than the fact that the two share an interest in at least one bill, I estimate whether or not the Member sponsors a bill the group is lobbying on. I expect the number of matching bills, or *bill overlap*, to be positively linked to the number of meetings between the two actors.

2.2.3 Members' Power in the Legislature

The second component of the theory of access posits that lobbyists have greater access to legislators who are relatively less powerful in the legislature. While all Members benefit from legislative and campaign assistance from lobbyists, there is considerable variability in the value that Members place on the various kinds of lobbyist-provided benefits. The basic job description of a Member of Congress is to participate, to varying extents, in bill sponsorship, committee hearings, floor debates, voting, and the distribution of earmarks, tax breaks, and other pork. For some Members, these legislative activities constitute the majority of their workdays. For others, there is considerably more time left over that can be expended by meeting with some of the hundreds of lobbyists who visit Capitol Hill every day.

Longer-serving Members have several important advantages over junior Members that make spending time with lobbyists notably less attractive for senior Members. First, because of their greater electoral vulnerability, Members early in their congressional careers are generally more interested than senior Members in maximizing their supportive constituency (Fenno 1978). Relative to freshmen and more junior Members, senior Members have had many more opportunities to take positions, advertise, and credit-claim (Mayhew 1974).

Established Members are better able to reach beyond family and friends to the outer concentric circles of the primary, electoral, and geographic constituencies (Fenno 1978). Relatedly, more senior Members have developed an astute understanding of their constituents' preferences. They have likely provided pork and constituent service to the state or district for years. The party of a legislator who has survived one or more terms almost certainly wishes to keep them in office. Thus, parties assist with reelection activities and fundraising. In other words, more senior Members have established ongoing fundraising machines.

Second, seniority gives Members a greater level of specialist knowledge and resources that makes them less reliant on lobbyists for information and legislative support. On a committee, long experience gives Members expertise in the policy areas under the committee's jurisdiction. More junior Members must focus on many dense issue areas until they develop a narrower expertise in a more manageable number of subjects. After they have been reelected a few times, Members can devote more time to crafting whatever they consider to be good public policy (Fenno 1978). They do not need to rely on outside sources, including lobbyists, for information about current law and its implementation, the merits and demerits of proposed policies, and the finer details of the policy as it was or could be adopted. While the Congressional Research Service produces reports on subjects of broad interest and supplies custom reports in response to Member requests, these may be too slow or too general for Members to use, especially when lobbyists generally are quick to be helpful and supply all requested information. Relative to more junior Members, it is undoubtedly the case that experienced Members have higher doses of what Denzau and Munger (1986) call legislative capability.

Third, seniority and the record of legislative accomplishments that seniority allows Members to establish create opportunities for Members to gain significant power in the legislature. Members in prestige and leadership roles have easy access to the political information they need, and they are sought after as employers by the most experienced and well-regarded staff on Capitol Hill. Like all professionals, congressional staff tend to move up the ranks as their skills and experience develop, from junior Members to senior, from House to Senate, and from less desirable to more desirable committees. This fact is important, as skilled congressional staff have been shown to be a valuable legislative resource (Goodman-Bacon 2018).

The advantages possessed by Members of Congress reelected multiple times reduce their need to rely on lobbyists for political and technical information. In contrast to freshmen Members of Congress, lobbyists have the time and motivation to focus on a narrow set of policies that exist or might exist. Lobbyists can provide legislators with needed insights about the likely direction of a policy debate or the electoral implications of particular decisions.

An example of the kind of information that is provided by lobbyists and valued – to various degrees – by congressional offices can be found in the lobby group's "leave-behind." When lobbyists attend meetings, they very often leave behind a one-page document explaining the group's immediate policy goals in quickly comprehensible bullet points (see Figure 2.1). When staff meet with lobbyists in the absence of the Member, as very often occurs, staff typically summarize the meeting for the Member afterward in person or in writing. Staffers who are newer to a policy issue may borrow liberally from the language of the leave-behind document when they prepare or sum up the meeting for their bosses. Most of the time this is a safe strategy, since staff usually possess a sense of whether the boss is likely to support the group's request or not. However, when Members are less knowledgeable about the issue, or their position has not yet been fully determined, and staff members present the issue to the Member exactly the way it is framed in the leave-behind, it creates a risk of biasing the Member in the group's preferred direction – without the Member understanding they are being co-opted.

More experienced staff and Members, meanwhile, do not need a leave-behind to know what the issue is. During their careers, they have probably been lobbied by others who prefer the same or even a different solution to the policy problem, and so they know the pros and cons of supporting the group's request. These Members may serve on committees with jurisdiction over the policy area. They may have voted on or even written legislation on the topic. Even if they are not experts on the subject, senior Members have ample access to lobbyists as well as more neutral experts who can provide alternative viewpoints as needed.

While more legislatively productive and powerful Members are very desirable targets for lobbyists to focus on, it is consequently much harder for lobbyists to get these legislators' attention. High-prestige Members receive many requests for lobby meetings. More senior members of committees devote more time and energy to their committee responsibilities, especially if they chair the committee. They have less time to be lobbied, and that lobbying time must be divided among all

PHARMACEUTICAL CARE MANAGEMENT ASSOCIATION

<u>Mandated PBM Disclosure Increases Prescription Drug Costs for Consumers and Employers</u>
(January 2009)

Mandated PBM Disclosure Would Increase Drug Costs

- Legislation requiring public disclosure of private PBM contract terms would increase managed drug spending by $127 billion over the next decade—an increase of 4.1 percent, according to a 2007 study by PricewaterhouseCoopers.[1]

- Congress rejected the inclusion of a PBM disclosure mandate as part of the Medicare Modernization Act when the Congressional Budget Office determined such a mandate would cost taxpayers $40 billion over 10 years. [2]

PBM Disclosure Mandates Have No Benefit to Consumers

- The Federal Trade Commission (FTC) has warned several states that legislation requiring PBM disclosure could increase costs and "undermine the ability of some consumers to obtain the pharmaceuticals and health insurance they need at a price they can afford."[3]

- In California, the Governor vetoed PBM disclosure legislation citing the FTC's warnings against such an approach.[4]

- "Consumers make purchasing decisions based on the price and value of goods and services, without regard to a vendor's cost of production," according to the FTC.[5] Basically, consumers want the best price and value for their prescription drugs and do not need the details of a PBM's complicated cost structure in order to make smart purchasing decisions.

- The FTC also warns that mandated disclosure would make it more difficult for PBMs to generate cost savings and may actually cause a decrease in cost savings. Such requirements would lead to an increase in healthcare costs that would ultimately fall on the shoulders of American consumers.

Too Much Disclosure Chills Competition

- The Department of Justice and the FTC issued a July 2004 report noting that "states should consider the potential costs and benefits of regulating pharmacy benefit transparency" while pointing out that "vigorous competition in the marketplace for PBMs is more likely to arrive at an optimal level of transparency than regulation of those terms."[6]

- "Just as competitive forces encourage PBMs to offer their best price and service combination to health plan sponsors to gain access to subscribers, competition should also encourage disclosure of the information health plan sponsors require to decide with which PBM to contract," according to the FTC.[7]

- Mandating public disclosure of price negotiation strategies and contract terms will damage competition by giving drug companies and retail pharmacies the upper hand in negotiations, thereby driving up drug costs for PBM clients and ultimately consumers.

Forced Disclosure Tramples Intellectual Property Rights and Contracts

- Forcing PBMs to publicly disclose the terms of business contracts violates the Takings Clause of the U.S. Constitution – effectively taking PBM property for public use without just compensation or legal protection.

- PBMs already appropriately address disclosure of financial arrangements in their contractual agreements with their clients. Clients also contract for audit rights to verify the accuracy of the disclosed information.

The Bottom Line

- PBMs are working everyday to make medicines more affordable for consumers. Any legislation that removes or dilutes the power of PBMs to negotiate deep discounts will only result in higher prices for consumers and higher profits for drug companies and retail pharmacies.

FIGURE 2.1 An example of a lobby group's "leave behind"

who request it (though not necessarily *evenly* across all who request it). Lobbyists thus face a trade-off: They can seek out meetings with high-importance legislators who may not be motivated to pay much attention to what the lobbyist has to say, or spend the same amount of time requesting and attending meetings with a larger number of lower-powered Members who may be happy to cooperate with the lobbyist, even though such Members have limited ability to carry out the group's legislative requests.

If higher-powered Members have greater ability to influence legislation than lower-powered Members, then for lobby groups, actually changing the language or votes surrounding a policy proposal becomes very difficult. This phenomenon is what I call the inverse pull of lobbying influence and legislator power.

2.2.4 Committee Membership

To compare Members' relative power in the legislature, I rely primarily on their committee assignments and their ranks on each committee. Seniority is embedded in these two factors, so I do not control separately for seniority in the chamber.

Committees are known as the workshops of Congress. Historically, committee members, and most importantly committee chairs, make the majority of decisions about what provisions a bill contains. While a number of scholars argue that the gravitational center of policy-making in Congress has shifted in recent years from committees to party leadership (Sinclair 2016; Curry and Lee 2020), committees still frequently write the first drafts of legislation. The distribution of issues and Members across committees allows legislators to focus on a narrow set of issues at a time. For example, serving on the Finance committee, which oversees the entire Medicare program, will make its members conversant with topics such as hospital ceiling hoists, the utilization rates of MRI machines, and employer-subsidized wellness programs.

Members' electoral incentives push them toward working on particular committees, as noted earlier. Especially early in their careers, Members request to serve on committees of particular interest to their constituents (Fenno 1978). Later, the Member may be more focused on gaining power and prestige in the legislature, and therefore may seek to be on Finance, Appropriations, or the House Rules committee (Fenno 1978). The House Rules committee is in fact an extension of the leadership's power to control the agenda and influence the outcome of legislation. Deering and Smith (1997) use these motivations to sort congressional committees into a few types. There is a significant literature that uses Members' requests to transfer between committees as an indicator of which committees are more or less desirable (Bullock 1973; Munger 1988; Munger and Torrent 1993; Groseclose and Stewart 1998; Stewart and Groseclose 1999); these studies generally reinforce the simple coding scheme of Deering and Smith (1997), which is therefore what I use here. Deering and Smith (1997) classify committees according to the benefits Members get from serving on them, as follows, in descending order of desirability:

1. *Prestige and influence committees* are those that most Members wish to be on because they have the most influence over public policy and attract the most attention. These committees are the two Appropriations committees; the two revenue committees, Ways and Means (in the House) and Finance (in the Senate), both of which control tax policy as well as many decisions about how that revenue is spent (such as all decisions regarding Medicare); the House Rules committee; and the two Budget committees. In addition, Members who are in leadership positions (i.e., majority or minority leaders and whips) are also counted as being on prestige committees.
2. *Policy committees* work in technically complex policy areas such as health care, housing, education, and foreign relations.[1]
3. *Constituent committees* are focused on particular constituencies, such as farmers, veterans, and Native Americans.[2]
4. *Unrequested or burden committees* are those that no one requests to be on, because their work is not publicly rewarding, such as committees dedicated to government operations and ethics.[3]

I expect that Members on prestige committees, and Members in leadership posts, will have less time available to meet with lobbyists than members of policy and constituent committees. The more elite members of prestige committees, as well as Members in the party leadership, have duties other Members do not have, such as counting and whipping votes and holding or attending party strategy meetings. Consequently, prestige committee members and those in leadership roles are likely to have more than the average number of meetings with fellow Members and staff. Members of policy and constituent

---

[1] These committees include those whose names contain the following phrases: Homeland Security, Labor, Banking, Commerce, Education, Energy, Financial Services, Foreign Affairs, International Relations, Health, Judiciary, Resources, Government Oversight, Intelligence, and the Joint Committees on Taxation and Economics.

[2] These committees include those whose names contain the following phrases: Merchant Marine, District of Columbia, National Security, Aging, Agriculture, Armed Services, Environment, Indian Affairs, Science, Small Business, Veterans, Transportation, and Public Works.

[3] These committees include those whose names contain the following phrases: Ethics, House Administration, House Oversight, Library, Post Office, Printing, Rules and Administration, and Standards of Official Conduct.

committees, meanwhile, have more reason than party leaders to meet with lobbyists who specialize in a subject area. And for members of the burden committees – who are mostly the more junior Members – developing one's skill set and reputation is likely to be facilitated by meeting with lobbyists more frequently, and with a broader set of lobbyists.

2.2.5 Member Rank on Committees

The highest-ranking member of a committee, known as the chairman or (far less often) chairwoman, has the most power on a committee. Depending somewhat on the internal rules of the committee, chairs set the agenda, decide what hearings and meetings will occur and when, select witnesses, speak first, control who is allowed to speak and for how long, and so on. The highest-ranking member of the minority party also has some power: Ranking members typically select their own witnesses, recognize members from their side to speak, and consent to certain decisions by the chair. But as distance grows between each member's seat and the center of the dais, committee rank decreases, and with it, the power to speak, vote, attract media attention, and influence committee decision-making.

Rank on a committee is mostly determined by the length of time served on the committee. When multiple new Members join a committee at the same time, as in a new congress, committees use tie-breaking rules, starting with length of service in the chamber. Thus, rank is an internally decided indicator of a member's ability to control what happens in committee.

A member's committee power varies over time in an upward direction as their seniority increases and as they are assigned to more prestigious committees, though it can stall or fall if their party loses majority status. Data on committee assignments come from Stewart and Woon (2017) with my gratitude.

To calculate the power of Members' committee assignments, I adapt the commonly used statistical formula for expected value, where expected value is equal to the value of the benefit multiplied by the probability of actually getting the benefit. My modified formula estimates committee power as the importance of the committee multiplied by the Member's rank on the committee. Since Members serve on multiple committees at a time, I then average the Member's committee power across all of his or her concurrent committee assignments. The resulting measure, *power of*

Member's committee assignments, is expected to be negatively associated with the frequency with which the Member meets with lobbyists.[4]

Figure 2.2 shows the relationship between Members' seniority in the House or Senate and my estimate of their committee power, highlighting the names of the Members' whose schedules I have. It shows that with greater seniority comes greater committee power. It also shows that the Members whose schedules I use in this chapter are collectively typical of the whole of Congress in terms of seniority and committee power status.

To summarize my expectations about the importance of Members' status in the legislature: Legislators with greater *committee power*, defined as being on more powerful committees (or in party leadership), and having higher ranks within those committees, should have fewer meetings with lobbyists than other Members. Perhaps counterintuitively from this, it follows that there is an inherent limitation on the ability of interest groups to influence the principal content of major legislation. And this is a reason to expect null effects of lobbying.

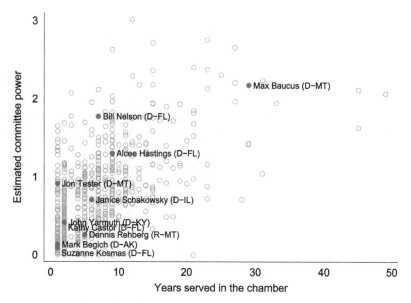

FIGURE 2.2 Relationship between seniority in Congress and estimated committee power

---

[4] Committee importance, committee rank, and committee power are all standardized so that the highest possible values are coded as 1 and lowest possible values coded as 0.

2.3 THE SALIENCE OF THE LOBBYIST'S REQUEST

We have discussed how a lobbyist's usefulness can increase their access to a Member, and that a lobbyist's usefulness is enhanced when the lobbyist is working on legislation authored by the Member, as well as when the lobbyist provides valuable campaign assistance to the Member. We have also seen that as a Member's power and prestige in the legislature increases, the Member is less available to be lobbied. The third component of my theory of access argues that if the salience of the lobbyist's issue is low for the legislator's constituents, a lobbyist's access to a legislator is likely to be greater.

Members are incentivized to introduce bills their constituents care about. The salience surrounding issues about which Members introduce bills and constituents care is, by definition, high. Yet mutual interest in a bill, and the policy knowledge of interested lobbyists, leads Members to have more meetings with the lobbyists working on the bill. The greater importance of usefulness over salience is due to legislators' tendency to prioritize position-taking and credit-claiming activities in order to enhance their chances of reelection.

But when a lobbyist does not want to draw public attention to their policy-seeking activities on an issue, they should seek meetings with Members who are *not* very interested in the issue. If we assume that Members tend to serve on committees that have jurisdiction over the issues and industries most relevant to their constituents, then lobbyists seeking to minimize scrutiny will be more likely to request meetings with those Members who are *not* on committees that have jurisdiction over the industry or the issues on which the lobbyist works the most. Such Members may be more open to persuasion than highly interested Members, especially if the legislator stands to obtain some other benefit from the lobbyist, such as campaign assistance or political information. Lower salience means the public is unlikely to notice a meeting between a lobbyist and a Member, making it less risky for the Member to perform legislative acts requested by the lobby group and for the lobbyist to provide campaign assistance that helps the Member. Lobbyists' behavior in this situation is the very definition of stealth lobbying.

2.3.1 Issue Overlap

To capture the overlap of issue interests between lobbyist and Member, I compare the issue areas a Member works in by virtue of his or her committee assignments. I rely on each committee's bylaws, which are posted on the committee websites. I matched these with the seventy-nine issue areas from which groups choose when they file lobby disclosure reports each quarter for each client. The *number of matching issue areas* is a count of the number of issue areas, among the seventy-nine, on which the lobbyist represents a client or employer *and* the Member served on a committee with jurisdiction over the issue between 2007 and 2010. However, I exclude from this variable any issue area on which the lobbyist and Member already exhibit *bill overlap*. I expect the number of matching issue areas, or *issue overlap*, to be negatively associated with the number of meetings.

2.3.2 Industry Overlap

As with a shared interest in the same issue, when a lobbyist and a Member share an interest in the same industry, salience is higher. To measure industry overlap, I matched each committee's jurisdictions, as listed in its bylaws, to the Center for Responsive Politics' 459+ industry codes. I expect *industry overlap*, defined as the number of industry codes that are both represented by the lobbyist and over which the Member has committee jurisdiction, to be negatively associated with the number of meetings between them.

To summarize my expectations for this chapter, I expect, primarily, that Members are more likely to meet with lobbyists who are useful to them. The usefulness of a lobbyist to a legislator is considered higher when the lobbyist gives the Member campaign assistance and when the lobbyist and legislator work on the same legislation. Second, I expect Members with greater committee power to have fewer meetings with lobbyists. And third, having controlled for overlapping bills, I expect the number of meetings to be greater when the salience of the lobbyist's issues and of their clients' industries is lower for the Member and her constituents.

2.4 DATA ON MEMBERS' DAILY SCHEDULES

To test my theory of access, I measure access very directly as the number of meetings between a lobbyist and a Member of Congress per unit time. I have therefore created a dataset out of the published schedules of a diverse set of Members of Congress over a four-year period.

While we cannot know for sure why some Members release their schedules and others do not, the selection of Members whose schedules have been captured include House Members (seven) and senators (four), men (eight) and women (three), representatives of larger states (California, Illinois, and Florida) and smaller states (Montana, Kentucky, and Alaska), whose seniority in the chamber ranges from zero to thirty-six years. There may be a peer-pressure effect: Democrats are more likely to publish their schedules than Republicans (nine versus two) and Members from two states, Montana and Florida, are especially likely to publish their schedules (four Members each).

There is some variation in how schedules are presented. Senators' schedules are much more detailed than House Members' schedules; the latter may even be a list of "visitors" rather than a minute-by-minute plan for the day. Meeting times are not always given, and for some Members travel itineraries are given while for others time spent traveling is just blocked off. There is also evidence that offices sanitize the published version of their schedules. For example, one Member repeatedly meets with an undescribed "Eric Newman," who on further investigation is a purveyor of cigars in the district. Evidently, the Member did not want to spread the word that they were taking meetings with the tobacco industry. Schedules do not identify lobbyists as such; more often they are described by the city or area in the state or district they are tied to, or for lobbyists from national organizations, the name of the organization, rather than any individual names, is mentioned. But this information is often enough for me to identify a lobbyist or lobbying client.

To convert the schedules into analyzable data, I first pasted the lists of Members, events, and dates into a spreadsheet and delimited them. Then, with the assistance of string matching for key words that were consistently connected with one of the following activities, I coded each event type as one of: congressional (e.g., "floor," "committee"), constituent ("city of," "constituent," "Florida Department of," "student(s) from"), party ("caucus," "Democrat," "whip"), press ("media," "editorial board," "WMNF [a local radio station]," "taping"), travel ("depart," "arrive," "travel"), personal ("family time," "personal time," "haircut"), and lobbying. I spent the majority of my coding time confirming that each event I coded as "lobbying" was in fact a meeting between an outside interest group or lobbyist and the Member or their office.

I then divided events into multiple observations, one for each guest or group mentioned on the schedule. This allows me to link individual lobbyists to the list of registered lobbyists filed by lobby groups with the House and Senate. In total, the data describe eleven Members' schedules and contain 21,503 person-events (or 20,619 events, if we ignore the number of attendants).

Next, to assess how available each Member is to lobbyists, I created a measure capturing the duration of each event. In most cases, and for all senators, I inferred duration by differencing the start time of the event and the start time of the following event. When there were gaps, such as at the end of the day, I used devices such as estimating when the day ended on other days or using the average length of similar events for that Member. These duration estimates are used in Figures 2.4 and 2.5. However, a significant minority of lobbying events were not discussions in the Member's office but took the form of receptions, luncheons, speaking engagements, tours, and briefings; I still coded these events as lobbying, though their durations are notably longer than the 15–30 minutes allocated for meetings in the office. As a result of this variation, and due more generally to the necessarily imprecise coding of the duration of time spent lobbying, in the models I instead use a count of the number of named people (or groups, if no individuals' names are given) the Member meets with, rather than the minutes scheduled.

2.5 A CLOSE-UP VIEW: HEALTH CARE LOBBYING

Senator Max Baucus was the chief architect of the legislation that became Obamacare. As such, it is convenient that he is one of the Members of Congress who made their schedules available. Therefore, I am able to divide Baucus's scheduled meetings with lobbyists according to whether the individual or group listed on the schedule is known to work on, or listed as meeting about, health care issues (Table 2.1).

As discussed in Chapter 1, Senator Baucus was the chairman of the Finance committee as it wrote health reform legislation, which was and is still regarded as the most powerful committee in Congress. As predicted by the inverse pull hypothesis, this status means Senator Baucus has less time to be lobbied than Members not on this committee. Baucus's schedule shows an average of four meetings per week with interest groups during the period of health reform, a rate significantly lower than the average of nearly seven meetings per week per Member of the full dataset. This difference supports the inverse pull hypothesis that Members who have the greatest power in the legislature are subject to so many demands that they do not spend a great deal of time with lobbyists. Meanwhile, the usefulness hypothesis predicts that Members will spend more time with interest groups working on the issues on which the Members are also

TABLE 2.1 *The most frequent health care visitors to Senator Baucus, 2008–10*

Lobby Group	Number of Meetings
Service Employees International Union	11
Pharmaceutical Research and Manufacturers Association of America	8
Advanced Medical Technology Association	7
America's Health Insurance Plans	6
American Hospital Association	6
American Medical Association	6
Business Roundtable	6
Catholic Health Association	6
Federation of American Hospitals	6
AARP (formerly the American Association of Retired Persons)	4
Physician Specialty Groups	3
Alliance for Quality Nursing Home Care	2
Amgen	2
DaVita Healthcare Partners	2
Delta Air Lines	2
Edison Electric Institute	2
National Committee to Preserve Social Security and Medicare	2

working. Baucus's schedule also supports this hypothesis: In the period between when Baucus first releases his "Call to Action" white paper and when the Senate votes on the Finance bill (the fourth quarter of 2008 through the first quarter of 2010), he reduces meetings with nonhealth lobbyists to 3.5 per week (Figure 2.3). Throughout the full period of 2007–10, Baucus has an average of 5.5 meetings per week with health lobbyists and four meetings per week with lobbyists working on other issues. Relative to the other Members whose schedules I have, this is more health meetings, but significantly fewer meetings overall: The average number of nonhealth meetings per Member per week is 6.8, while the average number of health care meetings per Member per week is 6.4. These differences show the increased importance to Baucus of meeting with groups working on an issue on which he is very focused.

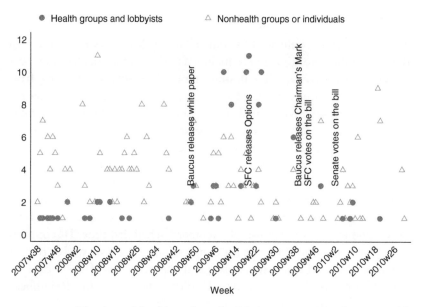

FIGURE 2.3 Number of health and nonhealth interest groups that met with Senator Max Baucus per week

Figure 2.3 shows in filled circles the massive increase in the number of meetings Senator Baucus takes with health care lobbyists during the most intense period of writing the bill. In 2008 before the election, Baucus meets more frequently with nonhealth interest groups than with health groups. After Obama's election, when it quickly becomes clear that health care would be the number one priority of the new president, health lobbyists turn their attention to Finance Committee Chairman Max Baucus. Their lobbying is most intense in the spring and early summer of 2009 as the Options and then the Chairman's Mark – all of which Baucus has control over – are finalized. During markup of the bill, health lobbyists give the very busy Baucus a break, and after the Finance committee votes on the health reform legislation in mid-October, the number of meetings with health groups drops dramatically while meetings with nonhealth groups return to their 2008 numbers. These patterns are consistent with the notion that the stealthiest lobbying occurs early in the bill drafting process: Later, when the legislation is debated by the full committee and reaches its apex in the media, the players are on display: lobbying cannot be stealthy – nor, therefore, can it be as effective.

2.6 DESCRIBING HOW MEMBERS ALLOCATE THEIR TIME

Figures 2.4 and 2.5 illustrate variance among Members regarding how they spend their working hours. Included in the graphs are all of the seven categories of activity, even if some types of events are missing from a Member's schedule. We see, for example, that Alcee Hastings does not list party or press activities while John Doolittle is the only House Member in the data whose schedule includes personal time. Senators, meanwhile, all schedule in personal time. Senators' schedules are explicit about how much time is spent doing congressional business, including votes and presiding over the Senate (a chore for freshmen Members).

Several observations can be made from these graphs. First, note that for all of the senators, and all but two House Members, congressional business is the most intensive use of Members' scheduled time. Discounting John Yarmuth, who does not list congressional business, we see that all but one of the House Members spend the plurality of their time on congressional business. For John Doolittle, who was the Republican Deputy Whip, party business takes more time.

Second, lobbying by outside interests constitutes a significant component of Members' daily schedules. After congressional business, meetings with lobbyists take more time than any other activity, or 22 percent of Members' scheduled time. If constituent events also count as lobbying, then lobbying takes 33 percent of Members' time.

Third, there is considerable variance across Members. Denny Rehberg spends 30 percent of his time in lobbyist meetings, relative to Max Baucus's 5 percent. John Doolittle spends 31 percent of his time on congressional business, while Max Baucus spends 72 percent of his time on congressional activities.

The confluence of multiple Members' schedules in a single state allows interesting comparisons to be made. Even holding constant the constituency, time period, and party, we see clear differences among Members. In Florida, Senator Bill Nelson most frequently visits with national groups such as the American Israel Public Affairs Committee (AIPAC), the Independent Insurance Agents & Brokers, the American Hospital Association, and space contractor Northrup Grumman (Figure 2.6). Nelson also meets frequently with NASA (Nelson was an astronaut who flew on the Shuttle), Florida citrus growers and farm bureaus, and the Moffitt Cancer Center. These repeat visitors illustrate several facets of Nelson's interests and role in the Congress – his position on the Finance committee as it was writing health reform, his personal interest in NASA

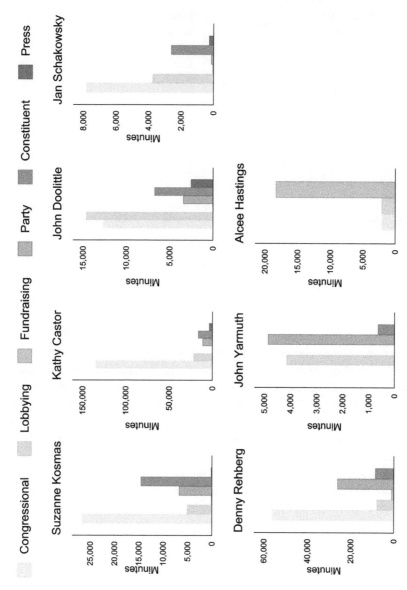

FIGURE 2.4 How House Members allocate their time, according to their published schedules

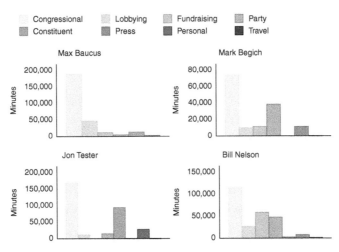

FIGURE 2.5 How senators allocate their time, according to their published schedules

(and its contractors), the large proportion of Jews interested in Israel in his state, and Florida's agricultural industry. The other Florida Democrats in the data have overlapping but quite varied meeting schedules, as seen in Figure 2.6. Only AIPAC and Planned Parenthood meet with all four Members. Representative Hastings meets with the Air Traffic Controllers Association ten times, while Representative Kosmas and Senator Nelson do not meet with this group. Universities in Florida meet with their local representative (and senator) frequently, but not with other Florida Members. This level of variation among Members of Congress from the same party and same state demonstrates that lobbyists choose their targets deliberately – and Members choose their visitors carefully as well.

Figure 2.7 shows that Montana's two Democratic senators are lobbied by two distinct groups: those from Montana and those representing the nation as a whole. Senator Jon Tester repeatedly visits with the most active Montana-focused lobbyists, including the two state universities, the major Indian tribe, the Montana Bankers, and the American Legion. Senator Max Baucus has no meetings with the universities, the bankers, or the Legion. Instead, his frequent visitors are the national business groups Business Roundtable, the US Chamber of Commerce, and the National Federation of Independent Businesses; the Service Employees International Union; and health care lobbyists from the Pharmaceutical Research and Manufacturers

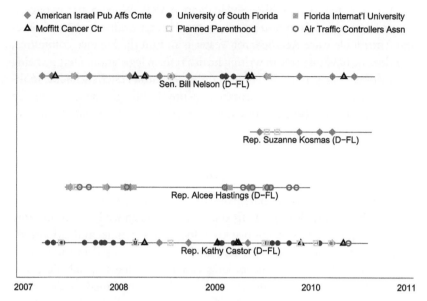

FIGURE 2.6 Scheduled meetings between lobby groups and Florida Members of Congress, among groups with ten or more meetings

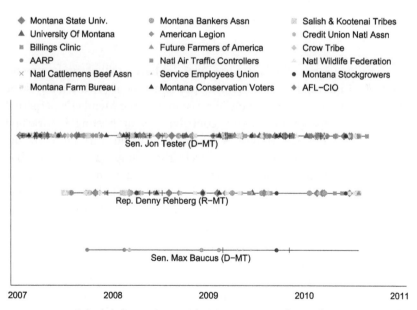

FIGURE 2.7 Scheduled meetings with Montana Members of Congress in the dataset, among these with ten or more meetings

of America, Blue Cross Blue Shield, and AARP. While Senator Baucus chairs the Finance committee as it writes the first draft of what becomes the Affordable Care Act, Senator Tester is not on the Finance committee, nor does he have any role in writing health reform legislation. Despite being in a different party and a different chamber, Senator Tester's schedule looks much more similar to Representative Denny Rehberg's, with a focus on local Montana concerns, than either of them resembles Senator Baucus's schedule.

2.7 EXPLAINING HOW MEMBERS ALLOCATE THEIR TIME

Beyond the observation that groups seem to target specific Members repeatedly for their lobbying efforts, what more can we learn about how lobbyists and Members choose to allocate their time and attention? Table 2.2 gives summary statistics for the variables used in the models presented in Table 2.3. The models test the Usefulness, Salience, and Inverse Pull hypotheses independently and in a combined model. Each Member is paired with each lobbyist or lobby group that ever visits them. The models uses negative binomial regression to predict the number of meetings the lobbyist in the dyad has with the Member in the dyad during the four-year period.

2.7.1 The Usefulness Hypothesis

The usefulness hypothesis predicts that lobbyists will secure a greater number of meetings with a Member per unit time if (1) the lobbyist or the lobby group provides financial assistance to the Member's perpetual reelection campaign by making contributions or hosting fundraising events and if (2) the lobbyist is working on a bill introduced by the Member. The models show definitively that campaign assistance has a positive and significant effect on the expected number of meetings between the Member and the lobbyist (Table 2.3). In the usefulness model, a single contribution or fundraiser is associated with moving the predicted number of meetings from 2.1 to 2.2, and at the maximum number of contributions or fundraisers, sixteen, the model predicts 4.7 meetings will occur.

What we cannot tell from this relationship is whether the lobbyist, having learned that a bill has been introduced, then requests to meet with the bill's author, or whether – more stealthily – the lobbyist requests the legislation before it is introduced. Since 2008, lobbyists have been

TABLE 2.2 *Descriptive statistics for the variables in the models*

	Min.	Max.	Mean	Med.
Total number of meetings between the Member and the group	1	28	2.1	1
Number of meetings between the Member and the group per year	1	9	1.2	1
Number of meetings between the Member and a named individual lobbyist	0	6	0.63	0
Number of contributions or fundraisers the group or lobbyist gives to the Member	0	16	0.27	0
Whether the group or lobbyist gives any contributions or fundraisers to the Member (yes/no)	0	1	0.09	0
Member sponsors a bill the group lobbies on (yes/no)	0	1	0.01	0
– Number of matching bills (*bill overlap*)	0	16	0.03	0
Member's committee oversees the lobbyist's industry (yes/no)	0	1	0.25	0
– Number of matching industries (*industry overlap*)	0	70	0.88	0
Lobbyist works on an issue over which Member's committee has jurisdiction, apart from matching bills (yes/no)	0	1	0.72	1
– Number of matching issue areas, apart from matching bills (*issue overlap*)	0	71	5.5	2
Power of Member's committee assignments (*committee power*)	0	1	0.14	0.08

required to report the bill number of all bills they are working on (before that, they instead reported vaguely that they were working on "tax law" or "health issues"). But the information is recorded only quarterly, and lobbyists still do not have to report details about specific meetings, such as whom they lobby, when, and what the meeting is about. Thus, it could easily be that the lobbyist persuades the Member to sponsor a bill that is later recorded under its bill number in the lobbyist's disclosure forms – and the lobbying disclosure data would not reveal this.

However, my data about Members' daily schedules allow me to identify which comes first – the bill or the meeting. To do this I compare, for those lobbyist–Member pairs that have any degree of bill overlap, the date the bill was introduced by the Member against the date of the meeting(s) between them. For 59 percent of the Member-group dyads that contain matching bills (thirty-three of fifty-six), the schedules show at least one

TABLE 2.3 *Predicting the number of meetings between a lobbyist and a Member of Congress*

	Number of meetings			
	Usefulness hypothesis	Inverse pull hypothesis	Salience hypothesis	Hypotheses combined
Number of contributions or fundraisers (*campaign assistance*)	**0.05** (0.01)			**0.04** (0.01)
Number of matching bills (*bill overlap*)	**0.10** (0.02)		**0.08** (0.02)	**0.11** (0.02)
Power of Member's committee assignments (*committee power*)		**−0.39** (0.06)		**−0.47** (0.06)
Number of matching industry codes (*industry overlap*)			**−0.03** (0.00)	**−0.02** (0.00)
Number of matching issue areas apart from bill areas (*issue overlap*)			**0.02** (0.00)	**0.01** (.00)
Constant	**0.72** (0.01)	**0.79** (0.01)	**0.67** (0.01)	**0.72** (0.02)
Ln alpha	**−0.99** (0.03)	**−0.99** (0.03)	**−1.01** (0.03)	**−1.02** (0.03)
Observations	7120	7120	7120	7120
Pseudo-R^2	0.00	0.00	0.00	0.01
Probability > chi^2	0.00	0.00	0.00	0.00

Notes: The models contain negative binomial regression coefficients. Standard errors appear below each estimate in parentheses. Bold coefficients are significant at $p < 0.01$. The universe is all Members and all lobbyists who appear in the published schedules between 2007 and 2010. As such, every lobbyist in the data met with a Member at least once. The unit of analysis is the lobby group–Member pair. Contributions from either the group's PAC or the individual are included in the number of contributions. Fundraisers are hosted by the group itself or by the individual listed on the schedule. Members' committee assignment power is defined as the prestige of each committee the Member sits on, on a four-point scale (as defined earlier), multiplied by the rank of the Member on that committee. *Committee power* is transformed so that higher numbers denote higher rank and more prestige.

meeting between the pair occurs *before* the introduction of the shared bill (and more may have occurred before the schedule data began). In fact, at least half of the 168 meetings in Member-group pairs in which there are matching bills occur before the bill is introduced. These pre-legislation meetings behind closed doors are a quintessential example of stealth lobbying.

2.7.2 The Inverse Pull Hypothesis

The inverse pull hypothesis argues that greater legislative power, as a function of Members' committee memberships and leadership status, is expected to affect the amount of time Members devote to meetings with lobbyists. Being lobbied requires the consent of the legislator, and legislators' time, as Fenno argued, is a scarce resource. Members of Congress, and their employed schedulers, agree to meetings with lobbyists if they have the time and motivation to do so. Thus, I argued that Members whose committee commitments are more intense should consequently have less time for meetings with lobbyists relative to Members with lighter committee responsibilities.

Committee power is defined, as explained previously, as the mean of the Member's committee prestige or power, multiplied by the reverse of their rank on the committee, so that for both variables larger numbers denote more power. We see in the inverse pull model of Table 2.3 that committee power is a significant negative predictor of the number of meetings the lobbyist will get with that Member. The most powerful Member in the data, Max Baucus, has on average one meeting per year with a given lobby group (Figure 2.7), while the two least powerful Members, Kathy Castor (Figure 2.6) and Jon Tester (Figure 2.7), hold up to nine meetings per year per group.

2.7.3 The Salience Hypothesis

The salience hypothesis predicts that lobby groups that would prefer not to attract public notice will seek access to Members for whom an issue is not very salient. When lobbyists and committee members have a lower number of issue areas and industries in common, notwithstanding any overlapping bills, the salience hypothesis predicts that the pair will have a higher number of meetings. This is stealth lobbying.

The third model of Table 2.3 shows that the number of industries (1) that the Member has committee jurisdiction over and (2) the group is involved in – a variable I label *industry overlap* – is, as expected, associated with a lower number of meetings between the two. As the number of overlapping industry codes is changed from zero to the maximum value, seventy, the predicted number of meetings decreases from 1.64 to 0.33 meetings.

Meanwhile, *issue overlap* – the number of issue areas (1) that the Member has committee jurisdiction over and (2) the lobby group publicly disclosed it was working on during the four-year time period – aside from issue areas in which there are overlapping bills – is unexpectedly associated with a greater number of meetings between the Member and group. The latter effect is negligible; however, the predicted number of meetings as we move from zero to the maximum of two (non-bill) overlapping issue areas changes from 1.91 to 1.97 meetings.

2.7.4 Hypotheses Combined

We can now evaluate for the first time how commonalities between legislators and lobbyists affect the probability of meeting together more often, and by putting all variables into the same model, we can determine whether each one is significant when also controlling for the others. Figure 2.8 displays visually the coefficients of the combined model, along with their 95 percent confidence intervals. We see first that campaign assistance, which is the combined number of contributions and fundraising events hosted by the lobbyist on behalf of the member, significantly predicts the number of scheduled meetings between the two, even while controlling for other things the two have in common. The model suggests that each additional contribution or fundraising event is associated with an average of 0.09 additional meetings, on top of the effects of common interests in bills, industries, and issue areas.

The effect of greater numbers of contributions or fundraisers is commensurate with the effect of having more bills in common. Figure 2.9 presents margins from the combined model illustrating that the effect of giving one or more contributions or fundraising events is statistically indistinguishable from the effect of working on one or more of the same bills.

Supporting the inverse pull hypothesis, the combined model illustrated in Figure 2.8 shows the expected negative effect of more powerful Members on the number of meetings a group secures with the Member. Regarding the salience hypothesis, *industry overlap* is negatively associated with the number of meetings granted, as predicted, while *issue overlap* is associated with an unexpected increase in the number of meetings. Industry overlap may thus be a better indicator than issue overlap of the salience of a policy for the Member's constituents.

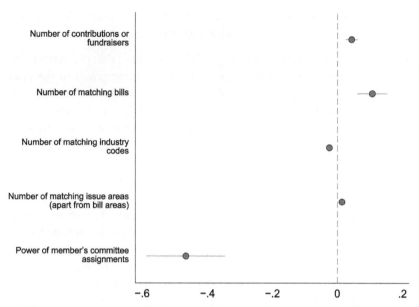

FIGURE 2.8 Factors that predict the number of meetings a lobbyist gets with the Member

Notes. *Markers show negative binomial regression coefficients surrounded by 95 percent confidence intervals. N = 7,120.*

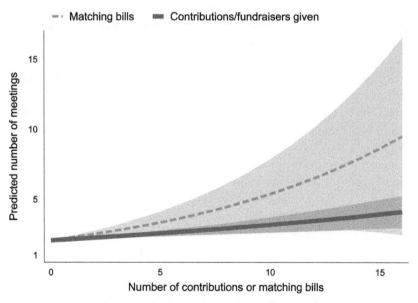

FIGURE 2.9 Predicted effects of the number of contributions from a lobbyist and the number of overlapping bills on the predicted number of meetings between lobbyist and member (based on the combined model)

2.7.5 Predicting Whether a Group Gets More Than One Meeting Per Year with a Member

Having studied Senator Baucus's schedule, I observed that the overwhelming modal length of time between visits by the same group to the same Members was 365 days, give or take just one or two days. This regularity occurs because many groups organize annual "fly-ins" for their group members and supporters flooding Capitol Hill with advocates from all over the country expressing the same message to as many Members of Congress as possible. The frequency of seeming fly-in lobbyist visits suggests that there may really be two categories of lobbyists – those who a Member will see on an annual basis and those who visit more frequently. If so, it suggests that there is something special about lobbyists who get in the door multiple times during the year. In addition, the difference between *some* campaign assistance, bill overlap, industry overlap, or issue overlap, and *none* of these things may be greater than the difference between a little of these things and a lot of these things. Dichotomous variables that describe whether an actor is in or out of a set often explain more than count or continuous measures when we analyze the influence of lobbying on policymaking.

To test these possibilities, I estimated a model that uses dichotomous variables instead of counts for the dependent variable and all explanatory variables. This logit model, illustrated in Figure 2.10, shows again that the presence of campaign assistance is a strong and significant predictor of securing more than one meeting per year with the Member. Lobby groups that contribute to or fundraise for Members of Congress are at least twice as likely to secure multiple meetings with that Member in a year, even controlling for overlapping bills, industries, or issues, as well as the Member's committee power. The strong effect of campaign assistance in this dichotomous model shows that while the number of contributions or fundraisers matters, even one contribution can increase the probability of securing additional meetings per year with the Member. And in addition to being highly significant, the effect of campaign assistance is almost as great as, and is in fact statistically indistinguishable from, bill overlap. It makes sense that if the bill was introduced as a result of meetings between the lobbyist and the Member, and if meetings are more likely to happen when contributions are made, then we should expect that contributions are correlated with bill overlap and that both are related to the incidence of meetings between the two actors.

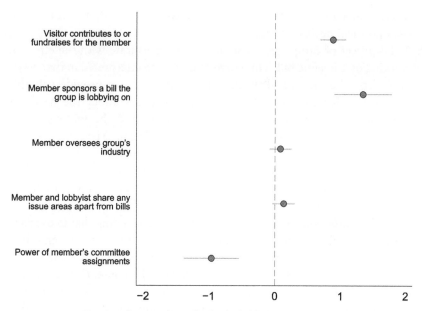

FIGURE 2.10 Factors that predict whether a lobbyist gets one or more than one meeting with the member
Notes. *Markers show logit coefficients surrounded by 95 percent confidence intervals. N = 7,120.*

2.8 DISCUSSION AND CONCLUSIONS

This chapter uses data never used before – the daily schedules of a diverse range of Members of Congress – to test the three key hypotheses of the book, regarding usefulness, the inverse pull, and salience. The dataset of Member schedules contains nearly 25,000 events, nearly 30 percent of which have been identified as meetings between lobbyists and Members of Congress.

The analysis shows that when a lobbyist provides campaign assistance to a Member of Congress, the Member is significantly more likely to grant a greater number of meetings with the lobbyist or group. Lobbyists who provide Members with campaign assistance are at least twice as likely to be granted more than one meeting per year with the Member relative to lobbyists who do not. In addition, more contributions or fundraising events predict more access. Each contribution or fundraiser is associated with an increase of 0.09 additional meetings. This significant relationship is a powerful indicator that money –

whether given first or after the fact – is associated with access to high-level political decision-makers.

The effect of campaign assistance is commensurate with the effect of working on the same bill. This correlation can be interpreted in two ways. Lobbyists who are knowledgeable about an issue can provide valuable technical assistance and information to Members about the need for legislation, the ideal details of the legislation, and the willingness of other groups and Members to support the legislation. Meetings between them are politically defensible, since the lobbyist provides to the legislator appropriate expertise and support. Alternatively, rather than seeking information and advice from a lobbyist, the Member may actually be responding to a request made by the lobbyist to offer the bill in the first place. The latter interpretation is supported by the finding that in dyads in which the lobbyist and the Member share an interest in the same bill, 59 percent meet *before* the introduction of any shared bills – suggesting that lobbyists stealthily request and influence the content of legislation that Members ultimately agree to sponsor. This tendency contrasts with the more common portrayal of lobbyists as status quo defenders reacting to legislative threats (as in Baumgartner et al. 2009).

For lobbyists not working on a bill introduced by a Member, what predicts the Member's openness to meet with them? And for those working on a bill the Member is sponsoring, how can stealthy lobbyists secure even more of a Member's precious time? The answer is campaign assistance. While the number of matching bills is estimated to be stronger than the number of contributions or fundraising events, it is clear that both are important.

Beyond legislative assistance and campaign support, consistent with the inverse pull hypothesis, Members are more likely to meet repeatedly with lobbyists when the prestige of Members' committee assignments, multiplied by the centrality of the Member to each committee, is lower (the inverse pull hypothesis). The results of the salience hypothesis are not as clear in these data: In the negative binomial model, *industry overlap* is negative, as expected, while *issue overlap* is positive, and in the dichotomous model neither *issue overlap* nor *industry overlap* is associated with whether the lobbyist gets more than one meeting per year.

Though scholars have mounds of data about interest groups' lobbying expenditures on different issues in a quarter, we still lack the specifics of which lobbyists meet with which Members, when, and how often. Given these limitations, the present data offer a new, previously unobservable glimpse into how federally elected representatives perform their duties.

Clever lobbyists and lobby groups find ways to make themselves useful to Members of Congress, providing both legislative support and campaign assistance. This chapter demonstrates that Members value the things that lobbyists provide, as evident in their greater willingness to meet with the lobbyists who provide them.

On the bright side, since more powerful Members are less accessible to lobbyist influence relative to less powerful Members, the analysis also suggests that lobbyists' ability to influence congressional policy outcomes is constrained. This finding supports my argument that the purpose of most lobbying is not to enact favorable laws but to secure private benefits found in low-salience legislation – especially if those lobbyists also provide contributions and fundraising.

3

The Strategic Behavior of Individual Lobbyists and Their PACs

For decades, scholars sought to evaluate the influence of lobbying by using the data available to them – political action committee (PAC) contributions. As we have seen, the literature on PACs has been inconclusive about the influence of these labor, public interest, and corporate groups on congressional votes (Lowery 2013). But like a person who searches for their keys under the streetlight because that is all they can see, identifying positive evidence of lobbyists' influence requires looking beyond the obvious. It requires moving into the dark.

In this chapter, I shine a light on recently available data that have scarcely been studied before. I use these data to infer lobbyists' intentions when making campaign contributions. I argue that in the early days of required reporting of individual lobbyists' contributions, lobbyists' stealth efforts were evident – if one looks carefully. Analysis of the new data suggests that whether or not lobbyists' contributions actually do buy anything, individual lobbyists behave as if their contributions might be buying something. Consistent with the usefulness hypothesis, the data hint that lobbyists target and time their contributions strategically to the politicians in a position to help them most – especially when they believe they will not be observed.

3.1 PACS AND CAMPAIGN FINANCE

In 2010, the average successful candidate for Senate spent almost $10 million on the campaign, and the average successful House candidate spent nearly $1.5 million.[1] To spend this much requires constant

---

[1] Center for Responsive Politics 2010. "Election Trends." www.opensecrets.org/overview/election-trends.php?cycle=2010.

fundraising. Making matters more difficult for the candidate, the relatively low limits placed on how much a PAC or an individual – indeed, any donor – can give directly to federal candidates' campaigns necessitate that the money must come from numerous different sources. Contrary to popular belief, federal candidates cannot be bankrolled by one or a few wealthy donors. In 2009–10, as health reform legislation was being drafted and debated, individuals could give no more than $2,400 total to any federal candidate's campaign. Even organizations that represent multinational corporations, whole industries, national labor unions, or other groups are limited to an amount that is today equal to less than a married couple can give – $5,000 per year. As such it requires many, many individual and PAC contributions to reach the amounts necessary to win.

But, you may say, what about SuperPACs? In *Citizens United* v. *FEC* (2010), the high court ruled that the "electioneering communications" rules established in the Bipartisan Campaign Reform Act of 2002 were unconstitutional infringements on free speech. The court decided that, like individuals, groups – corporations, labor unions, or any other organization – may spend unlimited amounts of money on campaign advertising. *Citizens United* led to a decision three months later known as *SpeechNow.org* (2010), in which an appeals court decided that if limits on the speech of organizations were unconstitutional, limiting contributions to such organizations also was unconstitutional, in view of the 1976 *Buckley* v. *Valeo* decision that campaign donations were protected as speech. Together, these court decisions enabled the creation of so-called SuperPACs – an unofficial term that describes the many political organizations now allowed to raise unlimited sums of money and spend as much as they want on election advocacy. So, while it is true that SuperPACs can spend unlimited amounts on campaign advertising (as long as they do not coordinate with the candidate), SuperPACs did not exist before the March 26, 2010, *SpeechNow.org* decision, and therefore there were no SuperPACs during the period in which health reform legislation was written and adopted.

To better understand the role played by PACs historically and today, the remainder of this section and the next provide a brief primer on PACs and campaign finance reform and hint at what campaign assistance might be overlooked if researchers focus solely on PACs.

3.1.1 Why Form a PAC?

PACs are formed by several types of organizations – companies large and small (Disney, Google, the J. H. Fletcher & Co. Mining Company), trade and professional associations (the American Medical Association, the National Association of Surety Bond Producers), labor unions (the AFL-CIO, the Brotherhood of Maintenance of Way Employees), and ideological groups (the League of Conservation Voters, the Value in Electing Women PAC). Yet most interest groups do not have PACs, and those that do are not a random selection of all groups (Grier et al. 1994; Hart 2001). The PAC population is dominated by business interests, especially those with greater profits and more employees (see Brady et al. 2007 for a meta-study of research on corporate political activity). Historically, business PACs, both firms and associations, constitute about two-thirds of the PAC population; in 2008 they comprised 63 percent of all PACs and contributed 69 percent of all PAC contributions.

Forming a PAC, then, seems to be a logical step for business organizations that have enough money to do so. The literature has little to say about the circumstances under which nonbusiness organizations choose to form PACs.

3.1.2 To Whom Do PACs Give?

A few general trends explain which PACs give to which candidates. First, we know that business groups in general like to split their PAC donations between Democrats and Republicans (Eismeier and Pollock 1984; Davis 1988; Kaufman et al. 1988; Powell and Grimmer 2016), though to the extent that they have a preference, business organizations tend to prefer Republican candidates (Gopoian 1984; Apollonio and La Raja 2004; McKay 2010). Meanwhile, labor unions give almost exclusively to Democrats (Sorauf 1988; Rudolph 1999; Apollonio and La Raja 2004), paying attention to Members' voting records on labor issues (Hurd and Sohl 1992; Jansa and Hoyman 2018) and tough races (Poole et al. 1987).

Beyond party, we know that organizations tend to favor those Members of Congress who work closely on the issues the organization is interested in. In particular, PACs often prefer to give to members of the committees that have jurisdiction over their industry (Grier and Munger 1993; Bennett and Loucks 1994; Grier et al. 1994; Loucks and Bennett 2011), and PACs overwhelmingly prefer incumbents (Poole and Romer 1985). These two patterns, along with the fact that so many business-oriented PACs give money to both parties, provide support for the notion that PACs' contributions are intended to facilitate groups' access to as many officeholders as possible.

Importantly, PACs contribute in ways that are different from how individuals contribute. A survey of individual donors contributing $500 or more to federal candidates found shared ideology to be the primary motivator (Francia et al. 2003). Still, about a quarter of individual donors surveyed acknowledged having more material motivations, such as that the candidate would or would continue to treat business "fairly" or be "friendly" to their particular industry (Francia et al. 2003, 68). Bonica (2016) showed that individuals who work at high levels of large corporations tend to contribute to candidates in ways that are more ideological and less strategic compared to the PACs that represent those corporations.

3.1.3 Campaign Finance Regulation during the Health Reform Period

The period between implementation of the Honest Leadership and Open Government Act (HLOGA) on January 1, 2008, and the Supreme Court's *SpeechNow.org* decision – which created SuperPACs – on March 26, 2010, was a unique period of maximum campaign finance reform. HLOGA, preceded by the Bipartisan Campaign Reform Act's 2002 ban on soft money and gifts to Members of Congress, and the lobbying disclosure requirements of the Lobbying Disclosure Act of 1995, had all increased transparency in lobbying and in the role of lobbyists in financing legislators' campaigns. But the *Citizens United* and *SpeechNow.org* decisions of 2010 – both of which loosened campaign finance restrictions – were not yet in effect.

HLOGA was adopted in response to government watchdog organizations and others who wanted to enhance transparency and accountability in election funding. In addition to the new requirement that lobbyists report their *personal* campaign contributions to Members of Congress and congressional candidates, as well as the contributions of any PACs under their control, HLOGA also ended gift-giving from lobbyists to Members and their staff, including travel, sports and theater tickets, free drinks, and meals of all kinds. These rules are enforced by the House and Senate Ethics Committees. The gift ban is strict, and exceptions must be requested in writing. Members and staff may not accept any gifts that exceed $50 or a combined value of $100 per year from anyone other than a family member, though exceptions are routinely made for wedding presents (Luneburg and Susman 2009). Registered lobbyists are not allowed to give anything of value to any Member or congressional staff member except "de minimus" items like pencils and coffee mugs.

As a result of the gift ban, gone are the days when Members could take corporate jets back and forth to the district or state; now they must pay the true cost of junkets (trips) – rather than the cost of an imaginary first-class ticket, as before. Congressmen, senators, and their staff members must pay face value for tickets to any Wizards game or Kennedy Center performance. The gift ban so disrupted interactions between Capitol Hill personnel and everyone else that no one on the Hill or K Street (where the plurality of lobbying firms are located) could claim ignorance about it. Moreover, no Member of Congress would want a journalist or member of the other political party to find out that they or a staff member accepted a banned gift: the threat of losing one's job far outweighs the benefit of a free dinner or plane ride. In effect, the ban is self-enforcing because no one wants to be found in violation of it. And in the modern political environment of interparty hostility and intraparty rivalry, violators will be identified quickly and publicly.

Without soft money, candidates had to rely completely on reportable and small contributions from individuals and PACs. Without lavish gifts to Members, lobbyists were left with only fundraising and direct contributions as means of showing support or building relationships. And without being able to donate to Members' campaigns without public detection, lobbyists' efforts to use money to curry favor with Members and staff were driven onto the public record. As a result, lobbyists' fundraising activities and personal contributions between 2008 and 2010 represent our best opportunity to detect lobbyists' previously secretive efforts to influence congressional politicians.

3.2 ACCESSING PUBLIC POLICY

Chapter 2 models the level of access that lobbyists have to congressional decision-makers. It takes a micro approach, focusing in on eleven Members of Congress and the lobbying that occurred over a four-year window. In this chapter, I take a more macro-level approach, focusing on *all* registered lobbyists' attempts to gain access to politicians during the time frame. Access helps explain numerous phenomena that are not well explained by simple notions that either "money buys votes" or, at the other extreme, "donors give ideologically." As an objective, access helps explain why so many donors prefer to give to members of particular committees (Hall and Wayman 1990; Evans 1996; Rozell et al. 2006;

Loucks and Bennett 2011), to the majority party (Cox and Magar 1999; Rudolph 1999), to their own congressional representatives (Wright 1985; Hojnacki and Kimball 1998; Miler 2010), to legislative leaders (Hojnacki and Kimball 1998; Poole and Rosenthal 2007), or to both political parties (Apollonio and La Raja 2004; McKay 2010).

Robert Walker, lobbyist and former Member of Congress, takes issue with the idea that contributions and fundraising are "buying access. It's just not the case" (Leech 2013, 25). "There's no quid pro quo in any of this," he states (Leech 2013, 22). But another lobbyist has lingering questions. "The issue, academically, to take a look at is what is being bought with the campaign contribution," says lobbyist and former president of the League of Lobbyists Michael Marlowe (Leech 2013, 9).

In Chapter 1, we discussed the fundamental problem of causal inference – that it is impossible to observe or create two identical situations in which the only difference is the absence or presence of the suspected cause. When a phenomenon of interest is impossible to observe, we instead look for the *observable implications* of that phenomenon (King et al. 1994). If campaign contributions are intended to buy access to Members of Congress, what observable implications would we see? Four implications are discussed in what follows. If lobbyists give politicians money in these four ways, we can infer that they are at least trying to buy favor with legislators and may be trying to buy policy success. If we do not see these patterns, it may be that campaign finance laws work: They keep contributions limited in number and amount so that no one person or interest group can "buy" a politician.

3.2.1 Implication 1: Maximized Contributions

If lobbyists donate as a means to increase the likelihood and frequency of their access to legislators, these contributions should be large and/or frequent. While we cannot be sure of lobbyists' budget constraints, we can compare their contributions before and after the health reform period, and we can also compare health care lobbyists to other lobbyists. We know from the literature that lobbyists draw high salaries, often higher than those of the Members of Congress they lobby (LaPira and Thomas 2017). The logic of maximization is derived from the usefulness hypothesis of this book, which holds that legislators are more responsive to entities that make themselves useful by supplying, among other things, campaign contributions, policy expertise, and political information.

3.2.2 Implication 2: Preference for Key Committee Members

Lobbyists trying to make themselves useful to legislators should pay particular financial attention to the politicians best positioned to help the lobbyist's clients. Like the logic of maximization, this logic of specification aims efforts to influence precisely at those decision-makers who have control over the relevant section, amendment, or bill and can maintain this control to the end when the legislation is passed. After the election of 2008, health care reform held primacy on the agendas of both the president and the Congress, and health care interest groups thus had an extraordinarily large incentive to try to influence the content of the legislation.

Two committees in particular – and one more than the other – were going to be the theaters for the creation of Obamacare. The Senate Finance Committee has greater jurisdiction than any other committee in Congress, including sole jurisdiction over Medicare and Medicaid. The committee also has control over any law enforced through tax collection, such as an individual or employer mandate for the purchase of health insurance. Finance is the Senate committee that pays for what the government wants to do – and health care reform would require an investment of nearly one trillion dollars over ten years. In 2008–10, the committee was known for its bipartisanship, as Democratic Chairman Max Baucus and Ranking Minority Member Chuck Grassley were regarded as having a good relationship, and Baucus in particular wanted a bipartisan bill. Only a collective proposal, he thought, would go far in getting public "buy-in" on legislation – without jeopardizing either party in the next election. Moreover, pivotal moderate-leaning Republicans such as Senators Snowe and Grassley were on the Finance committee, and their votes were critical to "get to 60" – the new norm for passing bills in the Senate. Al Franken's election victory in July after a lengthy recount battle made him the sixtieth Democrat, but it did not guarantee sixty votes, since party discipline in the Senate was far from absolute.

The Senate's Health, Education, Labor, and Pensions, or HELP, committee also deals with health policy, but its jurisdiction covers discretionary spending, such as funding for federally supported clinics for the poor and the creation of a savings plan for long-term care known as the CLASS Act (which was later eliminated before it went into effect). But HELP's long-serving chairman, Ted Kennedy (D-MA), had been diagnosed with

Senator Max Baucus, left, chairman, and Senator Chuck Grassley, ranking minority member, of the Finance committee in 2009 (Source: Senate Finance Committee website)

brain cancer and was frequently unavailable to lead the committee. The next most senior senator on the committee, Chris Dodd (D-CT), was in the midst of writing the complex "Dodd-Frank" legislation in response to the very recent financial crisis of 2007–08. Dodd, already the chair of the Banking, Housing, and Urban Affairs committee, was also facing a difficult and ultimately unsuccessful reelection campaign in Connecticut following his failed bid for president in 2008. Though Kennedy had a reputation for his circumspect political and negotiating skills, in his absence, Republicans on HELP were not deterred in voicing objections – especially since Baucus had indicated that he would be making compromises with Republicans.[2]

In contrast to the de facto three-fifths threshold required for a bill to pass the Senate, in the House, majority-party Democrats had thirty-nine Democratic votes to spare. The health reform bill put together by Speaker Pelosi across three committees (Energy and Commerce, Education and Labor, and Ways and Means) contained a wish list of liberal proposals

---

[2] Also see Skocpol and Jacobs (2010, 62–63) for the argument that Max Baucus was the central policymaking player on health reform legislation.

that Senate Democrats viewed as unpassable in the Senate. As a result, senators did not exhibit much deference to the Democratic House leaders. Further, the Democratic party majority in the House faced internal divisions. Liberals would have preferred a European-style single-payer system. In particular, by passing their bill before the Senate acted, the Democratic leadership hoped that their proposal for a strong public option modeled on Medicare would make its way into the final legislation. Conservative "Blue Dog" Democrats, meanwhile, raised concerns about high costs, increased taxation, and the burden on business. Although the institutional rules of the House granted the leadership considerable power, especially relative to the Senate, in order to pass a bill, the Democratic Speaker of the House Nancy Pelosi would need the support of the majority of the relevant committees plus at least some of the fifty-one Blue Dogs and eighty-six Medicare-for-All co-sponsors.

3.2.3 Implication 3: Tendency to Give at Particular Times

The literature suggests several key times during which legislators are most open to interest groups' preferences (e.g., Stratmann 1998; Box-Steffensmeier et al. 2005; Marshall 2010; Rocca and Gordon 2013; Zhang and Tanger 2017). In general, the best time to influence the content of a bill is before the bill is written. We know that humans have a bias toward the status quo, or the first-draft option, the default option. Thus, it is a heavier burden to change a bill than to influence how it is written in the first place.

Committees are the workshops of Congress, and committee markups are the workshops of committees. Committee markups occur after the chair puts forth a version of the bill, with varying levels of input from the ranking member and other committee members. Committee members then propose and debate changes to the bill, after which the committee votes to make or not to make each change. (Note, though, that there are variations in the rules governing committees, including the roles of the chair, ranking member, and rank-and-file members.) As such, committee markups are the most detail-dense opportunity for members other than the chair to influence the content of the bill.

Thus, in the case of Obamacare, lobbyists interested in adding, deleting, or changing parts of the bill should want to maximize access to legislators on the two key committees of jurisdiction, the Senate Finance and HELP committees, as they are marking up the bill. If they are unsuccessful in accessing and influencing committee members during markup, or even if they are successful, lobbyists' next best opportunity to influence the content and disposition of a Senate bill is when it goes to the Senate floor to be amended and voted upon.

3.2.4 Implication 4: Different Behavior for PACs

A fourth observable implication would be a difference in behavior between individual lobbyists and political action committees (PACs). Lobbyists are individual decision-makers, while PACs distribute the consolidated contributions of many individuals. As such the contribution choices of a PAC must be generally agreeable to its numerous supporters. Wright (1985) found that PAC money was raised (for the top five PACs) by individuals scattered around the country who crafted messages designed to appeal to citizens in particular industries or in support of particular policies or groups. Importantly, Wright argued, these were the people who would decide where the money would go, since they were the ones who raised it – and not lobbyists in Washington. This view is supported by numerous previous studies that suggest that a given PAC contribution does not typically focus on a single member, bill, or issue (Gordon 2001; Kroszner and Stratmann 2005). Rather, PACs tend to support electoral winners, a single party, or both parties (Poole and Romer 1985).

Others have argued, in contrast, that PAC contributions are strategically directed by the leadership of firms (Clawson et al. 1998; Goldstein 1999), unions (Baldwin and Magee 2000; Jansa and Hoyman 2018), or the organization's Washington lobbyists (Goldberg et al. 2020). In the HLOGA law, Congress acknowledged the possibility that lobbyists routinely work with PACs to direct campaign contributions strategically by requiring lobbyists to report the contributions of the political action committees whose contributions the lobbyist directs or controls. PACs have always been required to report their contributions, but the 2008 law treats contributions by lobbyist-controlled PACs almost as if they are coming from those lobbyists.

If we find that PACs behave in a manner that is less sensitive to the positions of legislators and the timing of their policymaking activities, while individual lobbyists exhibit greater responsiveness to activities by legislators, it would support the salience hypothesis, because PACs' contributions are highly visible, while those of individual lobbyists are not. This distinction would be especially pronounced in 2008 and 2009 before lobbyists were accustomed to disclosing details about their campaign contributions the way that PACs already were. If we find, on the other hand, that individual lobbyists behave similarly to the PACs they control, it would support the usefulness hypothesis, because it implies that organizational decision-makers use contributions to support helpful politicians – and to influence them to be supportive in return. By collecting and comparing data on the contributions of individual lobbyists and their PACs, I am able to evaluate for the first time the possibility that lobbyists are funneling campaign contributions toward incumbents who are in a position to help the lobbying group.

In sum, access-oriented lobbyists should (1) maximize contributions, (2) favoring particular Members in a position to be useful to them, (3) timed strategically. If lobbyists asking for legislative favors wish to keep this activity invisible from radar detection, then (4) individual lobbyists should act more strategically than PACs. If, however, lobbyists use PAC contributions to make themselves useful to Members of Congress, PACs and individual lobbyists may contribute in similarly strategic ways.

3.3 DATA ON THE CONTRIBUTIONS OF INDIVIDUAL LOBBYISTS AND THE PACS THEY CONTROL

The Lobbying Disclosure Act (LDA) of 1995 requires that lobbyists report information about their substantive lobbying efforts and associated expenditures. Anyone working as a lobbyist on behalf of a given client for at least 20 percent of their time and charging at least $3,000 in any given quarter must register. In-house lobbyists must file a disclosure form for the organization if their lobbying expenditures exceed $11,500 in a quarter. The information required includes the names of each individual lobbying for the organization (and whether each person is "covered" under the lobbying restrictions on former government employees) and the policy areas and specific topics on which each registrant lobbied for each client, along with the dollar expenditures each registrant spent on a client's or their employer's behalf during the quarter (most of which comprise the lobbyists' salaries or fees).

In addition to quarterly activity reports (known as LDA-2s), the 2007 HLOGA law requires that registered lobbyists submit, semi-annually, reports of their campaign contributions (known as LD-203s), whether or not they make any. The date, amount, payee, and honoree of every federal contribution of $200 or more must be reported, along with the name of the lobbyist, their employer, and the contributor (whether lobbyist or organization). Any organization or individual that "actively participates" in lobbying activities must report semi-annually all "FECA [Federal Election Campaign Act] contributions, as well as honorary contributions, presidential library contributions, and payments for event costs."[3] Lobbyists are also required to report the campaign contributions of PACs they establish, administer, direct, or control.

Annual studies by the Government Accountability Office (GAO) show that lobbyists' compliance with the disclosure laws has been fairly high. By comparing a random sample of 100 LD-203 filings to Federal Election Commission (FEC) data on contributions to federal candidates, GAO found in 2009 that 82 percent of the LD-203 reports were fully supported by documentation in the FEC data for all listed contributions. Of the remainder, 6 percent did not make any reportable contributions, while 9 percent were missing contributions. Extrapolating to the whole population, GAO estimated that as many as 98 percent of filed LD-203 reports were correct and complete in 2009, and fewer than 11 percent of registered lobbyists failed to file LD-203 reports. These numbers have been consistent since then.[4]

Starting in 2011, I began collecting the LD-203 data from the Senate Clerk's office. The Senate made these forms available only in .xml format at the rate of about one per week. I downloaded these raw data and parsed them. Next, I needed to link these data to information about lobbyists' clients, lobbying expenditures, and other lobbying activities. There is no common ID number that links individual lobbyists between the LD-203 (contributions) data and the LDA-2 (disclosure) data. Although the non-profit government watchdog organization the Center for Responsive Politics (CRP) maintains a database of carefully cleaned lobbying disclosure (LDA-2) reports, now available to the public at the website www .OpenSecrets.org, in 2011, CRP had not uploaded any LD-203 contributions, let alone matched them to their LDA-2 activities. Today, the full set of LD-203 disclosures is available only through the Senate's new application programming interface (API).

---

[3] "Actively participates" means participating in the "planning, supervision, or control of lobbying activities of a client or registrant when that organization (or an employee of the organization in their capacity as an employee) engages directly in planning, supervising, or controlling at least some of the lobbying activities of the client or registrant," according to the "Lobbying Disclosure Act Guidance" document provided by the House Office of the Clerk and the Senate Office of Public Records (accessed June 15, 2012).

[4] Government Accountability Office (2021).

In order to link lobbyists across the two sets of data, therefore, I used regular expressions (which allow precise matching of characters, names, and longer text) in Stata to match lobbyists' names and employers, followed by manual methods. Ultimately I was able to match more than 99 percent of the observations in which individual lobbyists were named to CRP lobbyist identification numbers (and some of the unmatched individuals were not actually registered lobbyists). I did further research to merge the records of individuals who had erroneously been given multiple identification codes by CRP. In 2021, after the Senate put all LD-203 information into an API, I used the field "Filer Type" to confirm that my use of regular expressions correctly distinguished individual contributions from lobbyist-controlled PAC contributions for more than 99 percent of the contributions.[5]

Lobbying organizations identify which issues they work on for each client each quarter from a list of seventy-nine topics. Of these, I classified four as being related to health: Health Issues, Medicare and Medicaid, Pharmacy, and Medical/Disease Research/Clinical Labs.[6]

I define the health reform period as starting with President Obama's victory on November 3, 2008, and ending when the companion bill to the Patient Protection and Affordable Care Act – the Health Care and Education Reconciliation Act of 2010 – was signed on March 30, 2010. This period is closely aligned with the quarterly filing of lobbying disclosure reports, starting with the fourth quarter of 2008 and ending with the first quarter of 2010. I use this time frame alignment to estimate whether or not each lobbyist worked on health reform in each of the three time periods before (i.e., the first three quarters of 2008), during (the last quarter of 2008 through the first quarter of 2010), or after (the last three quarters of 2010) the period of health reform legislation.

---

[5] Nine percent of the contributions I had coded as PACs were designated as individual lobbyists' reports in the API data, even though the listed "Contributor" was a PAC. I compared a random sample of these against the FEC database and found in all cases that they were indeed PAC contributions. I therefore consider these to be errantly reported as individual filings. Correcting for these, 99.7 percent of my "organization type" codes for contributions matched those of the API "Filer Type" code contributions.

[6] I considered using health-related industries, as classified by the Center for Responsive Politics, as my indicator of whether a lobbyist is a health lobbyist or not. In my estimation, for about 80 percent of registrants, the two variables were the same. The results are not substantively significantly different using the alternative measure and are equally supportive of my findings.

Next, to identify contributions to incumbent senators, I used regular expressions to search the Honoree and Payee fields for every observed variation on each senator's name. I then added information about each incumbent senator, including their class, party, and committee memberships, using information from the official Senate website. I estimate that about two-thirds of all lobbyist-reported contributions went to House candidates and about 30 percent went to the more than 100 eligible senators in each of the three time periods (before, during, and after health reform), excluding contributions to 2008 presidential and vice-presidential candidates (Senators Obama, Biden, Clinton, and McCain before the 2008 election).

In order to test hypotheses about who gives money to whom, it is ideal to have a dataset that includes not only all lobbyists' contributions but all *potential* contributions. Since previous scholars have not been able to identify registered lobbyists using FEC contributions data, researchers have not been able to control for those lobbyists who choose not to contribute, either at all or to a particular candidate. This means researchers compare the amount or number of contributions among contributors – totals that may have more to do with budget constraints or experience than with intention or influence – rather than a more meaningful comparison between contributors and noncontributors.

I avoid selecting on the dependent variable by generating one observation for every lobbyist and lobbyist-controlled PAC that filed an LD-203 contributions report, *paired with* every senator who was in office in the time period of 2008–2010. In each of these pairings, a contribution could exist, but may not. This allows my dependent variable to be whether or not the lobbyist contributes to the senator during the time period – and if so, how much they contribute.

As health reform gets underway, more than 900 individuals begin to lobby on health issues who did not lobby in the first three quarters of 2008, and another nearly 1,000 lobbyists add health to their existing issue portfolios. Only about 60 percent of the lobbyists in these data were active in all three time periods. Likewise, senators come and go as a result of elections, retirement, appointments, and death, and more than 20 percent of senators did not serve in all three time periods. It would not be accurate to consider a lobbyist who left Washington in 2009 to be abstaining from contributing to a senator in 2010, nor would it be appropriate to consider a senator who retired in 2008 to be an incumbent in 2009. I therefore used public records for senators, and LDA reports for lobbyists, to determine whether each lobbyist was active, and each senator was in office, at any point during each time period. I considered individual lobbyists to be eligible to report contributions starting in the period of time covered by their first semiannual report through the last report they filed between 2008 and 2010. I followed the same procedure for all registrants that reported making at least one contribution during the three years.

In this way, I generated two datasets, each containing three time periods. The individual-level dataset pairs each senator who serves in each time period with each individual lobbyist who is active in that time period. The registrant-level dataset pairs each senator who serves in each time period with each registrant that is active in that time period. I then merged these two "empty" datasets with my dataset of actual contributions, which I first separated by time period and filer type and aggregated into contributor-senator dyads. The resulting datasets link data on the campaign contributions of individual lobbyists and the PACs they control with their lobbying activities to develop the most complete picture that exists in the literature of *all* reported lobbying activity and contributions surrounding a specific policy issue.

3.4 DESCRIBING THE CONTRIBUTIONS

This dataset is different from those used by previous scholars because it contains the contributions of individual lobbyists, and the contributions of PACs controlled by registered lobbyists, rather than the contributions of PACs (Masters and Keim 1985; Poole and Romer 1985; Wawro 2001; Box-Steffensmeier et al. 2005; Barber 2016) or the contributions of individuals (Barber 2016; Bonica 2016). Because these data have never before been used to evaluate the effects of contributions on the behavior of Members of Congress, I first provide some descriptive inferences, before using statistical inference to better understand the data.

The data I downloaded in 2011 were messy, and I have endeavored over a long period of time to clean them. In 2021 I used a script to download them again from the Senate's API server, which allowed me to correct and extend some fields and to include additional fields. Even after this process, many contributions remained puzzlingly over the legal limits. Some of these were apparently typos with extra zeroes attached; others were not direct FECA contributions but honorary or meeting expenses. These payments are of unusual amounts and are not cash contributions, and so for unit homogeneity I have dropped honorary and meeting expenses.[7] I then used the

---

[7] The dropped observations include those mentioning in the Payee or Honoree fields (and not in the Contributor field), for example, Marriott, Hyatt, Foundation, Institute, advocacy,

Payee field to identify contributions to party committees, which have higher limits than contributions to specific candidates. This distinction, along with the distinction between individual contributions and those of lobbyist-controlled PACs, enables me to identify the maximum limit for each contribution.[8] I then reset values that were above the limit to the limit.[9] This recode affected 0.2 percent of the reported contributions.

My analysis of the HLOGA data indicates that about 17,500 unique lobbyists file LD-203 reports between 2008 and 2010. Of these, nearly half report making one or more contributions. After resetting excessive reported amounts to their legal limit, I estimate that individual lobbyists' contributions between 2008 and 2010 total more than $80 million, of which more than $25 million goes to incumbent senators between 2008 and 2010.

In addition to these individual contributions, lobbyists make a significant number of contributions on behalf of PACs that they establish, administer, or direct. I label these entities lobbyist-controlled PACs, because the lobbyist is involved in directing contributions to the campaigns of Members of Congress. Before the HLOGA law required lobbyists to disclose their personal contributions and those of any PACs they control, there was a debate about whether lobbyists were directing the campaign contributions of PACs to help buy influence, or at least access. The LD-203 data show for the first time that lobbyists do direct PAC contributions, and very frequently. More than two-thirds of the registrants listed in the data between 2008 and 2010 can be associated with one or more contributions during that time, either as organizations or as individuals working for those organizations. In total, lobbyist-controlled PACs report more than $800 million in federal contributions, delivering more than $140 million to incumbent US senators between 2008 and 2010.

---

council, consulting, Action Fund, vendors, etc. There were about 11,000 of these (2 percent of countable contributions).

[8] The limits for contributions from an individual to a candidate committee or party committee in the 2010 cycle were, respectively, $4800 (assuming two elections) and $30,400, and the limits for contributions from a PAC to a candidate or party were, respectively, $10,000 and $15,000.

[9] As alternatives to reducing contribution values to their legal limits, I also considered (1) dividing the excessive amounts by a number (either 1,000 or 100) to reach what I guessed was the actual amount contributed; (2) dropping them to $0 or $1; and (3) dropping a percentile of the contributions, such as the top 1 percent. Having tried these alternatives, which do not lead to any different conclusions, I have decided to drop excessive contributions down to the maximum allowed.

During the health reform period between President Obama's November 4, 2008, election and his signing of the companion bill into law on March 30, 2010, individual lobbyists contribute nearly $12 million to incumbent US senators, and lobbyist-controlled PACs give senators another $60 million. As we will see, the majority of this money comes from health lobbyists – even though the majority of lobbyists do not work on health issues.

3.4.1 Observing Implication 1: Maximized Contributions

Of the more than approximately 14,400 individual lobbyists I am able to link to specific issues during the health reform period, 23 percent work solely on health care issues, and another 22 percent work on health care issues as well as on other issues. I consider a lobbyist a health care lobbyist if they work *at all* on health care issues – whether this constitutes a portion or all of their portfolio – between 2008 and 2010.[10]

In 2008 before the election, the data show that about 39 percent of lobbyists work on health issues. During the last quarter of 2008 through the first quarter of 2010 – the health reform period – this number rises to 45 percent of lobbyists working at least partly on health care issues. As mentioned earlier, I identified nearly 1,000 lobbyists who shifted from not working on health care to working on health care as the issue got under way in Congress, and I found another 900+ previously unregistered lobbyists who began working on health issues for the first time during this period. The disproportionately high level of activity surrounding health care is remarkable, given that there were some seventy other issue areas that lobbyists could be working on, as well as major legislation like Cap-and-Trade legislation to address climate change and the financial sector reform bill known as Dodd-Frank. Yet we know from

---

[10] In addition to using a dichotomous variable measuring whether or not each lobbyist or lobbyist-controlled PAC worked on health issues, I considered two alternatives: (1) the *percentage* of clients for whom the lobbyist or lobbyist-controlled PAC worked on health issues (by counting clients per quarter per issue area) as well as (2) a dichotomous measure of whether the lobbyist worked *only* on health issues. But each of these would introduce a bias, since organizations that work solely on health care tend to employ their own lobbyists, in contrast to lobbying firms that work on many issues. We know from the literature and from these data that in-house lobbying organizations are less likely to make contributions than are employees of lobbying firms. The distinction between lobbyists who work at least *some* on health issues and those who do not work on any health care issues is therefore less biased than an alternative that treats lobbyists who work *only* on health care issues differently.

Baumgartner and Leech (2001) that lobbying activity across policy issue areas is highly skewed toward a small number of issues.

Even more compelling than the shift in lobbyists' attention to health care issues is the change in how lobbyists allocate campaign contributions. During the health reform period, the 45 percent of lobbyists in the data who work in whole or in part on health care provide about 69 percent of the money going to incumbent senators. Thus, individual health care lobbyists make more contributions to senators during this period than do lobbyists working on all other issues combined. Figure 3.1(a) shows the disproportionate contributions from health lobbyists during consideration of health reform legislation. (The quarterly filing deadlines of the Federal Elections Commission are included because as they approach, candidates often press donors to contribute so the candidate can make a strong showing when the amounts raised by each campaign are released.) Here we see strong evidence of the dominance of health reform issues during this time.

Figure 3.1(b) replicates the previous figure but for lobbyist-controlled PACs. In 2008 before the election, the data show that about 32 percent of lobbyist-controlled PACs are linked to lobbying registrants that work on health care, and this percentage rises to 40 percent during the six quarters of the health reform period.

As with individual lobbyists, lobbyist-controlled PACs working on health care issues give disproportionately: The 40 percent of unique lobbyist-controlled health PACs in the data contribute 64 percent of the money going from lobbyist-controlled PACs to incumbent senators during the health reform period. Thus health PACs, like the lobbyists who run them, exhibit a strong financial interest in making contributions to senators as health reform is being written.

3.4.2 Observing Implication 2: Preference for Key Committee Members

Next, we consider senators' committee assignments, which I hypothesized would lead certain lobbyists to favor particular senators over others. The data show that health lobbyists and the PACs they control both increase their contributions to key committee members after President Obama's election as health reform gets under way. Figures 3.2(a) and 3.2(b) distinguish key committee recipients from other senators. As shown in Figure 3.2(a), in each of the forty-four weeks of 2008 before Obama is elected, individual health lobbyists favor the fifty-seven senators who are not on the Finance or HELP committees writing health reform legislation.

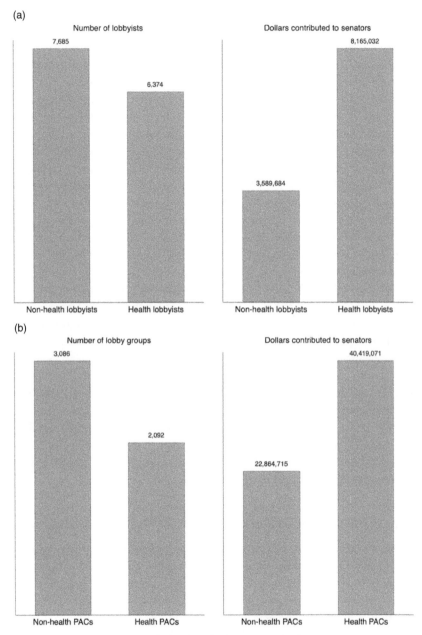

FIGURE 3.1 (a) Individual health lobbyists and their PACs contribute disproportionately to senators during the health reform debate. (b) Lobby groups working on health contribute disproportionately to senators during the health reform debate

(a)

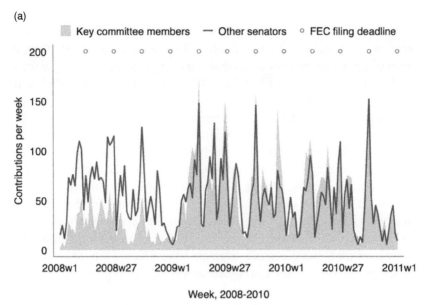

(b)

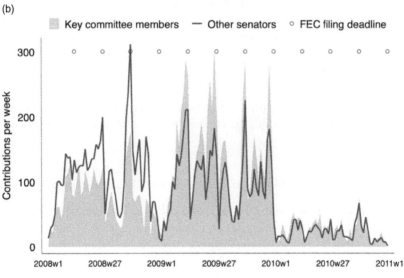

FIGURE 3.2 (a) Contributions per week to senators from individual health lobbyists to senators on and not on the key health committees. (b) Contributions per week to senators from lobbyist-controlled health PACs to senators on and not on the key health committees

Starting in early 2009, however, key committee members gain contributions from individual health lobbyists that surpass contributions to senators who are not on either committee. This heightened attention in the form of campaign contributions occurs in thirty-nine weeks, or 53 percent of the time, until the president signs the Affordable Care Act into law in March of 2010. After reform is signed into law, interestingly, health lobbyists' individual contributions remain high.

Figure 3.2(b) looks at the same data for lobbyist-controlled PACs and shows that, like individual lobbyists, PACs controlled by health lobbyists also give more money to key committee members than to other senators as health reform is being written. During the health reform period, PACs controlled by health lobbyists make more contributions to the key committee members than to other senators in fifty-seven of seventy-three weeks, or about 78 percent of the time. Contrary to the hypothesis that individual lobbyists are more strategic than PACs, lobbyist-controlled PACs' preference for key committee members is even greater than what individual lobbyists demonstrate.

Looking at Figure 3.2(b) you may notice, as I did when I made this graph, that early in 2010 there appears to a sharp drop-off in contributions from lobbyist-controlled health PACs to incumbent senators both on and not on the key health committees – a pattern not shared by individual health lobbyists. Weekly contributions from health PACs controlled by lobbyists fall from 461 in the fiftieth week of 2009 to just thirty-five in the third week of 2010. They do not approach numbers anywhere near their 2009 peaks throughout 2010. Was this an error in the data? We will return to this question later.

3.4.3 Observing Implication 3: Tendency to Give at Particular Times

We expected to see that lobbyists who are interested in influencing the content of health reform legislation would concentrate their contributions at key times in the legislative process. We see in Figure 3.1(a) that, as predicted, the lobbyists in these data who work on the issue of the day in 2009 are much more active contributors than those who do not work on health issues. Looking at contributions week-by-week, Figure 3.3(a) shows that in 2008 before the election, health contributions exceed nonhealth contributions in twenty-seven of forty-four weeks, or about 60 percent of the time. But starting after the election, when Senator Baucus releases his White Paper plan for health reform, until the final health reform measures are adopted in March of 2010, the average individual health care lobbyist makes more contributions to senators than does the average nonhealth lobbyist in seventy-two of seventy-three weeks, or 99 percent of the time. Comparison of these variations to the timing of consideration of the bill reveals that contributions to key committee members peak during key moments in the Finance and HELP committees' consideration of health reform – when the White House holds a health summit in the first quarter of 2009, when the Finance committee releases its first set of Options for Health Reform, when HELP releases its proposal and again when it votes, right before the Senate passes the bill, and again right before the vote on reconciliation in March of 2010. The timing of these contributions supports the theory that these lobbyists are using their contributions to encourage senators to remember them at important decision points.

Like individual lobbyists, lobbyist-controlled PACs also ramp up their contributions in early 2009. Figure 3.3(b) shows the same basic graph as Figure 3.3(a) but with lobbyist-controlled PACs instead of individual lobbyists. We see in Figure 3.3(b) that in 2008 before the election, PACs run by lobbyists who work on health care exceed the number of contributions from nonhealth lobbyists just seven of forty-four weeks, or 16 percent of the time. But during the health reform period, health-lobbyist-controlled PACs contribute more than nonhealth PACs in sixty-nine of seventy-three weeks, or 95 percent of the time that the Senate was writing and debating health reform legislation. The data also indicate, though it is not shown here, that the very same lobbying organizations increase their lobbying activity on health reform during this period relative to 2008 before the November election: Paired *t*-tests of LD-2 data reveal that individual firms lobbying on health reform increase their spending significantly in the active period of health reform compared to the period in 2008 before the election. So the increase in contributions from health lobbyists includes, in addition to a large number of new health lobbyists, a demonstrable change in the behavior of individual lobbying firms.

3.4.4 Observing Implication 4: Different Behavior for PACs

Although there are many more individual lobbyists reporting contributions (more than 17,000) than unique lobbyist-controlled PACs (about 53,00), the lobbyist-controlled PACs supply considerably more contributions – more than 410,000 of them between 2008 and 2010, worth more than $800 million (of which more than $140 million goes to incumbent senators). Individual lobbyists during this time make more

(a)

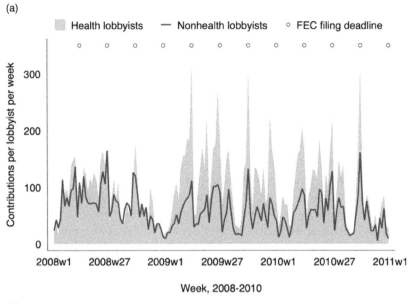

(b)

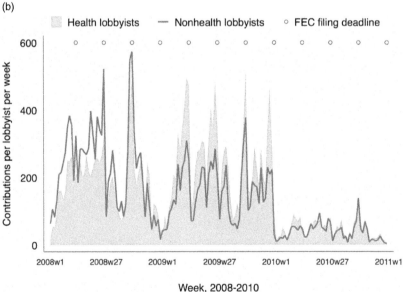

FIGURE 3.3 (a) Contributions per week to senators from individual health and nonhealth lobbyists. (b) Contributions per week to senators from lobbyist-controlled health and nonhealth PACs

than 110,000 contributions collectively worth more than $80 million (of which more than $25 million goes to incumbent senators). This difference in magnitude makes sense, since PACs have higher campaign contribution limits than individuals do, and because PACs have a whole fundraising operation, while individuals must pay out of pocket. Because they can afford it, the financial advantage of PACs may also mean they are not as selective or strategic as individual lobbyists. To the extent that lobbyists direct their PACs' contributions, however, we would expect these lobbyist-controlled PACs' contributions to be just as strategic as those of individual lobbyists.

The data provide mixed evidence of a strategic difference between individual lobbyists and the PACs they control. Both are responsive to the timing of health reform legislation: Contributions from health-oriented lobbyists and their PACs both increase in number and dollar total during reform relative to before, while contributions from non-health-oriented lobbyists and their PACs decrease in number and dollar total. And both pay attention to key committee members at key times: Individuals increase their contribution dollars to key committee members from 28 percent of incumbent senator donations before reform to 53 percent during reform; PACs increase the share of contributions going to key committee members from 37 percent before reform to 53 percent during reform. But individual lobbyists appear more sensitive than PACs to the fact that Finance, not HELP, would draft the majority of the bill: Individual health lobbyists shift about 12 percent of their contributions to Finance Committee members and 13 percent to HELP members during the health reform period, while health PACs increase their contributions to these key committee members by smaller amounts – 4 percent and 10 percent respectively – and favor HELP over Finance.

An interesting and significant difference between individual health lobbyists and their PACs can be seen in Figures 3.2(b) and 3.3(b), especially compared to Figures 3.2(a) and 3.3(a), and especially in 2010. Recall that in Figure 3.2(b) we saw a sudden drop-off in lobbyist-controlled PACs' contributions at the start of 2010, a drop that does not recover during the year – but that drop-off was among health lobbyists. Figure 3.3(b) shows that *all* lobbyist-controlled PACs sharply reduce their contributions in 2010 relative to 2009 and 2008. When I first graphed the data, I assumed I had made an error, but I could find none, and the data for individual lobbyists contained no evidence of this pattern. What might have changed early in 2010 to alter the behavior of lobbyist-run PACs in this way?

The Supreme Court's *Citizens United* decision on January 21, 2010, followed closely by its *SpeechNow.Org* decision on March 26, opened up the floodgates to unlimited, unregulated amounts of spending by organizations on behalf of federal candidates. No longer did lobby groups need to limit their federal contributions to $2,400 for individuals or $5,000 for PACs. The possibility that lobbyists who run PACs for their organizations may redirect these contributions to SuperPACs instead of to candidates' official campaign committees following these court decisions – and that individual lobbyists do not make this change – is a significant finding worthy of further research.

3.5 MODELING CONTRIBUTIONS ACTIVITY

To better evaluate what is going on, it is useful to have a statistical model of lobbyists' decisions about whether, when, to whom, and how much to contribute. Since FEC data do not designate whether or not a given contributor is a registered lobbyist, previous scholars have not been able to distinguish contributing obbyists from noncontributing lobbyists. The present study avoids this problem by creating dyads of possible contributions relationships between senators on one side and individual lobbyists and lobby groups' PACs on the other. For most lobbyist-senator pairs, no contribution occurs, because lobbyists frequently do not make contributions, and those who do give to a small selection of senators (perhaps in addition to House Members and challenger or open-seat candidates), not to all senators.

3.5.1 Variables

The unit of analysis is either the lobbyist-senator dyad or the registrant-senator dyad. Two alternative dependent variables are used. First is a dichotomous indicator of *whether the lobbyist/PAC contributes to the senator* in that time frame. Second is a continuous variable, *average dollars per weeks contributed*, which reflects the combined contribution dollars going from a lobbyist to a senator during the time period, averaged by week (so the difference in the length of time periods does not play a role). The continuous variable provides more information than the dichotomous variable does and can be considered a measure of the intensity of the lobbyist's interest in contributing to the senator. But the amount of money donated may just reflect irrelevant factors such as the income of the lobbyist or PAC. As such, we evaluate both variables. I use logit analysis to predict the dichotomous dependent variable, and I use ordinary least squares (OLS) to predict the continuous dependent variable.

The models test the four implications about health lobbyists – (1) that they act differently from nonhealth lobbyists, (2) that they favor key committee members, (3) especially during key moments in the legislative process, and (4) that they contribute in a manner that reveals greater sensitivity to political events relative to PACs. To evaluate whether health lobbyists favor key committee members, I create an interaction term that multiplies whether the lobbyist in the dyad works on health issues (in whole or in part) by whether the senator is on the Finance or HELP committees. All constituent parts of these interactions are also included (Brambor et al. 2006). The key explanatory variables are thus *health lobbyist, Finance member, HELP member, health lobbyist X Finance member*, and *health lobbyist X HELP member*.

Regarding the effect of the time period on health lobbyists' contributions, I do not test this directly because, as mentioned earlier, the sets of lobbyists, registrants, and senators differ over time. For the same reason, I do not test directly whether PACs behave differently from individual lobbyists. Instead, I run separate models for all three time periods, both for individual lobbyists and for lobbying registrants, and compare the results.

I include important control variables in the models as well. *Number of clients from senator's state* records the number of clients the lobbyist represents that are from the senator's home state as indicated in lobbying expenditures reports. Each client is counted just once in each time period for each registrant. This indicator of constituent ties in the models controls for the known tendency for donors to give to their own congressional representatives (Wright 1985; DeGregorio 1997). I also include a measure of the registered lobbying organization's spending on lobbying from LDA-2 disclosures: *Logged lobbying expenditures* measures the lobbying organization's capacity to make campaign contributions. The natural log (ln) of expenditures is used, since it is reasonable to expect a curvilinear relationship in which increasing expenditures have decreasing marginal returns. Because the same senators appear repeatedly in the dataset, I use fixed effects for each senator in the data.[11] Doing so controls for senator-specific variables that do not vary across lobbyists but may well influence whether the lobbyist or registrant gives to a candidate, such as whether

---

[11] I also considered using two-way clustered standard errors, as developed by Cameron et al. (2011) and used in Chapter 4. The results were not significantly different.

the senator is currently running for reelection, whether they are in a leadership position, and whether they are in the majority party. (I mention these three factors because when each is run as a predictor variable, it tends to be significant.) The use of fixed effects also means that the models allow senators to whom no lobbyist or PAC contributes to drop out (most often, they are not running for reelection).

Figures 3.4(a) and 3.4(b) show the results of the logit estimation of whether any contributions exist in the dyad. Figures 3.5(a) and 3.5(b) present OLS regression coefficients predicting total dollars contributed in the dyad. Full model specifications appear in Table 3.1.

3.5.2 Maximized Contributions

Our first implication holds that lobbyists maximize their contributions when their issue is on the congressional agenda. As expected, individual health lobbyists, whether in 2008 before the election, during the health reform debate, or in 2010 after the legislation is signed, contribute significantly more to senators per week if they are involved in health issues than if they are not. While also controlling for the other variables in the models, the log-odds that an individual health lobbyist gives to a senator are 34–74 percent greater for individual health lobbyists than for other lobbyists, and individual health lobbyists give senators 3–6 percent more dollars per week than nonhealth lobbyists do (Figure 3.5(a), line 1). Among lobbyist-controlled PACs, those that work on health care issues give senators 17–76 percent more money to senators than nonhealth PACs (Figure 3.5(b), line 1), but these health-lobbyist-controlled PACS are actually no more likely than PACs whose lobbyists work on other issues to donate to senators (Figure 3.4(b), line 1). It thus appears that health reform mobilizes individual health lobbyists to give and to give more and increases the probability that lobbyist-controlled health PACs contribute to senators – but it does not increase the amount of money that lobbyist-controlled health PACs contribute.

3.5.3 Preference for Key Committee Members

The usefulness hypothesis implies that key committee members in the Senate should receive the most financial attention from healthcare

TABLE 3.1 *Predicting lobbyists' campaign contributions to senators before, during, and after the Senate's consideration of health reform legislation*

	Individual Lobbyists						Lobbyist-Controlled PACs					
	Whether any contribution occurs in the dyad			Average dollars per week contributed			Whether any contribution occurs in the dyad			Average dollars per week contributed		
	Before	During	After	Before	During	After	Before	During	After	Before	During	After
Health lobbyist/ PAC	1.34 (0.04)	1.74 (0.05)	1.50 (0.06)	0.06 (0.01)	0.06 (0.00)	0.03 (0.01)	0.87 (0.02)	1.03 (0.02)	1.11 (0.06)	0.76 (0.11)	0.57 (0.05)	0.17 (0.04)
Health lobbyist/ PAC x Finance	1.40 (0.11)	1.34 (0.07)	1.22 (0.08)	-0.00 (0.01)	0.06 (0.01)	0.07 (0.01)	1.33 (0.06)	1.25 (0.05)	1.15 (0.10)	0.51 (0.20)	0.40 (0.10)	0.26 (0.07)
Health lobbyist/ PAC x HELP	1.39 (0.10)	1.19 (0.06)	1.08 (0.08)	-0.00 (0.01)	0.04 (0.01)	0.01 (0.01)	1.40 (0.06)	1.42 (0.06)	1.12 (0.10)	0.25 (0.21)	0.72 (0.10)	0.06 (0.07)
Finance member	1.91 (1.32)	37.32 (21.84)	1.82 (0.46)	0.00 (0.03)	0.11 (0.02)	0.06 (0.03)	2.27 (0.67)	18.51 (4.96)	51.99 (52.53)	-0.05 (0.53)	2.37 (0.30)	0.81 (0.21)
HELP member	1.41 (1.03)	1.81 (1.28)	0.04 (0.04)	0.02 (0.03)	-0.02 (0.02)	0.00 (0.03)	1.07 (0.36)	1.24 (0.42)	0.22 (0.07)	-0.14 (0.53)	-0.21 (0.30)	-0.04 (0.21)

(continued)

TABLE 3.1 (continued)

	Individual Lobbyists						Lobbyist-Controlled PACs					
	Whether any contribution occurs in the dyad			Average dollars per week contributed			Whether any contribution occurs in the dyad			Average dollars per week contributed		
	Before	During	After	Before	During	After	Before	During	After	Before	During	After
Logged lobbying expenditures	1.17 (0.00)	1.20 (0.00)	1.18 (0.01)	0.01 (0.00)	0.01 (0.00)	0.01 (0.00)	1.29 (0.00)	1.35 (0.00)	1.27 (0.01)	0.40 (0.01)	0.21 (0.00)	0.06 (0.00)
Number of clients from senator's state	1.08 (0.00)	1.06 (0.00)	1.05 (0.00)	0.04 (0.00)	0.05 (0.00)	0.04 (0.00)	1.03 (0.01)	0.99 (0.01)	1.06 (0.01)	1.32 (0.09)	1.44 (0.04)	0.63 (0.02)
Constant	0.00 (0.00)	0.00 (0.00)	0.00 (0.00)	-0.19 (0.02)	-0.14 (0.02)	-0.12 (0.02)	0.00 (0.00)	0.00 (0.00)	0.00 (0.00)	-4.24 (0.38)	-2.60 (0.21)	-0.72 (0.15)
N	1262261	1450137	1238981	1262261	1506453	1290073	439166	551775	463044	439166	562285	497526
(Pseudo-)R²	0.16	0.14	0.12	0.01	0.01	0.00	0.14	0.17	0.11	0.02	0.02	0.01

Notes: "Average dollars per week" models use OLS regression with fixed effects for the senator. "Whether any contribution occurs in the dyad" models use logistic analysis with fixed effects for the senator and present odds ratios. The unit of analysis is either the lobbyist–senator dyad (under Individuals Lobbyists) or registrant–senator dyad (under Lobbyist-Controlled PACs). Models predict, as indicated, either the total dollars contributed per week, averaged across the number of weeks in each time period, or whether any contribution occurs in the dyad during the time period. "Before" refers to the period in 2008 before the election (except that logged lobbying expenditures and the number of clients from the senator's state cover the first three quarters of 2008). "During" begins with the election of President Obama on November 4, 2008, and ends when the president signs the second of the two health reform bills on March 30, 2010. "After" covers the period in 2010 after the bills are signed. Bold coefficients are statistically significant at $p < 0.05$.

(a)

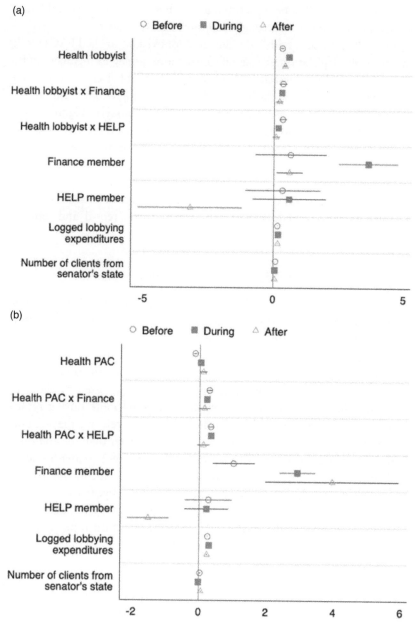

FIGURE 3.4 (a) Factors that predict whether or not a lobbyist contributes to a senator before, during, and after the health reform debate

(b) Factors that predict whether or not a lobbyist-controlled PAC contributes to a senator before, during, and after the health reform debate

Notes. *Markers show OLS coefficients surrounded by 95 percent confidence intervals. Models include fixed effects for the senator.*

lobbyists as the bill is being written and debated. The data on lobbyists' campaign contributions strongly support this hypothesis.

In 2008 and 2009, both individual and lobbyist-controlled PACs working on health legislation give significantly more money to members of the Finance and HELP committees relative to other lobbyists and other senators. This can be seen in the logit models (Figures 3.4(a) and 3.4(b), lines 2 and 3) as well as in the ordinary least-squares models (Figures 3.5(a) and 3.5(b), lines 2 and 3). As further evidence that these contributions are motivated by the health reform agenda, in 2010 after health legislation is signed, lobbyists' contributions to key committee members tend to decrease in both number and likelihood, except that individual health lobbyists continue to give disproportionately to Finance members (Figure 3.5(a), line 2), as senators considered whether to "repeal and replace" the law.

3.5.4 Tendency to Give at Particular Times

The third observable implication in this chapter holds that, beyond favoring key committee members, lobbyists should donate more at key points in the development of legislation. Specifically, we expect individual and lobbyist-controlled PACs working on health care to pay more financial attention to members working on the legislation during the time that they are working on it. This implication is somewhat supported by the data. Individual health lobbyists are more likely to contribute during reform compared to before (Figure 3.4(a), line 1). Before reform, the log-odds that a health lobbyist contributes are 34 percent greater than for nonhealth lobbyists, and during reform, the log-odds are 74 percent greater for health lobbyists than for nonhealth lobbyists. The total amount contributed is 3–6 percent greater per week for individual health lobbyists than for nonhealth lobbyists. In addition, as reform gets underway, individual health lobbyists who are already in the habit of donating direct 6 percent more money per week to members of the committee authoring the bill, the Senate Finance Committee (Figure 3.5(a), line 2).

As health reform gets underway, lobbyist-controlled health PACs increase the amounts of their contributions (Figure 3.5(b), line 1), if not the likelihood (Figure 3.4(b), line 1). These groups donate about 76 percent more than nonhealth lobbyists before reform and 57 percent more during reform (Figure 3.5(b), line 1). Interestingly, lobbyist-controlled PACs across all issue areas significantly increase their contributions to Finance members during the health reform period, (Figures 3.4(b)

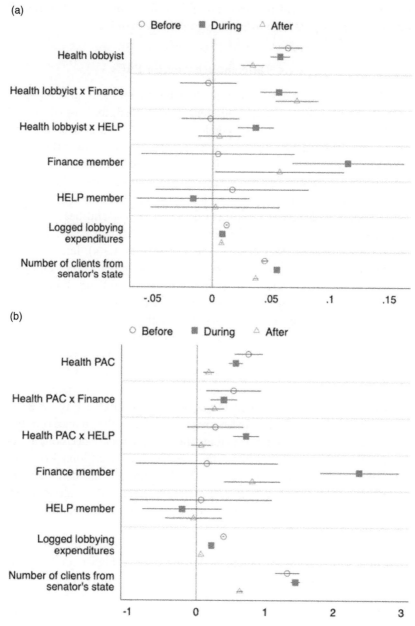

FIGURE 3.5 (a) Factors that predict the total dollars a lobbyist contributes to a senator before, during, and after the health reform debate
(b) Factors that predict the total dollars a lobbyist-controlled PAC contributes to a senator before, during, and after the health reform debate
Notes. *Markers show logit coefficients surrounded by 95 percent confidence intervals. Models include fixed effects for the senator.*

and 3.5(b), line 4), and this fact diminishes the seeming effect of health lobbyists directing PAC contributions to Finance members.

3.5.5 Different Behavior for PACs

The fourth implication is that individual health lobbyists and lobbyist-controlled health PACs behave differently. In general, lobbyist-controlled health PACs – displayed in figures ending in "b" – act in ways that are very similar to individual health lobbyists. Both contribute more than their non-health counterparts and both favor key committee members over other senators. But a number of noteworthy differences emerge from the models.

First, lobbyist-controlled PACs exhibit less sensitivity to timing than individual lobbyists do. After President Obama is elected and health reform begins to take shape, the probability that an individual health lobbyist donates to a senator significantly increases (Figures 3.4(a), line 1), while lobbyist-controlled health PACs are no more likely than other lobbyist-controlled PACs to contribute to senators. (Figures 3.4(b) line 1). Relatedly, individual lobbyists pay particular financial attention to key committee members, especially during and after the health reform period, and they favor Finance committee members over HELP committee members (Figure 3.4(a), lines 2-3, and Figure 3.5(a), lines 2-3). Lobbyist-controlled PACs also contribute more to key committee members, but they favor HELP members over Finance members (Figure 3.4(b), lines 2-3, and Figure 3.5(b), lines 2-3). This difference suggests that lobbyist-controlled PACs are less responsive than individual lobbyists are to the fact that the Finance committee, not the HELP committee, is making the vast majority of decisions about health reform.[12] After the legislation is signed, individual lobbyists show a sharp drop in their contributions to HELP members while continuing to support Finance members (Figure 3.4(a), lines 2 and 3), while lobbyist-controlled health PACs drop their contributions to all members (Figure 3.4(b), lines 2 and 3).

Given that about 12 percent of health care lobbyists during the health reform period were new (either newly registered lobbyists or lobbyists new to health issues), it makes sense that some of them did not know at the beginning which Senate committee would have ultimate control over the bill. Before the bill was drafted, it would have been natural for lobbyists to

---

[12] The Finance Committee had greater jurisdiction over the bill than the HELP committee did, as acknowledged by Professor John McDonough (2011), a senior staff member for HELP during this time.

think that the primary committee to write it would be the committee with "health" as the first word in its name. Yet, individual lobbyists seem to catch on to the greater importance of Finance much more quickly than lobbyist-controlled PACs do. Even after the legislation is signed, individual health lobbyists continue to exert pressure (in the form of greater contributions) on members of the Finance committee as it faces numerous attempts to repeal and replace the law it had written (Figure 3.4(a), line 2, and Figure 3.5(a), line 2), while at the same time lobbyist-controlled health PACs are no more likely to donate to Finance members than to other senators (Figure 3.4(b), line 2).

The four graphs and twelve models present a large number of findings, so I have summarized them in Table 3.2, along with the observable implications of the theory that the models test.

3.5.6 Control Variables

Regarding the control variables in the models, first, home-state connections are a significant factor in predicting whether or not and how much a lobbyist or their PAC gives to a senator. During the health reform period, as the number of clients that share the senator's home state increases from zero to one, the predicted total the lobbyist contributes increases by about 60 percent, and at the maximum number of clients during the reform period – fifty-two clients, the predicted contributions are nearly three times as much as when no clients are from the senator's state. For lobbyist-controlled PACs, when the registrant moves from zero clients from the senator's state to one, the predicted dollars donated per week move from 1.4 to 2.9, and at the maximum number – eighty-seven clients from the home state – the model predicts total contributions that are orders of magnitude greater than if none of the registrant's clients were from the senator's state.

Second, the more an organization spends on lobbying, the more likely are its lobbyists to make personal contributions to senators. During the health reform debate, for individual lobbyists, the model predicts that individual lobbyists whose logged lobbying expenditures are at the 75th percentile contribute about 40 percent more money than those at the 25th percentile. Among lobbyist-controlled PACs, registrants at the 75th percentile contribute about 50 percent more money than those at the 25th percentile. The greater tendency of groups that spend more on lobbying to also contribute greater funds to senators' campaigns is fully consistent with anecdotal accounts that well-paid lobbyists believe contributing is essential (e.g., Leech 2013, 42).

TABLE 3.2 *Summary of model findings*

Observable implication	Individual health lobbyists	Lobbyist-controlled health PACs
1. Health lobbyists act differently from nonhealth lobbyists.	Yes. In 2008–10, health lobbyists are more likely to give and to give more to senators than nonhealth lobbyists.	Somewhat. In 2008–10, health PACs give more, but are not more likely to give, to senators than nonhealth PACs.
2. Health lobbyists are more likely to give to key committee members than to other senators.	Yes. In 2008–10, health lobbyists are more likely to give and to give more to key committee members (especially Finance members) than to other senators.	Yes. In 2008–10, health PACs are more likely to give and to give more to key committee members than to other senators.
3. Health lobbyists are more likely to give at key times, especially to key members.	Somewhat. Health lobbyists are more likely to give during reform than at other times. During reform health lobbyists increase the amount of their contributions to Finance and HELP members, but not the likelihood of contributing to them.	Somewhat. Health PACs give senators more money than nonhealth PACs in all three time periods and give more to HELP members (but not Finance members) during reform than before. But they do not increase their contribution dollars during reform.
4. Individual health lobbyists are more sensitive than health PACs are to who is working on the legislation and when.	Yes. During and after reform, individual health lobbyists favor key committee members over other senators and favor Finance members over HELP members.	Yes. During reform, health PACs are more likely to give, and to give more, to HELP members than to Finance members.

Finally, the fixed effects for each senator are most likely to be significant during reform, and they are least likely to be significant afterward, providing further evidence of the strategically timed nature of lobbyists' campaign contributions. Although the models control for being on the Finance committee, the fixed effects parameters (which are not included in the table) show that some members of that committee are still marginally more likely to be associated with greater contributions (including Senators Baucus, Lincoln, Menendez, Rockefeller, and Schumer). Majority Leader Reid also receives disproportionately more contribution dollars relative to other senators. Among HELP members, only the chairman of the committee, Senator Dodd, receives significantly more contributions than other senators.

3.6 DISCUSSION AND CONCLUSIONS

In contrast to previous studies, the analysis in this chapter uses, as an explanatory variable, lobbyists' *personal* campaign contributions, and the contributions of PACs controlled by registered lobbyists, rather than contributions from PACs generally. These data yield new insights about lobbyists' attempts to curry favor with different senators. The analysis shows that lobbyists working on health reform are more likely to contribute to senators, and especially to key committee members, as the bill is being written and debated, relative to other senators and other times. PACs whose contributions are directed by health lobbyists give more to senators throughout 2008–10, and health PACs are more likely to favor key committee members, especially HELP members, compared to other lobbyist-controlled PACs and other senators.

The combination of health lobbyists' contributions to the right senators at the right times is evidence that lobbyists may use money strategically to do several things of which we should be suspicious. First, lobbyists may be using campaign contributions to curry favor with the key legislators drafting a very significant piece of legislation. Whether the contribution is a plea for attention (by all accounts the scarcest commodity in Washington), an attempt to bribe (albeit with relatively small amounts of money and leaving a publicly visible paper trail), a way of saying thanks for doing something to help the lobbyist (whether this is a policy favor or simply willingness to take a meeting), or a sincere wish for the Member's continued electoral success, we will likely never know. Yet my analyses of variations in donation patterns (1) between health lobbyists and nonhealth lobbyists at different times in the development of health reform legislation, (2) between the two health-writing committees and other senators, and (3) between individual lobbyists and lobbyist-controlled PACs, together suggest that lobbyists are maximizing, timing, and targeting their campaign contributions to senators strategically.

Some have argued that the low dollar limits on individuals' and PACs' contributions prevent this money from influencing legislator behavior (e.g., Milyo et al. 2000). While there remains, as discussed in this chapter, a federal limit on the amounts of money an individual and a PAC can contribute to federal candidates' campaign committees, there is no limit on the number of lobbyists an interest group can mobilize to donate to specific legislators. As such interest groups are at liberty to greatly multiply the dollars that a set of interests can contribute to Members' campaigns. We also saw evidence that as Supreme Court decisions to allow unlimited expenditures on campaigns took effect, lobbyist-controlled PACs suddenly curtailed their contributions to senators' official campaigns, presumably shifting those dollars to Super PACs. Like a squeezed balloon, outside groups' attempts to influence Congress create a new spending bulge nearby.

This chapter shows that interest groups commonly exceed the limits put on PACs by amassing contributions from the lobbying firms and individual lobbyists they hire. By isolating lobbyists' potentially transaction-oriented contributions, as distinct from the ideologically driven contributions of members of the general public, these new data shed light on the stealthy, strategic behavior of lobbyists who, by definition, seek to access legislators and influence legislation.

It can be very difficult to identify and distinguish the various reasons for lobbyists' contributions (Lowery 2013), as we have discussed. Yet, this chapter reveals the predictability of lobbyists' contributions based on their interest in the hottest legislation of the day. The analysis supports the possibility that financial contributions from lobbyists are intended as transactions rather than ideological commitment. The findings do not necessarily mean that the purpose of lobbyists' campaign contributions is to "buy" desired policy outcomes – but they do strongly support the notion that lobbyists use contributions to attract attention from, increase access to, and possibly elicit reciprocal actions by powerful US senators.

4

Stealth Fundraising and Legislative Favors

> I don't know a politician who enjoys fundraising.
>
> Senator John McCain, quoted in Cassata (1996)

Despite the understandable reluctance of most people – and politicians – to cold-call asking for money, fundraising is imperative to getting into Congress and staying there. Depending on the timing of elections and the safety of the incumbent's seat, Members of Congress must "dial for dollars" nearly every working day in call centers across the street from the House and Senate office buildings. The Republican House Campaign Committee in 2013 recommended that Members spend four hours per day on "call time" – twice as much as on constituent meetings and legislative work (Shevlin and Doran 2016). Speaker of the House Nancy Pelosi said she attended some 400 fundraisers in 2011 (Glass et al. 2012) – more than one per day. Like telemarketers, Members of Congress are given lists of names and numbers and scripts to read. A *60 Minutes* hidden-camera report described the scene:

About a dozen tiny offices, equipped with a phone and computer, line a corridor. This is where Members of Congress sit behind closed doors and plow through lists of donors dialing for dollars. Outside in the main hallway is a big board where the amount each Member has raised for the party is posted for all to see and compare. "It is a cult-like boiler room," [said House Member David Jolly (R-FL)].

Another Member from the Democratic side, who said that the constant pressure to fundraise was among the reasons he retired in 2012, said about the call center he used, "It smells like a gymnasium locker room after a few hours. It's awful, it's like a sweatshop" (Dennis Cardoza [D-CA.] quoted in Shevlin and Doran 2016). It is easy to understand from this that Members of Congress would rather be doing something else – legislating, helping constituents, or just about anything else – rather than spending so much time raising money. And yet, especially after *Citizens United* allowed any organization to spend unlimited amounts of money on political advertising, raising $18,000 per day is essential for keeping one's job (Shevlin and Doran 2016). It is understandable that Members in this position would be frustrated, as demonstrated in a voice mail left during one of these calls:

This is Eleanor Norton, Congresswoman Eleanor Holmes Norton. I noticed that you have given to other colleagues on the Transportation and Infrastructure Committee. I am a senior Member, a 20-year veteran, and I am handling the largest economic development project in the United States now, the Homeland Security compound of three buildings being built on the old St. Elizabeth Hospital site. ... I was frankly surprised to see that we don't have a record, so far as I can tell, of your having given to me, despite my long and deep work, essentially in your sector. I'm simply candidly calling to ask for a contribution. I'm asking you to give to the Citizens for Eleanor Holmes Norton, PO Box 70626. (Glass et al. 2012)

This voice mail message is revealing for several reasons. It exhibits the implicit norm that federal building contractors should contribute to members of the committee that has jurisdiction over federal building contracts. It was shared publicly by someone we assume to be a building contractor who had donated to numerous other (mostly white male) members of the committee but had not donated to this (Black female) member, despite her being the fourth or fifth highest-ranking majority member on the sixty-person committee.[1] And it shows, more broadly, how tight the connection is between congressional fundraising and legislative benefits for those lobbyists who help in the fundraising effort.

In this chapter, I argue that stealth lobbyists share the fundraising burden borne by Members of Congress by hosting fundraising events for them. Members do not have to plan the event or invite guests; they just show up, say a few words, shake a lot of hands, and maybe get a bite to eat. Compared to the sweatshops of party-provided Capitol Hill cubicles, being honored at a fundraiser would seem to be a welcome gift – and one that does not even have to be reported.

The call lists provided to Members dialing for dollars consist of previous donors to the campaign, friends and family of donors, and, eventually, donors to any candidate of the same party. These are cold calls to people whom the Member generally does not know. By contrast, fundraising events are attended by Washington insiders – mostly lobbyists who have

---

[1] We do not know the date the recording was made, but if she is a twenty-year veteran, she would have been the fourth- or fifth-highest ranking Democrat on the committee in 2012.

met the Member in the past or are likely to meet him in the future. The candidate is surrounded by friendly faces – a phenomenon that thrills politicians, especially in contrast to the windowless cubicles described earlier. The candidate does not even have to say, "Will you donate $XXXX to my campaign?" because the donation is built into the price of admission to the event.

This chapter presents a glimpse into the fundraising world of incumbent Members of Congress. I argue that the great demands on Members' time, and the relatively low limits placed on campaign contributions, mean that fundraisers hosted by lobbyists are even more valuable to Members of Congress than contributions. To assess this expectation, I present data about fundraising events that occurred over a ten-year period. Many of these events were hosted by lobbyists interested in health reform legislation and for the benefit of senators working on health reform legislation. I analyze these data and link them to actual actions Members took on behalf of the hosts of these fundraisers. The data show that when interest groups or their lobbyists host a fundraiser for a senator, the senator is significantly more likely to introduce in committee an amendment requested by the fundraising group, relative to other groups and senators. We see in this chapter a significant and normatively troublesome link between interest groups' fundraising activity and legislative effort by the beneficiaries of those fundraisers.

4.1 THE IMMENSE PRESSURE TO FUNDRAISE

For Members of Congress, contributors are necessary, rare, and valuable. But any one contributor cannot secure an electoral victory; rather, it takes many contributions from different groups, lobbyists, and others to build up a candidate's war chest sufficiently to mount a viable reelection campaign. In 2009–10 as health reform was being written, donors could give just $2,400 per donor per candidate. It takes many, many of these maximum contributions for Members to amass the amount needed to have a reasonable chance at winning. The median senator running for reelection spent $8.6 million in 2010 (among these, the median loser spent even more – $16.5 million). In the House, the median incumbent running for reelection spent $1.2 million (among these, the median loser spent $2.4 million).[2] And the numbers keep going up: In 2018, winning in the

---

[2] The data described in this paragraph are summarized from CRP data and available at www .opensecrets.org/elections-overview/winning-vs-spending.

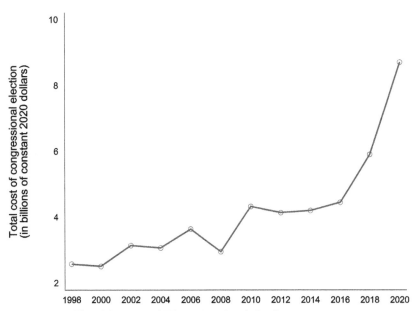

FIGURE 4.1 The rising cost of US congressional elections
Notes. *Figures include spending for all congressional candidates by candidates, parties, PACs, and observable outside organizations. Source: Center for Responsive Politics, "Total Cost of Election (1998–2020; Adjusted for Inflation)."*

House required a war chest of nearly $1.5 million, and the median Senate seat cost more than $11 million. Figure 4.1 shows the inflation-adjusted total costs of federal election campaigns.

Yet raising all of this money is not really optional. In 2010 the candidate that spent more money beat the opponent in 86 percent of House races and 78 percent Senate races. And in 2016 these numbers were up to 95 percent and 85 percent. In a two-person race, money does not always buy victory: but it usually does.

Given this pressure, fundraising is a constant occupation for Members of Congress, as witnessed in the party-run "sweatshops" described earlier. In comparison, the chance to go to a restaurant or Capitol Hill townhouse and be surrounded by lobbyists who (at least pretend to) respect the Member and make them feel good at a fundraising event must be a very appealing alternative.

Especially since HLOGA in 2008 ended the popular practice of lobbyists paying for Members' breakfasts, lunches, dinners, sports tickets, and so on, lobbyists have fewer opportunities to ingratiate themselves to politicians and their staff. This change from previous norms cut down on lobbyists' ability to talk to legislators about their issues without staff or anyone else being there to monitor or interrupt. From the perspective of lobbyist Howard Marlowe:

Between the emails, and the tweets, and the video conferences with the district, it is hard to get [Members'] attention in the office. So if I could get them out to the cafeteria, or to the Monocle or something like that for lunch, it would be absolutely great. But instead, because of HLOGA's gift ban, I can see the legislative person only at the campaign fundraiser, and Members of Congress take advantage of that. (Leech 2013, 8)

We can infer that Members pressure lobbyists to host fundraising events for them, and it looks like lobbyists are willing to comply. The number-one type of fundraiser-host in the data presented in this chapter is a lobbyist. For these lobbyists, hosting fundraisers has major benefits, which may include rare opportunities to have the ear of a national decision-maker.

Few legislators and lobbyists welcome the increasing role of fundraising in campaigns – and by extension, in policymaking. Senator Evan Bayh specifically cited the pressure to fundraise as one of his reasons for retiring from the Senate in 2011: "It's not uncommon for a Member of the Senate to have a fundraising breakfast, a fundraising lunch, and a fundraising dinner, and then when the Senate breaks for the week to go home, more fundraisers" (quoted in Klein 2010). Indeed, my data show the modal times for fundraisers to be held are breakfast (8:30 am), lunch (noon), and the end of the workday (6 pm). This schedule allows Members to fundraise at times when they are not expected to be in the office or committee room – and to attend multiple fundraisers a day.

The growing intensity of fundraising in Washington led veteran lobbyist Howard Marlowe to express "concern about the new tendency to mix legislative policy and political funding":

Fifteen years ago Congresswoman Jones would have said, "I'm having a difficult race. I only won by 65 percent last time. I've got a real rough race this time. I really need your support." Today, it would be Ms. Jones saying, "I'm helping you out. What's *your* issue?" She will go around the room and ask each lobbyist who paid to come to the fundraiser what they want. (Leech 2013, 7–8)

4.2 THE BENEFITS OF FUNDRAISERS

Despite the tacit preference of legislators and lobbyists not to engage in constant fundraising activity, fundraising events do have real benefits for both. I outline four of these next.

4.2.1 Getting Around Contribution Limits

In the United States, private donors supply *all* funding to congressional candidates. Campaigns are expensive, principally because television ads are expensive (and are not publicly subsidized). Yet, individual and group donations to congressional campaigns are limited by law to $5,000 or less per candidate per election. These low limits mean successful candidates must do an incredible amount of fundraising.

Fundraising events have an amazing multiplier effect on the contribution dollars a candidate can accumulate in a short period of time. Fundraiser hosts know this, and typically bundle all the contributions solicited at the event and present them to the politician, in effect taking credit for the whole bundled amount – even while a direct contribution of this amount would be illegal. Fundraising events help politicians to reach their fundraising goals in considerably less time, and successful fundraising can give politicians an edge in the next election.

4.2.2 Providing a Subsidy to Legislators

Lobbyists are not permitted to pay for the costs of fundraising events, such as space rental, food, and invitations, but lobbyists can and frequently do invest their time and other nonfinancial resources into fundraisers. Fundraiser hosts identify willing donor-guests, arrange the hospitality, issue invitations, collect the contributions, and deliver them to the candidate or her representative. These lobbyist-provided services free up the Member to allocate more time to the issues in which they are interested. Just as organizations aim their lobbying efforts at legislators who are already inclined to pursue the group's policy goals (Denzau and Munger 1986; Hall and Wayman 1990; DeGregorio 1997; Hojnacki and Kimball 1998; Esterling 2004; Hall and Deardorff 2006), we can assume that lobbyists also elect to host fundraisers for legislators who have the capability and inclination to act on the lobbying group's objectives. In this way, fundraising lobbyists help Members to devote the scarcest resource on Capitol Hill – attention (Baumgartner et al. 2009) – to the lobby group's policy priorities.

4.2.3 Increasing Lobbyists' Access to Members

By all accounts, access to Members of Congress is difficult for lobbyists to come by, as we saw in Chapter 2. A third benefit to fundraisers for lobbyists is that hosting them provides virtually guaranteed, semiprivate access to targeted politicians. As lobbyist Howard Marlowe noticed:

Some lobbyists lobby by fundraising only. Those lobbyists can get to regularly see Congresswoman Jones and all the other people that they're raising money for in the fundraising environment. They get to know the Members of Congress at the fundraisers. They get to talk all the time. (Quoted in Leech 2013, 8–9)

4.2.4 Eluding Notice

A fourth advantage of fundraisers is that they do not have to be reported, and as such, they are almost totally unmonitored. HLOGA sought to increase the transparency of fundraising by requiring committees to report the "bundled contributions" of individual registered lobbyists who raise large amounts of money for a campaign. But for several reasons, this change in the law has had little effect on behavior. There is a threshold below which bundles need not be disclosed ($16,000 in 2009), and fundraisers hosted by multiple lobbyists can divide the total raised among all of the hosts (or increase the number of hosts) in order to avoid reaching this threshold amount. While the mean number of hosts per fundraiser in these data is two, 3 percent of fundraisers are hosted by ten or more named hosts – meaning these events could raise $160,000 for a single politician and still not be reported. In addition, if the lobbyist is not explicitly credited for the bundle by the campaign, it is not considered bundling, even if the lobbyist organized the event. The data show the effects of these seeming loopholes: Between 2009 and 2015 only 133 congressional campaign committees reported receiving any bundled contributions, while in the 2012 cycle alone there were 3,151 campaign committees in operation – suggesting that the bundling reporting requirement is capturing only a small fraction of the fundraising events that occur.[3]

The opacity of fundraising activities has prevented scholars and the public from examining who is hosting them, who is benefitting, and what the lobbyist or group gets in exchange. Fundraising events are, in short, an important, mostly overlooked opportunity for lobby groups to pressure, or even to buy, their way to preferred public policies.

---

[3] Two instances of bundling by lobbyists for senators on the committee are treated as fundraising events in the analysis.

4.3 THE BENEFITS OF AMENDMENTS

As we will discuss in this chapter and in the next, in 2009, members of the Senate Finance Committee working on health reform legislation had an opportunity to introduce their own individual amendments to the legislation before they voted on it and sent it to the full Senate. Like fundraising events, microlegislation in the form of amendments offered in committee provide lobbyists and legislators an excellent opportunity to quietly trade favors. I describe four such benefits next.

4.3.1 Amendments Provide Groups with Private Benefits

For the interest groups that request them, amendments almost always mean financial benefits, regardless of whether they represent business, professional associations, consumers, nonprofit organizations, or patient groups. The text of amendments often makes clear who would benefit from the microlegislation. Examples can be seen in amendments that would:

- increase the premium discount that employers can use to reward employees for participating in wellness programs, requested by the Retail Industry Leaders Association;
- allow patients to use Medicare-funded hospice care even if they do not have a terminal illness, requested by the National Hospice and Palliative Care Organization;
- provide access to home infusion therapy services for Medicare beneficiaries, requested by the National Home Infusion Association;
- provide mandatory funding to allow for full national implementation of aging and disability resource centers, requested by National Association of Area Agencies on Aging; and
- fund the "best possible training" for home health and other workers who provide hands-on care, requested by the Paraprofessional Healthcare Institute.

While amendments can be based in ideological or practical policy preferences held by the senator, such as Senator Schumer's "level playing field" public health insurance option or Senator Kyl's proposal to strike all cuts to the Medicare Advantage program, more often, the amendments benefit a narrow set of private interests.

4.3.2 Amendments Provide Lobbyists and Legislators
with Career Benefits

For the individual lobbyists who represent those groups, amendments help achieve professional goals of getting legislative results for clients. Having written evidence of her influence over a particular senator can help a lobbyist in their future efforts to attract and retain clients or to elicit promotions or new job offers. Even if an amendment has no realistic chance of being included in the law, the lobbyist benefits from having it introduced. The lobbyist can always blame a crowded agenda, deal-making, or the other party if the amendment fails to be adopted.

For the legislator, amendments can enhance reelection chances by providing another opportunity, if they want it, to take positions, advertise, and claim credit (Mayhew 1974). For example, amendments allow Members to take a stand against Medicare fraud, to speak up for midwives, to show off their commitment to reducing hospital-acquired infections, or to encourage employer-sponsored wellness programs. Members of Congress are skilled at framing their amendments in a defensible way that does not make them look like they were requested by particular lobby groups – though the groups know they are the result of the lobbyists' efforts.

4.3.3 Amendments Are Unconstrained

In the Senate Finance Committee as it was working on health reform legislation, any member could offer as many amendments as they wanted. Since these were all submitted in writing, and only a fraction was discussed on the record during markup, these amendments were not limited or discouraged in any way. For instance, Senator Hatch introduced three very similar amendments to limit noneconomic damages in health care lawsuits to $250,000, $500,000, or $1,000,000, respectively, demonstrating that there was no marginal cost to the senator or other disincentive to offer additional amendments.

There is one technical constraint on amendments that might limit them, but in practice it does not. Senate Finance Committee rules require senators to accompany their amendments with cost-savings measures that would offset any additional costs to the Treasury. In practice, however, senators provide general ideas rather than legitimate and specific provisions. As examples: "Amendment will be offset by closing corporate tax loopholes." "Offset: A commensurate increase in the annual insurance fee." Or just "Offset: To be determined."[4] The fact that these amendments were nonetheless offered and given an amendment number by committee staff is an indication that senators were not constrained by this rule.

Lobby groups, too, seem to feel no limitations in requesting as many amendments as senators are willing to entertain – and if one senator declines, they can just shop around for a different senator.

4.3.4 Amendments Encourage Reciprocation

A third benefit to amendments is that they may – and might even be designed to – elicit fundraising assistance. As implied by Congresswoman Norton's leaked voice mail message, under certain conditions, Members *expect* to receive campaign contributions, and even to be honored at fundraising events, as a result of the legislation they provide to lobbyists. Relatedly, Members who benefit from a lobby group's contributions or fundraising efforts might feel a reciprocity norm that they should return the favor.

In summary, microlegislative amendments are a mutually beneficial mechanism that allows senators to earn the good will of lobby groups and helps lobbyists to achieve professional goals – and may also encourage the lobby group to host a fundraising event to benefit the obliging senator. The constant need for Members of Congress to raise vast sums of money in order to keep their jobs, combined with the low cost of offering amendments that benefit the lobbyists who help Members raise this money, support the hypothesis that *when a lobbyist hosts one or more fundraisers for a senator, the senator is more likely to advocate for one of the lobby group's preferences as an amendment to legislation, relative to other senators and other lobbying groups*. This expectation is inspired by the usefulness hypothesis introduced in Chapter 1.

4.4 UNUSUAL DATA

In this chapter, I am able to make extraordinary inferences by combining three rare sources of data in a way that previous scholars have not been able to do. These unique data comprise (1) written comments submitted by lobby groups, (2) amendments offered by senators on the Finance committee, and (3) a database of invitations to Washington fundraising events, all of which I describe next.

---

[4] Another reason that offsets are so vague is that when a Member conceives of a cost-saving provision that will be palatable, the legislator keeps it confidential so that others do not use it.

4.4.1 Lobby Groups' Written Preferences

Seeking to avoid the debacle of the last serious health reform effort in 1994, Senator Baucus and, to some extent, Ranking Member Chuck Grassley pursued an open, bipartisan, negative-lobbying-proof process. In the spring of 2009, the committee released a series of three volumes of "Options for Health Reform," which contained a wide range of possible elements of health reform legislation. In an unusual move, committee leaders solicited comments from the public (read lobbyists) on these proposals, which they would use to inform a draft of the bill. The committee had published proposals for comment in the past, but only rarely. My position as a congressional fellow gave me access to more than 500 letters submitted by nearly 900 lobby groups. These letters provide an important window into what lobbying groups want, because researchers seldom have access to detailed data about exactly what public policy outcomes groups are seeking – making it difficult if not impossible to assess their success (Lowery 2013). As a result, US interest group scholars have very rarely analyzed the content of lobby groups' arguments to Members of Congress (Burstein 2014, ch. 6).

The letters themselves contain various indications of stealth lobbying. First, despite the dominance of business-oriented groups among lobbyist registrations, it is not-for-profit groups that submit the plurality of comments to the Senate Finance Committee on health reform, as seen in Table 4.1. About 56 percent of the groups submitting comments are charitable or advocacy groups (501(c)(3) or 501(c)(4)), while a smaller number, some 43 percent, come from business-oriented groups, including trade and professional associations (often 501(c)(6)). Yet these nonprofit groups are not necessarily the purely charitable public interest groups connoted by the label "nonprofit." Frequently, while the legal status of the group is nonprofit, it represents individuals and businesses that are very much profit-seeking – and this is by design.

Business firms often prefer to use trade associations than to do their own lobbying. The association provides political anonymity to the businesses it represents. For smaller businesses, lobbying by proxy is easier and cheaper than lobbying on one's own behalf. Congressional Members and staff know that the "peak association" – the largest and most active association for an industry – represents dozens if not hundreds of firms or professionals. Organizations such as the American Medical Association (AMA), the American Hospital Association (AHA), America's Health Insurance Plans (AHIP), the

TABLE 4.1 *Types of groups that submitted comments about health reform legislation to the Senate Finance Committee*

Group type	IRS definition of type[a]	Examples in the data	Number of these identified in the data
501(c)(3)	Religious, educational, charitable, scientific	Child Welfare League of America, Clinical Immunology Society, Atrius Health	434
501(c)(6)	Business leagues, chambers of commerce, real-estate boards	American Assn. for Homecare, US Chamber of Commerce, Florida Hospital Assn.	161
Firm	IRS requires 10-K if publicly traded	Sonic Healthcare, Novo Nordisk, Sierra Benefit Solutions	99
Other business groups and coalitions	n/a	Provider Roundtable, Coverage That Works Coalition, Stand for Quality Coalition	54
Nonprofits and nonprofit coalitions	n/a	Women & Health Care Coalition Disclosure Project	34
501(c)(4)	Civic leagues, social welfare organizations	AARP (formerly the American Association of Retired Persons), National Association of Counties	28
501(c)(5)	Labor organizations	American Farm Bureau Federation, AFL-CIO	4
501(c)(9)	Voluntary employee beneficiary associations	Cook Group Incorporated, Service Employees International Union	3
Government	n/a	Calif. Dept. of Public Health, New Mexico Medicaid	3

[a] *Source:* IRS Publication 557, 2013.

Advanced Medical Technology Association (AdvaMed), and the Pharmaceutical Researchers and Manufacturers Association (PhRMA) are treated as the business elites with which government actors negotiate.

Like peak associations, coalitions are useful in that they can mask the self-serving purpose of groups' requests. These coalitions tend to use fanciful names, such as the Coverage That Works coalition, the Stand for Quality coalition, and the Access to Medical Imaging coalition. Many of these are seemingly ad hoc collections of different groups under a single letterhead and are brokered by lobbyists working at lobbying firms (Heaney 2006).

As further evidence of their stealth nature, the submitted letters are frequently written not by the organizations themselves but by "hired gun" contract lobbyists. We know this because the contact person is usually listed along with an email address at a lobbying firm, even if the letter is signed by someone who works for the group. While it may be perfectly reasonable for a group to ask its hired lobbyist to write such a letter, the practice reveals that many letter authors are not authentically describing from their point of view the problems they think need legislative action but are instead being packaged by a paid professional.

4.4.2 Committee Members' Amendments

In the lead-up to marking up the bill, committee members began to add, subtract, or change details of what the bill would do. Across twenty-two committee members (excluding the chairman, who does not offer amendments because he controls the bill), a total of 564 amendments were introduced for consideration by the full committee. This is a much higher number than usual owing to the high salience of health reform. Even more unusual was Senator Baucus's decision to publish all 564 amendments on the committee's website – a move the committee had never made before.[5] Baucus cited this choice as among his committee's efforts toward transparency in pursuing health reform legislation.

4.4.3 Fundraising Activity

Since 2005, the Sunlight Foundation, a nonprofit government watchdog group that has now been absorbed into the Center for Responsive Politics

---

[5] This is according to Chairman Max Baucus as captured in the transcript.

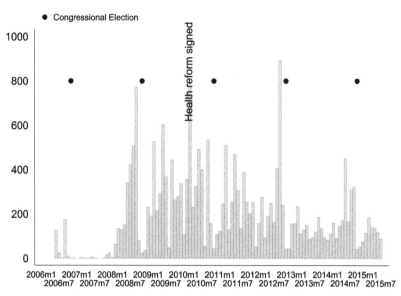

FIGURE 4.2 Number of fundraising events captured in database, by month

(CRP), has collected anonymously submitted invitations to the many fundraising events that occur virtually every day on and near Capitol Hill. These are an important and uncommon source of data, especially since there is no obligation to report details about fundraisers to any public authority. The invitations, which the Sunlight Foundation converted into fields in a spreadsheet, contain more than 22,000 distinct congressional fundraising events between 2005 and 2015. We cannot be sure what portion of the population of fundraisers it captures; certainly, it underreports fundraising events. Still, these are the best data available on fundraising events.

Figure 4.2 shows that fundraising peaks just before congressional elections in even-numbered years. The month health reform is signed into law, however, the number of fundraising events exceeds any other time that is not right before an election. What to infer from this? The most innocent explanation is that Members of Congress were so occupied by health reform legislation that fundraising events slowed down in the final stages, and to compensate, fundraising surged after the law was adopted. A less benign explanation is that lobby groups that were happy with how health reform had turned out sought to reward the legislators who had provided requested legislation or who had voted the way groups wanted.

4.4.4 Key Explanatory Variable: Group Hosts a Fundraiser for the Senator

The time period I use extends from 2006 to 2015, as shown in Figure 4.2. This extended time frame allows for the possibility that a health lobbyist hosts a fundraiser for a senator after the bill is passed, or that a senator remembers a fundraiser held before consideration of the legislation began.

I divided events hosted for multiple senators and hosted by multiple lobbyists so that the unit of observation is the senator-host dyad. Multiple events within the same dyad were reshaped into new variables (dyadfundraiser1, dyadfundraiser2, etc.). Some hosts are the clients of lobbyists, or groups that lobby on their own behalf (e.g., National Stone, Sand, and Gravel Association [ROCKPAC], REALTORS Political Action Committee [RPAC]); others were lobbying firms, known as registrants (e.g., Akin, Gump, Strauss, Hauer & Feld Civic Action Committee). About half of the individual hosts were registered lobbyists; the rest could not be identified, except for certain politically interested celebrities (e.g., Ben Affleck, Condoleezza Rice).

The matching of individuals who hosted fundraisers with individuals who lobbied was an iterative process done by identifying the most likely true matches first. CRP's *OpenSecrets.org* website very helpfully provides unique identifiers for lobbyists, which allowed me to disambiguate multiple lobbyists with the same or similar names. But the hosts of fundraisers may be listed under slightly different names. I first matched individual lobbyists to individual fundraisers by first and last name. I then tried the most common nickname or alternate spelling in place of the first name (e.g., Val instead of Valerie, Steven instead of Stephen). I moved through alternative names until no more matches could be made. Similarly, I standardized the names of organizations that hosted fundraisers, using the CRP's version of the group's name. CRP also provides the names of "parent" groups, which I used to consolidate spending and lobbying activity (unless multiple "child" groups submitted separate letters to the committee regarding health reform).

I used CRP's cleaned versions of Lobbying Disclosure Act data to link each individual lobbyist to the lobbyist's employer (in the case of in-house lobbyists) or clients (in the case of firm lobbyists). For a lobbyist to be matched to a client, the lobbyist had to personally work for that specific client, and not just for a firm that represented the client.

To fully gauge the effects of fundraising on Members of Congress, the data should contain instances of fundraising as well as, importantly, instances of not fundraising. Without including groups that did not fundraise for the senator, we cannot determine whether the fundraising made the member more likely to take an action that benefits the group. By pairing every member of the committee with every organization that submitted comments to the committee, we can make more robust inferences about the effects of fundraising on actions by the senator. I therefore create a dyadic dataset of 866 organizations ×22 committee members = 19,052 dyadic observations.

4.4.5 Dependent Variable: Amendment-Offering

If a legislator offers an amendment in committee that is requested by an interest group, this is an indicator that the senator is making an effort on the group's behalf. Letter writers typically comment directly on one or more of the proposals highlighted in the Options for Health Reform documents promulgated by the committee; some groups also specify particular changes, additions, or subtractions they would like to see. The letters generally do not specify that a senator should introduce this substance as an amendment to the draft bill, at least in part because the draft bill had not yet been written and could still contain the change the lobbyist is advocating. Still, the letters included in the sample all contain interest group preferences that could reasonably be introduced as amendments to the draft bill.

To match amendments to legislative requests, I first identified in each letter any and all specific requests that were *not* legislative provisions suggested by the committee in its draft Options for Health Care Reform. Many letters had no specific additional requests.

Like students trying to avoid plagiarizing, senators intentionally alter the language given to them by interest groups. Identifying matches was an inductive process in which the objective was, first, to amass a long list of all potential matches, and second, to reduce this list down to near-certain matches. Importantly, identifying matches of group requests and offered amendments was blind to interest groups' campaign contributions.

Unusually, one senator, Jeff Bingaman, explicitly listed specific groups as having endorsed his eight amendments. For all other amendments, I started by using plagiarism detection software. As has also been performed by a number of scholars recently (Corley 2008; Wilkerson et al. 2015), plagiarism detection software facilitates the matching process. Using the free software WCopyFind, I compared the amendments (as a corpus) to the letters. The software was set to identify any common phrases of between two and six words, allowing between one and four imperfections, and ignoring punctuation and letter case. I read each of these to distinguish insignificant coincidental language ("the Department of Health and Human Services") from substantive policy overlap.

In a second stage of match identification, I chose key words from each *request* and searched all the amendments for those key words, and I read each of these to determine if they were a substantive match. I also created key words from each *amendment* and again used WCopyFind to identify these key words in any request. Following this was a reductive process of extracting, from a list of all *potential* matches, a set of *definite* matches between what the group wanted and what the senator puts in an amendment. To make this determination, I selected the phrases from the letters that closely matched phrases selected from the amendments. In cases in which I had doubts about whether an amendment and a letter were describing the same policy solution, I used the Internet to learn more about the group's positions and the legislator's preferences and used this information to determine true matches.

A match counted only if the group affirmatively made a request that was *not already in the Options*. In these cases, the group, not the committee staff, originated the provision, and this phenomenon is fundamentally different from expressing a position about a provision that committee staff have already considered.

Finally, I reviewed the three columns of (1) interest group language, (2) amendment language, and (3) Options language (if any), and I evaluated whether the amendment and letter were a definite or probable match. Matches were only definite if I determined that the group's requests and the amendment were *almost certainly* describing the same proposal. Table 4.2 offers some examples of the matches produced by this procedure.

4.4.6 Control Variables: The Lobby Group

I collected and linked various independent variables that describe each interest group's political activities and other factors associated with lobbying power. Data for these variables come from numerous sources: the Senate's database of registered lobbyists' activities and expenses and its separate database of registered lobbyists' campaign contributions; several databases on nonprofit organizations (provided by GuideStar, the Foundation Center, and the Urban Institute); the Securities and

TABLE 4.2 *Examples of letters matched to amendments*

Excerpt from letter	Excerpt from amendment
[We recommend] developing additional HCBS enhanced matching options, including a 5-year period for improving the HCBS/institutional care balance, with greater enhanced matching for new HCBS beneficiaries in the least balanced states initial expense, and reduced matching for states that fail to meet balancing targets.	This amendment provides a modest, targeted, 5-year-limited increase in federal matching payments (FMAP) for Medicaid covered home and community-based services (HCBS).
Committee should consider recommending the removal of cost-sharing for all appropriate immunizations (i.e., recommended by the Advisory Committee on Immunization Practices [ACIP]).	No cost-sharing (e.g., deductibles, copayments) under Medicare for all USPSTF recommended preventive care services and immunizations recommended by the Advisory Committee on Immunization Practices (ACIP).
[We] urge that the credit be structured so that it could be applied against the payroll taxes paid by both for-profits and non-profits.	Non-profit entities that meet the eligibility requirements of the small business credit would be eligible to receive the credit.
[the law] should establish by law a transition pathway of updates linked to the Medicare Economic Index, to complete replacement of the SGR [sustainable growth rate] by 2015.	The amendment would eliminate the sustainable growth rate formula and provide an update to physicians and other health care providers covered by the Medicare physician fee schedule equal to or based on the Medicare Economic Index (MEI).
We urge the Committee to consider increasing the premium discount to allow a 50 percent premium reduction for healthy lifestyle programs authorized under the existing HIPAA regulation.	This amendment codifies the current regulatory framework of allowances for premium deduction under HIPAA, immediately raising the allowed percentage reduction in premium (or rebate or a modification of a co-pay or deductible) from 20 percent to 30 percent and allowing the Secretaries of HHS, Department of Labor and Treasury the discretion to take the percentage up to 50 percent for adherence to or participation in a reasonably designed program of health promotion and disease prevention.

(continued)

TABLE 4.2 *(continued)*

Excerpt from letter	Excerpt from amendment
[We] recommend considering an increase in FMAP for HCBS services beyond 1 percent. . . . consider conditioning the receipt of the proposed 1 percent FMAP increase on successful submission by each state of a workforce development plan	This amendment provides a modest, targeted, 5-year-limited increase in federal matching payments (FMAP) for Medicaid covered home and community-based services (HBCS).
. . . provide more flexibility to small businesses to become more active in wellness programs . . . The Committee's proposal to provide employers with 50 or fewer employees with a credit limited to $400 per employee with no sunset requirement is policy in the right direction.	Under this amendment, a tax credit would be allowed for 50 percent of the costs paid by an employer for providing a "qualified wellness program" during a taxable year. The amount of the credit would be limited to an amount not exceeding $200 for each of the first 50 employees, plus $100 for each additional employee beyond the first 50 employees.
Without standardized expectations from state-to-state, there is a great probability of confusion on the part of consumers and manufacturers due to non-standardized definitions and reporting requirements.	This amendment would pre-empt any state (or political subdivision of a state) physician payment disclosure law or regulation to prevent the unnecessary need to potentially comply with potentially 51 different disclosure requirements.
Providing a full credit up to 10 employees provides help to the businesses that generally need it the most. The credit needs to be capped at some level of employees and phased out to ensure that no business is immediately cut-off because it has added employees. Instead a phased-out credit ensures that the tax benefit is gradually reduced with the growth of the business. . . . the average wage of full-time employees at businesses with fewer than 10 employees is over $30,000 meaning that in many cases the value of the credit is already cut in half.	This amendment would modify the Chairman's Mark so that employers whose employees have average annual full-time equivalent wages from the employer of less than $30,000 would qualify for the full credit. The credit would phase out for an employer for whom the average wages per employee is between $30,000 and $40,000 at a rate of five percent for each $500 increase of average wages above $30,000.

(continued)

TABLE 4.2 *(continued)*

Excerpt from letter	Excerpt from amendment
[We] urge the Committee to include legislative language currently being drafted by Senator Cantwell under the name of "Project 2020" in the health reform package. Project 2020 offers a fully developed legislative plan to take these three critical and tested programs to scale nationally, providing the necessary infrastructure, dedicated funding, technical assistance and evaluation.	The amendment modifies the Aging and Disability Resource Center (ADRC) section in the Chairman's Mark to increase the total ADRC authorization to a total of $727 million for the years 2010 through 2020 years. This funding expands the Mark's current proposal to allow for full national implementation of the ADRC pilot project.

Exchange Commission's Edgar database of publicly traded companies; and aggregated data produced by CRP.

Group's lobbying expenditures. A group's total expenditures on lobbying is the variable most often used to control for lobbying intensity. This variable captures the amount spent by the group, including any lobbying firm it hires, during the four quarters of 2009 (coinciding with the start of the Congress in January to the final Senate vote in late December). Most of the money spent on lobbying expenditures goes to the salaries or fees of the lobbyists, since no gift-giving is allowed to government officials. Lobbying expenditures are not only an indicator of a group's capacity to lobby, they also are a proxy for how many individuals a client devotes to lobbying in a particular issue area and how much time is spent on that issue area. These data are reported by lobbying registrants to the House and Senate and are cleaned and made accessible by CRP. I linked them to the groups that submitted comments to the Finance committee using regular expression string matching followed by manual checking.

Group's annual revenue (ln). Larger organizations and companies represent more people than smaller organizations. As a result, legislators are likely to pay more attention to bigger, wealthier groups, even if they do not lobby intensely by hosting a fundraiser. I use publicly available sources to measure group revenue.[6] In all, I have annual revenue amounts

---

[6] To measure group revenue, I collected either an IRS form 990 (for nonprofit groups) or 10-K or 8-K (for publicly traded companies). These public documents include the organization's

for 826 out of 866 organizations included in the analysis. For the remaining forty organizations, I impute *revenue* based on a regression of revenue on these variables: lobbying expenditures, PAC contributions, lobbyists' contributions, and whether the organization represents business. (Dropping the observations with missing revenue data does not change the results.) I use the natural log (ln) of revenue given that the differences among lobby groups at the low end are likely more consequential than differences at the high end.

Number of health lobbying firms the group uses in 2009. While some organizations may contract with a single lobbying firm for all its needs, others may focus on those lobby firms with a particular interest in health care issues, and some may even hire multiple lobbying firms that work on health care issues. This variable is a count of unique registrants used by the lobby group client in 2009.

Total number of requests made by the group or its coalition partners. The sheer number of requests made by each group is an important variable to control for because of the possibility that the more (or less) a group asks for, the more it is likely to get. Helpfully, in most cases the letter writer makes it straightforward to count the number of requests, for example, by using bullet points, giving comments in table format, or otherwise clearly delineating requests (e.g., "First ... Second ... "). The total number of requests made is controlled for so that we may evaluate whether there are diminishing – or increasing – marginal returns to scale on lobbyists' requests.

4.4.7 Control Variables: The Dyad

Group is from the senator's state. Given the importance in the literature of Members' ties to constituents and their employers (e.g., Arnold 1990; Hall and Wayman 1990; Schiller 1995), I consider whether the interest group is headquartered in the senator's state. Groups' headquarters location comes from the letter to the committee or from its federal tax filing.

Contributions from group to senator. In addition to the key explanatory variable, which is a dichotomous indicator of whether or not the

---

annual revenue. I use the 2008 or 2009 annual revenue amount to describe the group's revenue. The decision to use 2008 or 2009 depends solely on when the data were collected. A few letter writers represent private firms that are not publicly traded and therefore do not produce 10-Ks; for these few businesses I look for online mentions of the organization's approximate revenue.

lobby group or any of its lobbyists contribute to or host a fundraiser for the senator, I am also interested in the total amount of contributions given by the group to the senator in the dyad. For each senator–lobbyist dyad, this variable is the total of money the lobby group gave to the senator, plus any contributions from the individual to the senator, plus any contributions made from employees of the group to the senator. These data come from the FEC, the Senate Office of Public Records, and the Center for Responsive Politics, respectively, and were discussed in greater detail in Chapter 3.

4.4.8 Control Variables: The Senator

The literature seeking to explain the nature and level of Members' activity in Congress is disparate. Variables found to help explain Member activity include seniority (Kessler and Krehbiel 1996; Anderson et al. 2003), party status (Schiller 1995), committee membership (Schiller 1995; Jeydel and Taylor 2003), staff capacity (Schiller 1995), economic or industry activity in the represented district or state (Hall and Wayman 1990; Schiller 1995), and personal characteristics such as gender (Lazarus and Steigerwalt 2009; Volden et al. 2013) and race (Bratton and Haynie 1999; Gamble 2007). Collectively the literature has shown that all of these factors can affect Members' level of participation, but not in consistent ways. For example, Finance members are more likely than other senators to introduce bills, while Foreign Relations members are less likely to do so (Schiller 1995), and junior Members of Congress introduce more bills in general (Schiller 1995), but fewer of these bills are reported out of committee (Anderson et al. 2003). No study I am aware of has focused exclusively on the decision to offer an amendment in committee, though it is one of numerous actions examined by Hall and Wayman (1990) and Evans (1996).

To control for Member effort apart from fundraising and favors, I considered three variables related to the Member:

Senator's conservatism. A senator's party and political ideology may affect the senator's willingness to offer amendments to pending legislation. For example, amendments may be offered to restrict or expand the scope of government, or they may be offered by the minority party to object to the chairman's preferred version of the bill. This is measured using the widely used DW-NOMINATE method developed by Poole and

Rosenthal (2007), which calculates ideological distance as a function of how often each member votes with or against the party.

Senator belongs to HELP *committee.* Another consideration is the competing demands on senators. In particular, as discussed in Chapter 3, the Senate Health, Education, Labor and Pensions (or "HELP") committee was writing a health care bill alongside the Finance committee. HELP has jurisdiction over discretionary budget items, as opposed to the Finance committee's broad jurisdiction over tax policy, Medicare, and Medicaid. I expect that Finance members who were also on the HELP committee might be more sensitive to the needs of certain groups, and therefore would be more likely to offer amendments to the Finance committee bill.

Senator is up for reelection. Finally, Senators up for reelection, which is one-third of them in a given even-numbered year, may be more willing to entertain the requests of interest groups that are in a position to help them win reelection (McCarty and Rothenberg 1996; Bronars and Lott 1997; Stratmann 1998).

While including senator-specific variables in the model sheds light on which legislator traits are associated with greater willingness to offer amendments requested by lobby groups, an alternative strategy is to use fixed effects for senators that allows unspecified variation within a senator across lobby groups. I test both alternatives – senator-specific traits and fixed effects for senators – in the models in this chapter.[7]

4.5 METHOD

Each organization that submitted comments, and each organization listed on the letterhead of a coalition, was included in the sample, for a total of

---

[7] In addition to the three senator-specific variables used in the models in this chapter, I considered several other control variables. Regarding senators, seniority in the legislature or on the committee, membership on other committees (beyond HELP), gender, and race were all collinear with the three senator-specific variables I do use, and I did not expect them to exert an independent effect on the decision to offer an amendment. Regarding groups, I considered including the relative number of positive versus negative lobbying requests (Baumgartner et al. 2009; McKay 2012a), whether the organization represented business interests, and whether the employees of an organization, rather than their employers, might be donating to Members directly. All of these were either collinear with the PAC and lobbyists' personal contributions, not substantively important, and/or contained too much missing data for me to use in the models.

866 organizations.[8] All twenty-two of the members of the committee, excluding Chairman Baucus, offered amendments. Thus, the sample consists of 866 × 22 = 19,052 dyads, of which 224 contained an amendment-letter match. The dependent variable is coded as 1 when there is a substantive match between a request made by an interest group and an amendment offered by a senator and 0 otherwise.

Of the 866 organizations, 152 were found to be involved in fundraising for one or more of the twenty-two senators on the Finance committee. An organization is considered a fundraiser for the senator if, for the lobby group that writes the letter, any of the following is true: (1) the *group* is listed as hosting a fundraiser benefitting a senator, (2) an *in-house lobbyist* for the group hosts a fundraiser for a senator, or (3) a contract lobbyist whose *client* is the group hosts a fundraiser for a senator. The decision to treat all fundraiser hosts equivalently biases somewhat toward a null finding, since contract lobbyists have many clients, and any legislative benefit they get from fundraising may go to another of the lobbyist's clients that does not submit a letter to the committee.

To assess the effects of fundraising activity in a dyad with success in getting a senator to offer an amendment requested by the group, I use logit models with errors clustered on both the senator and the interest group, except in the fixed-effects model.[9] Two-way clustering yields more conservative estimates than clustering on either dimension alone.

4.6 ANALYSIS AND INFERENCE

When a lobbyist fundraises for a Senate Finance Committee member, the odds that the senator offers an amendment requested by the group are nearly six times greater than the odds if no fundraiser occurs in the dyad. Adding in various controls, the odds that the senator offers an amendment requested by the group is still more than twice as likely than without a fundraiser. Table 4.3 presents models that show, respectively, (1) no control variables, (2) group-specific control variables, (3) senator-specific control variables, (4) dyad-specific control variables, (5) all control variables (this is the main model), and (6) all control variables except senator-specific, for which we

---

[8] Results are substantively similar when treating the coalition, rather than the group, as the unit of analysis.

[9] Following Thompson (2011) and Cameron et al. (2011), and using a program written by Mitchell A. Petersen and Jingling Guan (Petersen 2009), this method clusters errors separately in each dimension and also runs the model without clustering; then adds the former and subtracts the latter.

TABLE 4.3 *Logit models of the likelihood that a lobby group will have one of its policy requests introduced as an amendment to the health reform bill by a senator on the Senate Finance Committee*

	No controls (1)	Group-specific factors (2)	Senator-specific factors (3)	Dyad-specific factors (4)	Group, senator, and dyad-specific factors (5)	Group- and dyad-specific factors with senator-fixed effects (6)
Group or its lobbyists host a fundraiser for senator	1.76 (0.27) [5.78]	1.15 (0.34) [3.15]	1.80 (0.26) [6.04]	1.75 (0.27) [5.77]	1.17 (0.33) [5.75]	1.26 (0.25) [3.51]
Group's 2009 lobbying expenditures ($1,000s)		−0.00 (0.00)			−0.00 (0.00)	−0.00 (0.00)
Number of health lobbying firms the group uses in 2009		0.19 (0.03)			0.19 (0.03)	0.19 (0.03)
Total number of requests made		0.04 (0.01)			0.04 (0.01)	0.04 (0.00)
Group's annual revenue (ln)		0.01 (0.04)			0.01 (0.04)	0.01 (0.03)
Senator belongs to HELP committee			−0.09 (0.29)		−0.07 (0.32)	
Senator up for reelection in 2010			−0.03 (0.25)		−0.06 (0.28)	
Senator's conservatism (DW-NOMINATE)			−0.26 (0.31)		−0.24 (.34)	
Group's contributions to senator ($1,000s)				0.00 (0.00)	0.00 (0.00)	0.00 (0.00)
Group is from the senator's state				0.73 (0.45)	0.88 (0.45)	0.88 (0.48)
Constant	−4.76 (0.17)	−5.62 (0.71)	−4.73 (0.18)	−4.78 (0.17)	−5.60 (0.69)	

(continued)

TABLE 4.3 *(continued)*

	No controls (1)	Group-specific factors (2)	Senator-specific factors (3)	Dyad-specific factors (4)	Group, senator, and dyad-specific factors (5)	Group- and dyad-specific factors with senator-fixed effects (6)
Observations	19,052	19,052	19,052	19,052	19,052	18,186
Probability > Chi²	0.00	0.00	0.00	0.00	0.00	0.00
Pseudo R2						0.14

Logit coefficients are displayed with standard errors in parentheses later. Brackets surround odds ratios for the key explanatory variable. The unit of analysis is the senator-group dyad. There are twenty-two senators on the Finance committee (minus the chairman, who does not offer amendments) and 866 groups that submitted their policy preferences. In Model 6, one senator is dropped for having no group-requested amendments. Bold coefficients are significant at $p < 0.05$.

use fixed effects. Model fit statistics suggest that all six models are statistically different from the null model, though they still leave considerable variance unexplained.

In the first model, in the absence of any control variables, odds ratios (shown in brackets) indicate that the odds that a senator offers an amendment are almost six times as likely when the group hosts a fundraiser for the senator. In the second model, the association is still strong and significant while also controlling for lobbying factors. Two of the three variables that capture lobbying intensity – the number of registered clients working on the group's behalf regarding health care policy and the number of requests made in the group's letter – are both positive and significant in this model but not as large as the relationship between fundraising and amendment-offering. Lobbying expenditures are not a significant predictor of lobbying success for these organizations, and when controlling for lobbying intensity, the effect of groups' annual revenue is not significant in predicting the group's legislative success.

The third model considers senator-specific effects, but none of these is significant when controlling for fundraising. In the fourth model, we see that contributions to the senator from the group or its lobbyists matter – but even controlling for the amount contributed from the group to the senator, hosting a fundraiser is associated with more than twice the odds that the senator offers an amendment requested by the group. The effects of contributions will be further explored in Chapter 5, but this difference between the relative power of contributions and fundraising is further evidence of what we saw in Chapter 2 that suggests that fundraising assistance is more valuable to senators than contributions.

The fifth and sixth models put all variables together, and the results are illustrated in the coefficient plots given in Figures 4.3 and 4.4, respectively. Even while controlling for lobbying intensity, campaign contributions, senator traits, home-state advantages, and the annual revenue of the group, when a group interested in health care reform hosts a fundraiser for a senator on the Finance committee during any of the ten years between 2006 and 2015, the odds that the senator offers an amendment requested by the group are at least three and a half times as great, and this effect is significant at $p < 0.001$.

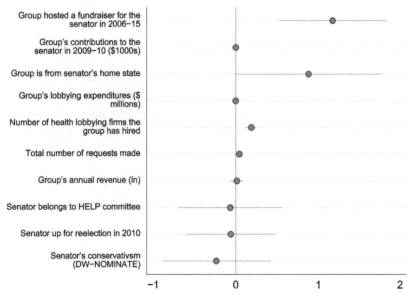

FIGURE 4.3 Factors that predict whether a senator offers an amendment requested by the group, with group-, senator-, and dyad-specific variables **Notes.** *The figure displays logit coefficients and 95 percent confidence intervals for Model 5, which includes group-, senator-, and dyad-specific factors.*

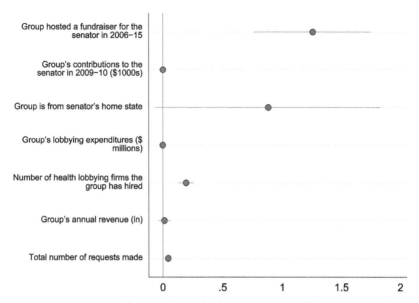

FIGURE 4.4 Factors that predict whether a senator offers an amendment requested by the group, with fixed effects for senators
Notes. *The figure displays logit coefficients and 95 percent confidence intervals for Model 6, which includes group- and dyad-specific factors and uses fixed effects for senators.*

Among control variables, we first see that whether the group is from the senator's state is a positive but not a significant predictor of amendment success for the group. This result is surprising evidence that, in spite of a long line of studies demonstrating that Members favor constituents over nonconstituents (e.g. Fenno 1978; Arnold 1990; Hall and Wayman 1990; Schiller 1995), Members may favor the lobbyists who host fundraisers for them even more.

Groups with higher revenue are not significantly more likely than other groups to have amendment success when controlling for the other variables in the models. In robustness checks, a model that substitutes for revenue an indicator for business interests also shows no significant effect for business. However, business is correlated with lobbying expenditures ($\rho = 0.14$) as well as the number of health lobbying firms hired ($\rho = 0.21$), and when these two variables are left out of the model and business is included, business is a significant predictor of amendment success. The significance of business interests and nonsignificance of high-revenue lobby groups suggest that senators were more inclined to look out for business interests, whether big or small, and did not treat high-revenue nonprofit interests (such as the AARP) the same as high-revenue business interests. This possibility is consistent with the argument in Chapter 1 that Democrats were eager to please business interests from the start, to avoid the massive and successful negative lobbying campaign against the Clinton health reform proposal of 1993.

None of the three variables that describe senators is a significant predictor of amendment success, and when we take these out and instead use fixed effects for the senator, the model (Model 6) looks very similar to the model that includes them (Model 5). By using a fixed-effects model in Model 6, we can infer that the odds that a group that fundraises for a senator are about three and half times the size of the odds if the group lobbies but does not fundraise for the senator.

The timing of fundraising events for Finance committee members as they draft and mend the legislation provides further evidence of fundraisers as legislative subsidy. Figure 4.5 shows the distribution of senator-group fundraiser pairs in these data over time. The bars show the number of dyads per week in which the group hosts a fundraiser for the senator. (The y-axis is logged to show detail.) The diamonds designate fundraiser dyads in which the senator eventually offered an amendment requested by the group. The figure suggests that the timing of the fundraiser relative to the

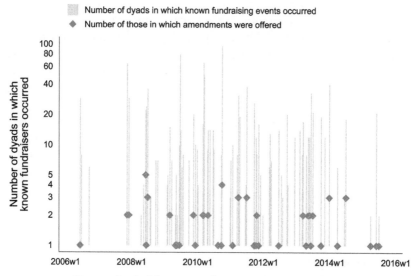

FIGURE 4.5 Known fundraising events for Senate Finance Committee members hosted by lobby groups that submit comments to the committee, by date

timing of amendment-offering is unimportant, as fundraising lobbyists are equally likely to see amendment success whether the fundraiser is before or after the committee markup in the fall of 2009. And while a quid pro quo expectation might hold that fundraising activity would be at a peak during the critical period in which amendments are offered in the Finance committee, during the markup, the groups in these data hold *no* fundraisers for committee members. This pattern is entirely consistent with the usefulness hypothesis that during the intensive period of bill markup, lobbyists do not host fundraisers for Members to attend, allowing Members to concentrate on lobby groups' concerns at the most critical time.

4.7 DISCUSSION AND CONCLUSIONS

US senators who are thinking about reelection, even six years into the future, must constantly raise money toward that goal. Millions of dollars are needed to discourage opponents and to reach voters. Yet, fundraising is not an activity enjoyed by many politicians – or any politicians, if you believe John McCain. At the same time, elite legislators – such as senators crafting a complex bill that would affect virtually every American and have significant consequences for the lobbyists engaged in the most-lobbied policy area in Washington – are involved in countless meetings, hearings, briefings, press interviews, and communications about the legislation they write. These duties reduce the amount of time legislators have to raise money. Importantly, this slack is picked up by lobbyists. Individual lobbyists and lobby groups put in the time and effort to host fundraising events that benefit these elite legislators. Not coincidentally, these same lobbyists often have an interest in the legislation that the benefitting politicians are in the midst of writing, adjusting, approving, or blocking.

This chapter demonstrates that lobbyists seeking particularistic benefits from health care legislation in 2009 and 2010 were more likely to be successful in securing these benefits if they hosted one or more fundraisers for the senator who offers in committee an amendment requested by the group. Importantly, the dyadic analysis presented means that it is not just that lobbyists who host fundraisers are generally more successful: The data show that when a lobby group hosts a fundraising event for a senator, *that* senator is more likely to offer an amendment requested by *that* same group. And by using a fixed-effects model for senators across 866 interest groups, we see that it is not just that senators who offer group-requested amendments are also the beneficiaries of more lobbyist-hosted fundraisers. Rather, groups that host fundraisers for a given senator are more likely than groups that lobby the senator but do not host a fundraiser to see a requested amendment offered by the senator.

The timing of fundraising does not seem to matter in these data. Fundraisers that occur as early as 2006 and as late as 2015 are associated with a greater likelihood that the benefitting senator offers an amendment requested by the group. And alternative models varying the time frame during which fundraisers occurred (e.g., limiting them to 2008–10 when health reform was being considered by Congress) do not produce significantly different results. This long time horizon is evidence of the stealth nature of fundraisers' lobbying activity.

Is it likely that senators would have offered their amendments in the absence of the fundraising event, perhaps because they thought it was a good idea? Because the language in the amendments is so similar, and often identical, to the language in interest groups' request letters, we can infer that these amendments are at least partly a function of the lobbying effort and were quite possibly encouraged by the money that went along with it. For the senator, amendment-offering in committee is an inexpensive, even costless, way to perform a legislative favor for a lobbyist that hosts a fundraising event for the senator. In the language of Denzau and Munger (1986), the supply price of amendment-offering is low. Likewise, for the lobbyist, hosting a fundraiser may be a cost-effective thing to do. As mentioned by some of the lobbyists interviewed by Leech (2013), fundraising events give attending lobbyists opportunities to keep abreast of what is happening with legislation, as well as the chance to get face time with politicians and congressional staff – a benefit that may increase the lobbyist's subsequent access to those offices. Indeed, some of the hosts in these data host twelve or more fundraisers for a specific senator in a two-year period.

However, though the costs of fundraising for senators seem attractively low, for the public, the cost may be high. The amendments examined here, if enacted, could be worth millions of dollars for the firms that benefit from them. Though only 154 of the 564 proposed amendments were adopted into the bill, the amendments that I link to interest groups' requests as described here are twice as likely as other amendments to be included in the bill and therefore in the law. From this, we can conclude that interest group–requested amendments had a real effect on policy outcomes in the form of obscure details in Public Law 111–148. The analysis suggests that the pressure on legislators to constantly raise money encourages them to seek fundraising help from lobbyists, and one way that they may increase the funds elicited is to introduce low-salience amendments in line with the lobbyist's requests. As summarized by experienced lobbyist Howard Marlowe:

A lobbyist might use money to say, "Look, would you introduce this amendment for me, or will you make this speech or this argument?" Is it illegal? No, not at all, but it needs to be looked at more. I think we need to learn what, if anything, lobbyists are buying. (Leech 2013, 8)

5

Stealth Lobbying, Stealth Contributions, and the Affordable Care Act

Baucus, the Senate Finance Committee chair whose transparency made McKay's work possible, was unsurprised to find that text from lobbyist letters ended up in his bill. "I've seen that happen from the get-go, from when I first arrived in Congress," Baucus said.

Reported in Koerth (2019) after the publication of related research (McKay 2018)

As Senator Baucus put it in his folksy Montana way, lobby groups and Members of Congress have long worked together to craft legislation that benefits organized interests. But political scientists have faced considerable challenges in determining just how common these relationships are and to what extent they are fueled by campaign money. I argue that clever lobbyists, working in stealthy conditions, achieve benefits for their organizations that do not attract negative public attention for either the legislators or the lobby groups. Lobbyists make themselves useful to Members, and Members introduce low-salience legislation requested by lobbyists. Yet collectively, these quasi-exchange relationships are like needles in a haystack of perfectly defensible legislative and constituent-oriented interactions and activities.

The theory of stealth lobbying holds that lobbying is most effective when lobbyists secure low-salience legislation without attracting public notice, and this practice allows Members to stealthily provide legislation in exchange for much-needed campaign contributions. In previous chapters we have seen the importance of campaign assistance in helping lobbyists achieve access to politicians; we have observed lobbyists targeting and timing contributions so that they go to the most powerful legislators at the most opportune times; and we have linked fundraising events to microlegislation. In this chapter, we will conduct the most direct examination yet of the possible influence of campaign contributions over the content of legislation.

The chapter introduces data about the details of what groups wanted in health reform legislation and how they used their personal money to help get it. The data are shaped into three different units of analysis designated by Roman numerals I, II, and III. Each of these can be thought of as testing one of the three themes of the book – salience, usefulness, and null effects, respectively.

5.1 TESTING THE SALIENCE HYPOTHESIS: GROUP SUCCESS IN COMMITTEE

The salience hypothesis holds that lobbyists are more influential when the salience of the legislation and of the surrounding policymaking is low. We have seen examples of lobbyists' efforts to be influential under conditions of minimal scrutiny, as in more frequent meetings with legislators, the greater tendency of individual lobbyists to contribute strategically to legislators relative to PACs, in unreported fundraising events, and in microlegislation requested during committee consideration of a bill. This chapter directly tests the effects of salience on lobbyists' and legislators' behavior by comparing conditions of low salience to conditions of high salience. This first level of analysis for this chapter, therefore, tests the salience hypothesis by evaluating the influence lobbyists exert at different stages of the development of health reform legislation in 2009.

Microlegislation is a perfect example of low-salience legislation requested in a low-salience environment: It affects only a narrow set of interests and is typically written in a way that is uninteresting and irrelevant to observers such as journalists and the public – probably deliberately. The language is likely to be technical and arcane, if not impenetrable, and to contain references that the layperson will not understand.

Importantly, the salience theory holds that both the policy proposal and the setting in which it is considered are both low-salience. Although Congress works on important matters every day it is in session, media coverage of Congress tends to be episodic. The public has a low opinion of Congress, and, as such, mainstream national media outlets cover Congress only when it is doing something exceedingly important, such as rescuing the economy or the banks, flirting with a government shutdown, or making the biggest change to health care in a generation. Since journalism in the United States is incentivized almost entirely by ad revenue, the story must be "sexy" enough to engage casual consumers of the news (Hamilton 2004). Newsrooms, then, if they cover Congress at all, tend to cover key times in the consideration of congressional legislation: the beginning, when proposals successfully reach the policy agenda, and the end, when votes occur and laws are decided upon. There is little interest on the part of the general public in the sausage-making process that occurs as legislation is written, amended, and deliberated over.

Committees, as the workshops of Congress, make an excellent venue for lobbyists to pursue low-salience microlegislation. Hall and Wayman (1990) and others (Kingdon 1984; Wright 1990; Hojnacki and Kimball 1998) have argued that the influence of money in Congress is most likely to be found in committee, rather than on the floor. Lobbying members of a committee that has jurisdiction over issues of interest to the lobbyist is simply more efficient than approaching Members not on the committee, since committees comprise the legislators most interested in a set of issues (Shepsle 1978). Some have noted that lobbying in committee can help to obscure or even hide potentially unsavory relationships between legislators and lobbyists. As Hall and Wayman remark, "the less public, often informal nature of committee decision making suggests that Members' responsiveness to campaign donors will receive less scrutiny" (1990, 801).

In particular, committee markup of legislation (also known as executive session), creates an opportunity for lobbyists to influence the language of a bill. Shortly before markup, draft legislative language, which typically has not been seen by committee members before this point, is laid out by the chair. Members are then invited to make amendments to it. Depending on the governing rules of the committee, the chair allows a subset of the amendments offered in writing to be discussed orally in markup deliberations to be recorded in the transcript. The remaining amendments mostly die quietly – though sometimes, undiscussed amendments find their way into the bill anyway, as in the case of the Becton Dickinson request detailed in Chapter 1. Amendments that are not discussed in committee markup and are not adopted into the legislation are typically *never* a part of the public record. This matters, because if Members and lobbyists assume an amendment will not be made public, they are likely less focused than they would be in other stages on avoiding the appearance of money-induced bias. The low salience of committee markup, and the even lower salience of amendments discussed during markup, allow the provisions in these amendments to go almost entirely undetected by political opponents. In this way, amendment-offering in committee enables Members to advocate proposals that benefit lobby groups, and in particular, those lobby groups that support Members' perpetual reelection campaigns.

As we discussed in Chapter 4, several factors beyond salience make an exchange of money for favors more likely during the amendment stage than at other times. First, for lobby groups, the amendments typically confer a valuable benefit to a particular group. For example, the amendments offered here would "expand," "expedite," "include," or "incentivize" some group's preferred outcome. On their face, the language of committee documents and legislation does not always reward certain groups, but in its effects it almost always does. Second, persuading a Member to offer an amendment in committee is a lower hurdle to clear than getting an item onto the full committee's agenda or securing a preferred policy outcome. An interest group that wants a certain amendment offered need only convince one committee member to do so. That member is the only veto point, and lobbyists have multiple alternative committee members to turn to if the first effort fails. From the point of view of the senator, amendment-offering is a "no-lose" game: Members have no reason not to offer as many amendments as they want. And third, even if the reward for the lobbyist's client is narrow or low-probability, the experienced lobbyist stealthily derives personal professional benefits by taking credit for getting the client's request offered as an amendment.

5.1.1 Dependent Variables for Analysis I

The first unit of analysis is the 866 groups that submitted comments in response to the Options for Health Reform promulgated by the Senate Finance Committee in 2009. There are three dependent variables at this level of analysis, which describe three successive stages of legislative development. These stages are first, the Chairman's Mark; second, committee amendment-offering; and third, the committee report. The dependent variables at the group-level analysis are thus *group success in the mark*, *group success in getting an amendment offered*, and *group success in the report*.

5.1.1.1 Analysis I, Stage 1: Success in the Mark
To measure success in getting a group's preferences into the chairman's first draft of the bill (known as the Chairman's Mark), I first identify each provision from the committee's Options for Health Reform document

that appears in the lobby group's letter.[1] I compare the list of Options to the provisions in the Mark to determine whether the group's preferred option is successful or not. *Success in the Mark* is defined as the percentage of a group's "asks" that appear in the Chairman's Mark draft proposal. Some of the requests are negative; that is, groups registered their objections to a proposal, and this was treated as a request that the committee not include a provision. Given that this dependent variable is a proportion, I estimate it using a generalized linear model (Papke and Wooldridge 1996; Baum 2008).

5.1.1.2 Analysis I, Stage 2: Success in Getting an Amendment Offered

In the second stage of legislative development, *success in getting an amendment offered* describes whether or not any of the group's requests are found in an amendment offered by a committee member to the Chairman's Mark. After the chairman releases the mark, groups may turn their focus to the twenty-two Members of the committee who can suggest additions, deletions, and other changes to the legislation. The process for identifying matches between groups' letters and senators' amendments was detailed in Chapter 4. This dichotomous dependent variable is estimated using a logit model.

5.1.1.3 Analysis I, Stage 3: Success in the Report

After the public markup session occurs, but before the chairman finalizes the legislation for the committee to vote on, committee members have an interesting opportunity to stealthily persuade the chairman to insert, delete, or change parts of the legislation, all outside of public view. The Becton Dickinson amendment described in Chapter 1, for example, was accepted not in the formal markup session but afterward in unrecorded interactions between Senator Menendez and Chairman Baucus or their staff surrogates. In these data, while sixteen provisions appear in the report that are absent from the original Chairman's Mark, only two of these are introduced by senators on the record during markup. Thus, many amendments are being quietly adopted by the chairman into the bill without any publicly observable communication about them.

The dependent variable *success in the report* reflects the number of a group's requests that are realized in the committee's agreed version of the bill, as a proportion of the total number of requests the group makes. Success in the report includes successes in the mark that were not undone

---

[1] I am grateful to Toni P. Miles for this important suggestion and her related coding work.

during markup, as well as accepted amendments and any changes the chairman makes in his "Chairman's Modifications" to the mark. Like *group success in the mark, group success in the report* is a proportion between 0 and 1, and I use a generalized linear model to estimate it.

The process of drafting, soliciting comments, adjusting, amending, and then finalizing and voting on the legislation in committee is illustrated in Figure 5.1. Moving left to right, we see first that the Chairman releases a series of three Options for Health Reform. Next, groups submit comments to the committee and its staff via email. Third, the Chairman narrows in on a smaller subset of options in his Chairman's Mark proposal. Next, senators offer amendments to the Chairman's Mark. Lastly, the chairman finalizes the legislation and the committee votes it up or down.

5.2 TESTING THE USEFULNESS HYPOTHESIS: SUCCESS IN THE SENATOR-GROUP DYAD

The usefulness hypothesis asserts that lobbyists who make themselves useful to Members of Congress will have a better shot at persuading them to pursue lobbyists' desired policy objectives, including microlegislation. As we saw in Chapter 2, lobbyists provide several kinds of benefits to Members that Members find useful, especially information, both technical and political, and campaign contributions.

The line between technical and political information is fine, and lobbyists draft arguments that make both in a single letter. Sophisticated lobbyists subtly tailor their requests to the priorities of individual legislators. For example, nurse midwives seeking a higher Medicare reimbursement rate for attending a childbirth might, when talking to a female Member of Congress, emphasize the less medical, more personal assistance that midwives provide women who are giving birth. When approaching a budget hawk, the midwives might point out that midwife-attended births are significantly cheaper than obstetrician-attended births, and so the government would save money by recognizing nurse midwives as equal providers and allowing them to bill independently of obstetricians. Approaching a member whose district has a large Medicaid population, the midwives might provide the useful technical information that 40 percent of all births in the United States are paid for by Medicaid. If the lobbyist can subtly insert a political message that a proposal would be particularly helpful to the Member's state or district, so much the better. Notably, this message-tailoring is helpful not because it alters Members' opinions or policy

FIGURE 5.1 Flow of legislative activity on the Senate Finance Committee's health reform bill in 2009

stance, but because it helps them *justify* their decision-making to constituents, journalists, and colleagues.

In addition to making themselves useful by providing helpful information, individual lobbyists and lobbyist-controlled PACs collectively make tens of thousands of campaign contributions per year to congressional candidates. As we learned in Chapter 3, between 2008 and 2010, individual lobbyists report making more than $80 million in federal contributions and lobbyist-controlled PACs contribute another $800 million. The data suggest that lobbyists donate this money in ways that appear to be sensitive to the issue at the top of the congressional agenda by targeting key lawmakers at key times. This chapter builds on these findings by linking lobbyists' contributions to the information those lobbyists conveyed to key lawmakers. By investigating whether donating lobbyists are more likely than nondonating lobbyists to achieve a greater proportion of their organization's policy goals in the legislation that becomes the Affordable Care Act (ACA), we can draw inferences about the effectiveness of lobbyists' campaign contributions.

5.2.1 Dependent Variable for Analysis II

To test the usefulness hypothesis, the second unit of analysis is the senator-group dyad. As in Chapter 4, I pair every senator that served on the Finance committee during consideration of the health reform bill with every lobby group that submitted a letter regarding the draft legislation. There are two reasons to shape the data into dyads. First, revisiting our discussion of causal inference, we need in our data observations in which contributions were given as well as observations in which contributions were not given, to ascertain whether contributing has significantly different effects on legislators relative to not contributing. Second, creating dyads between lobby groups and senators allows us to examine whether contributions from a group to a senator affect the likelihood that *that* senator offers an amendment requested by *that* group, compared to all the other senator-group pairings.

There are 22 senators × 866 groups for a total of 19,052 group-senator dyads. (Contributions to Baucus are excluded here because as chairman he did not offer any amendments.) Most of these dyads contain neither a contribution nor an amendment. But it is important for us to understand the conditions under which contributions might be associated with micro-legislative policy goals, even if these are rare events. The models in the dyadic analysis use logit to predict the dichotomous dependent variable *dyadic amendment success*, defined as whether or not the member in the dyad offers an amendment requested by the group in the dyad.

5.3 LOOKING FOR (NULL) EFFECTS: SUCCESS FOR THE LEGISLATIVE PROVISION

We have discussed how challenging it is for researchers to demonstrate that lobbying or campaign contributions have an effect on legislators' policy decisions (Smith 1995; Baumgartner and Leech 1998; Burstein and Linton 2002; de Figueiredo and Richter 2014). An important insight into why the effects of lobbying are so intangible is provided by Baumgartner et al. (2009). Their study of ninety-eight federal policy proposals over a four-year period found that more than 90 percent of the time, lobbying by one side is counteracted by lobbying by the other side. Using a resources index comprising PAC money, lobbying expenditures, business financial resources, group membership numbers, and the number of covered officials (i.e., those who formerly worked in Congress or high in the executive branch), the authors found that the two "sides" of a policy proposal tend to offset each other. Thus, an individual group's chances of winning on a given issue were only about fifty-fifty, no better than a coin toss. Because both sides tend to contain both wealthy and less wealthy interest groups, if half of those win and half lose, then it appears that resources do not matter, when, the authors argue, it probably does. On those rare occasions when the sides had unequal levels of resources, however, Baumgartner et al. (2009) find that the side with greater resources won (five times) more often than it lost (three times).

In a similar study, Heinz et al. (1993) gathered data from 776 lobbyists working on seventy-seven policy proposals at the federal level during the late 1970s and into the 1980s. I evaluated their data with an eye toward explaining which side of the issue won. Like Baumgartner et al. (2009), I found that the side with greater resources was not significantly more likely to win, but that certain traits of lobbyists were correlated with greater levels of success for those lobbyists. These winning traits were related to groups' resources, including more intense lobbying (more days in Washington per month, dispatching more lobbyists), participation in PAC contributions, and having more contacts in government (McKay 2012b).

Applying these findings to the present data, it makes sense to evaluate each side of a proposal as a unit and then identify net differences between them in terms of campaign contributions and sheer numbers. Then we can gauge whether winning is more closely related to having more lobbyists or having greater resources.

5.3.1 Dependent Variable for Analysis III

Here, for the first time in the book, we consider whether each *side* of the policy debate is successful as a function of the combined campaign donations of lobbyists for and against particular components of the legislation. To test the null effects hypothesis, the third unit of analysis is the 254 provisions specified in the Options.

There are two dependent variables in the provision-level analysis. *Provision success in the mark* indicates that the provision appears in the mark, and *provision success in the report* denotes that the provision appears in the report.[2] Of the 254 health reform provisions commented upon by interest groups, 122 are successful in the mark and 134 are successful in the report.

5.4 UNPRECEDENTED TRANSPARENCY

The creation and negotiation of American health reform legislation in 2009 under President Obama offers an ideal opportunity to detect the influence of interest groups' money and efforts. As part of the chairman's intent to be open and solicit all views, Senator Baucus took several atypical actions that facilitate my analysis of interest group influence on what became the ACA.

5.4.1 Lobby Groups' Comments

First, as mentioned in Chapter 4, Baucus created a dedicated email address so that lobby groups and others, including individuals, could submit comments on the proposals. The committee had solicited public comments before, but doing so was an ad hoc decision made quite rarely. Communication to Members of Congress is read, logged, and shared with staff members for response, and Washington organizations are familiar with the open-letter style of communicating, in which the addressee is specified but the letter is written in the public style of talking points. Still, it

---

[2] It would not be appropriate to model whether the provision appears in any amendment, because provisions that appear in the Options are by definition not eligible to be considered successes for any one group.

is possible that less experienced letter submitters did not fully understand that their letters could be made public. Indeed, at least one letter is stamped by the author as "Confidential." Further, the comments were provided to me by the committee; on this occasion the committee did not publicly release them.

5.4.2 Senators' Amendments

Second, as discussed in Chapter 4, Senator Baucus published on the Internet all of the 564 amendments to the legislation submitted by members of the Finance committee before they were discussed in committee markup. Yet despite Baucus's unprecedented willingness to publish proposed committee amendments, his decision was not covered in any of the newspapers that circulate Capitol Hill (*Roll Call*, *The Hill*, and *Politico*). Thus, these amendments may well have been written by Members and staffers who did not fully anticipate that they would be posted for the world to see. It is fair to say that congressional staff were writing for an audience of a particular set of senators and staff rather than the broader public.

5.4.3 Lobbyists' Personal Contributions

A third novelty was the recent HLOGA law, which requires bundled contributions to be reported as well as the campaign contributions of individual lobbyists and the contributions of any PACs they might control. Registered lobbyists who do not make any contributions are also required to file LD-203 disclosure forms. The newness of this reporting regime in 2008 meant that 16 percent of 2009 lobbying disclosure reports contained examples of lobbyists who failed to submit LD-203 disclosures of campaign contributions, according to the Government Accountability Office (2010). Given that the first semiannual report of lobbyists' personal contributions to congressional candidates was due in July of 2008, lobbyists in 2009 were not in the habit of reporting their personal contributions, their bundling activities, or the contributions of the PACs they were directing.

Combining these increases in transparency, it seems reasonable to infer that lobbyists may not have been immediately aware that their contributions would ever be linked to their legislative requests. The low visibility of each of committee amendments, interest group requests, and lobbyists' personal contributions, and the high value to interest groups of the microlegislation contained in committee amendments, together create conditions that increase the likelihood of observing the stealthy influence of interest groups over legislators and legislation.

5.5 EXPLANATORY VARIABLES

Having laid out the six dependent variables that the models seek to explain, we now turn to the explanatory, or independent, variables used in the models.

5.5.1 Key Explanatory Variable: Campaign Contributions

In contrast to many previous studies that rely wholly on PAC contributions, this book uses three kinds of campaign contributions from lobby groups: personal contributions from in-house lobbyists, personal contributions from lobbyists working on contract for the group, and contributions from PACs. I matched contributions from contract lobbyists to *all* of the clients they represented during the time frame of 2008–10, and combine these into a single variable that captures all lobbyists' contributions made to senators on the committee during the whole of 2009 or 2010.

In the group-level analysis, whether a *group or its lobbyists contribute to a Finance member* is a dichotomous variable that indicates that anyone in the group makes any of the three sources of contributions to any member of the Finance committee. In the dyadic analysis, whether the *group contributes to the senator* indicates that the group in the dyad, or any of its lobbyists, contributes to the senator in the dyad. In the provision-level analysis, *contributions advantage* is defined as the combined contributions to Finance committee members of lobby groups that support the provision, minus the combined contributions to Finance committee members of lobby groups that oppose the provision. Since contract lobbyists often represent multiple clients interested in the same legislative provision, I created unique contribution IDs to avoid double-counting the contributions of lobbyists working on contract.

5.5.2 Control Variable: Constituency

We know that legislators tend to favor their own constituents in policy-making (Fenno 1978; Arnold 1990). However, a growing segment of the literature finds evidence that Members of Congress may also favor political supporters more strongly than ordinary constituents (Miler 2007;

Giger and Klüver 2016; Kalla and Broockman 2016). As such we need to control for whether the Member should be representing the group because it is in the district or state. To evaluate the influence of constituents we use a single variable that indicates whether or not the *group is from a Finance member's state*, or in the dyadic analysis, whether or not the *group is from the senator's home state*.

5.5.3 Control Variable: Resources

As Senator Baucus wrote the first draft of the bill, we know that he sought to please business organizations, to be bipartisan, and to avoid losing, the way Democrats had done on the issue of health reform in the 1990s (McDonough 2011). Because some groups represent more individuals or a broader segment of the economy, these groups should have a more powerful impact on senators than smaller and less wealthy organizations, particularly in the first stage of getting preferences into the Chairman's Mark. *Group's annual revenue (ln)* is the logged dollar amount of the group's budget or revenue for the year 2008 or 2009 (depending on when the data were collected). I use the natural log of revenue dollars because the raw numbers are unwieldy but still generate the same substantive conclusions. Revenue was collected from publicly available sources as described in Chapter 4. This number is imputed in a small number of cases (4.6 percent; also detailed in Chapter 4).

5.5.4 Control Variables: Lobbying Intensity

Lobbying as persuasion is distinct from campaign contributions as inducements or tokens of appreciation. To better distinguish between these two possibilities I use several variables that reflect lobbying intensity.

Group's lobbying expenditures captures the amount spent by the group, including any lobbying firm it hires, for all of 2009 and 2010. It is logged in the group-level case and it is stated in millions of dollars in the dyadic case; this decision makes no difference to the significance of the variable.

Number of health lobbying firms hired by the group provides a window into a group's level of lobbying activity that may be more informative than the dollar value of lobbying expenditures, since lobbying expenditures are totaled across all issue areas, so we do not know how much large organizations are spending on health care lobbying versus other issues. Using CRP's standardized names for registrants and clients, I count, for each lobby client that submits comments to the Finance committee, the number of registrants working on health care issues in 2009.

Total number of requests made by the group is a count of requests in each letter, following the logic that the more a group asks for, the greater the chances that at least one of its requests will be granted.

Whether or not the *group has an office in the Washington area* is coded 1 if the organization is listed as being headquartered in Washington, DC (or its suburbs in Virginia and Maryland), or if it uses a lobby firm headquartered in Washington.

The final lobbying intensity variable is *numbers advantage*, which is used only in the provision-level (III) analysis. It is defined as the number of lobby groups that support a provision, minus the number that oppose the provision. No lobby group is counted more than once, even if a client uses more than one lobbying firm.

5.5.5 Omitted Variables

I considered a variety of other variables that I do not use in the analyses presented. I describe these next along with the reasons I have chosen not to use them in the models.

Group type. Many studies have considered whether business organizations are more successful than other kinds of groups. However, group type was not a significant predictor of greater success at any of the three stages of development when also controlling for the other variables in the models. In the data analyzed in this chapter, business is not even correlated with legislative success ($\rho = 0.13$ or less). It appears from this that on the issue of health reform, at least, senators are just as interested in the preferences of nonprofit groups, such as the AARP, disease organizations, and the YMCA, as in the preferences of insurance companies, drug companies, doctors, and hospitals. Business groups in these data are more likely than nonbusiness groups to make contributions, however, and we will see that contributions are a significant predictor of greater success. But only about one-third of the business organizations in this sample make any contributions to Finance committee members.

Preference direction. Whether each request in the letter is positive ("do this") or negative lobbying ("don't do this") (McKay 2012a) had no bearing on success and thus is not used in the models.

Senator-specific variables. I considered various factors unique to each senator that may have had an influence on the senator's willingness to offer amendments requested by groups, including the timing of their possible reelection (McCarty and Rothenberg 1996; Bronars and Lott 1997; Stratmann 1998), their estimated voting ideology (Poole and Rosenthal 2007), and whether or not a senator belonged to the other committee working on health reform legislation, that is, the Health, Education, Labor, and Pensions, or HELP, committee, albeit at a much less substantial level. But by using a model with fixed effects for senators, which essentially compares senators to themselves as interest groups vary, these differences are all subsumed in the fixed effects.[3]

Group contributes to Baucus. I considered whether or not the group contributed to the chairman in the 2010 election cycle. Since by all accounts Senator Baucus and his staff determined which legislative provisions did and did not go into the Chairman's Mark document, it is possible that lobby groups' contributions to Baucus have a greater effect than contributions to other members of the committee. However, this effect was not significant and so I do not include it in the models.

Employee contributions. When an individual contributes more than $200 to a federal candidate, this contribution must be disclosed to the FEC. The CRP aggregates these contributions by the donor's employer (as listed by the donor) and links them to the recipient and any committees on which the recipient serves. But only 10 percent of the groups that submitted comments to the Finance committee can be linked to reported employees' contributions to committee members, so I do not use employees' contributions in the models.

Coalition membership. Finally, some sixty letters are submitted by coalitions, or groups of groups, as discussed in Chapter 4. Dealing statistically with coalitions is a challenge, because coalition members vary on explanatory variables, such as group revenue, but generally share values of the dependent variable, level of influence. Statisticians call this arrangement of observations, which share the values of a dependent variable but vary on predictor variables, a "micro-to-macro" multilevel modeling situation. The statistics literature has focused mainly on the reverse situation, macro-to-micro hierarchical modeling. Croon and van Veldhoven (2007), who were among the first to propose a micro-macro multilevel modeling strategy, recommend treating the lower-level unit as the unit of analysis (in this case, the interest group) rather than the higher-level unit (the coalition), as doing so reduces the size of the standard errors. Croon and van Veldhoven (2007) alternatively recommend a latent variable

---

[3] Substituting these variables for the variables with which they are collinear does not substantively change the results.

model approach, which I considered. However, these random-effects models were substantively the same as the models that do not account for coalitions' preferences; thus for ease of presentation they are not reported here. In addition, an indicator variable designating whether the group belongs to any coalitions was not positive and significant in predicting success in any of the models.

5.6 ANALYSIS

This chapter argues that exchanges of legislative goods for monetary contributions are most likely to occur when the exchange has a lower-than-normal probability of being noticed. The results of each of the three levels of analysis can be summarized as follows. At the group level (I), lobbyists' influence appears to be strongest in the amendment-offering stage, when public scrutiny is lower and the lobbyist's probability of success is greater relative to the earlier drafting stage and the later finalization stage. At the dyad level (II), when a lobbyist contributes to a senator, that same senator is more likely to offer microlegislation requested by that lobby group relative to other groups and other senators. At the side level (III), when considering all lobbying and contributions together, while it is difficult to see the influence of campaign contributions, since there are contributions on both sides of a policy proposal, the data hint that when no strong majority prefers to adopt or not to adopt a proposal, money matters more. Together these findings offer strong evidence that the influence of lobbyists is greatest over low-salience microlegislation in comparison to publicly visible, macro-level policy battles that involve many groups.

5.6.1 Results for the Salience Hypothesis (I): Group Success in Committee

Table 5.1 presents the models for the first, or group-level, analysis, and Figure 5.2 illustrates the coefficients.

5.6.1.1 *Success in the Mark*

Success in the mark is illustrated with open circles in Figure 5.2 We see, first, that when a *group or its lobbyists contribute to a Finance member*, the group is significantly more likely to increase its success in the mark compared to groups that do not financially contribute. Predicted probabilities from the model indicate that when a group contributes to any member of the Finance committee, it can expect about 41 percent of

TABLE 5.1 *Predicting lobbyists' success at sequential stages of committee consideration of the health reform bill*

	Success in the mark (GLM)	Success in getting an amendment offered (logit)	Success in the report (GLM)
Group or its lobbyists contribute to a Finance member	**0.629** (0.134)	**1.384** (0.288)	**0.629** (0.141)
Group has an office in Washington area	**0.369** (0.151)	0.240 (0.304)	0.099 (0.160)
Number of health lobbying firms hired by group	−0.048 (0.075)	**0.442** (0.210)	**−0.133** (0.063)
Group's lobbying expenditures (ln)	−0.001 (0.002)	−0.003 (0.005)	0.000 (0.003)
Group is from a Finance member's state	0.002 (0.167)	−0.597 (0.327)	−0.101 (0.179)
Total number of requests made	**0.050** (0.009)	**0.061** (0.011)	**0.059** (0.009)
Group's annual revenue (ln)	**0.066** (0.029)	0.016 (0.052)	0.028 (0.028)
Constant	**−2.701** (0.565)	**−3.900** (0.889)	**−1.824** (0.557)
Number of clusters	310	310	310
Observations	866	866	866
Pseudo-R^2		0.245	
Scaled deviance	517.981		591.504
Scaled dispersion	0.604		0.689

Notes: Cells contain generalized linear model (GLM) coefficients (first and third models) or logit coefficients (second model), with standard errors below in parentheses. Bolded coefficients are significant at $p < 0.05$.

what it asks for; when its group does not contribute, it receives on average only 22 percent of what it asks for. This effect is significant when also controlling for constituency effects, the group's revenue, and lobbying intensity.

Groups from a Finance member's state do not secure a greater proportion of their requests in the mark than groups headquartered somewhere

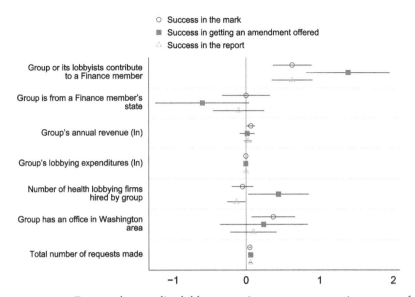

FIGURE 5.2 Factors that predict lobby groups' success at successive stages of committee consideration of the health reform bill
Notes. *Markers show coefficients for the three models as indicated, surrounded by 95 percent confidence intervals. N = 866 groups.*

else. This is understandable, since this variable is meant to capture constituent effects, and if those effects are unique to each senator-lobby group dyad, then we would not see them here.

Higher levels of a *group's annual revenue* are associated with greater interest group success in the mark. Predictive margins indicate that groups with revenue amounts at the 25th percentile typically see about 26 percent of their requests realized in the mark while those at the 75th percentile see about 31 percent of their requests in the mark. This finding is consistent with the argument that Baucus's first draft of the law focused on pleasing large interest groups, such as AARP, the American Hospital Association, and the American Medical Association, whose support he saw as vital to getting a bill passed (McDonough 2011).

Four variables aim to distinguish the intensity of lobbyists' efforts from the contributions they make. The availability of so many different measurements of lobbying intensity will tend to increase the standard errors of each, meaning that while a positive finding would be significant among these collinear variables, we could not infer that lack of significance for all four variables is necessarily an indication that lobbying does not matter.

Group's lobbying expenditures and the *number of health lobbying firms hired by the group* are not significant predictors of greater success in the mark when controlling for contributions. This result could suggest that money, in the form of campaign contributions and fundraising, is more effective than substantive arguments, as proxied by dollars spent lobbying, in influencing the content of the bill. But it may be simply that including both of these competing variables diminishes the effects of each. Groups that have an *office in the Washington area* are predicted to achieve about 35 percent of their requests in the mark, compared to an average of 26 percent for groups without a Washington-area office. This finding is likely because Washington-based groups tend to be more professionalized and are likely to have been more conversant with the Options the committee was considering relative to groups that do not have a permanent Washington presence. Finally, the more a group asks for, the more it seems to get. Groups in the 75th percentile for the *total number of requests made* have about 28 percent of their requests met in the mark, while groups in the 25th percentile have about 22 percent of their requests met in the mark. By including this variable, the models control for the tendency of some groups to comment on every proposed policy, most of which they like, while other groups confine their comments to just those proposals they would prefer to be changed or dropped.

5.6.1.2 Success in Getting an Amendment Offered

In the second stage of the legislation, the effects of lobbying and contributions activity become even more pronounced. Now that the entire committee, rather than just the chairman, has a formal opportunity to state their preferences for the bill, we see that groups that offer campaign contributions to committee members are significantly more likely to have at least one of their requests offered as an amendment to the bill. This model, depicted in solid squares in Figure 5.2, predicts that when a lobby group contributes to any member of the committee, the odds that the group sees one of its requests introduced as an amendment by a senator are four times the odds if the group does not contribute, controlling for the other variables in the model. Put differently, the predicted probability of *success in getting an amendment offered* moves from 4 to 22 percent when the group contributes to a committee member.

The variable intended to capture constituent effects, *group is from a Finance member's state*, is not a significant predictor of success in getting an amendment offered. This suggests that for lobbyists attempting to secure a piece of microlegislation, campaign contributions may be more useful than home state connections. However, it may also be that a lobby group's headquarters matters only if it is in the state of the senator in the dyad, rather than in the state of any member of the committee.

In contrast to success in the mark, success in getting an amendment offered is not significantly predicted by a *group's annual revenue*. This finding is consistent with the fact that Baucus sought to include the preferences of key interest groups at the beginning of the process (McDonough 2011), even if, as the legislation developed further, the preferences of larger groups were not more powerful than those of smaller groups.

Regarding the intensity of lobbying, the *number of health firms lobbying for the group* is positively and significantly associated with greater *success in getting an amendment offered*. This makes sense, as the higher the number of lobbyists working for the group on health care issues, the more instances there are likely to be of lobbyists coming up with ideas for microlegislation – and the more money there is to accompany such requests. Meanwhile, *lobbying expenditures* and having an *office in Washington* are not associated with greater *success in getting an amendment offered*.

5.6.1.3 Success in the Report

At the third stage of legislation, *success in the report*, we see again that contributions matter. This model is presented in open triangles in Figure 5.2. Predicted probabilities indicate that the groups in these data increase the portion of their requests found in the report from about 26 percent to about 43 percent when the *group contributes to a Finance committee member*. In contrast, *group is from a Finance member's state* is not at all helpful in securing more of the group's preferences in the report.

The group's *annual revenue, lobbying expenditures*, and having an *office in the Washington area* do not appear to matter much at this stage, while the *total number of requests* the group makes has a positive effect on the group's success in the report. The *number of health lobbying firms* the group hires is also not a predictor of greater success in the report. The latter result may be due to the correlation between this variable and the other variables that capture lobbying intensity.

5.6.2 Results for the Usefulness Hypothesis (II): Success in the Senator-Group Dyad

Having established from the group-level analysis just discussed that groups that make campaign contributions to senators tend to achieve more of their expressed policy goals, we can now drill deeper to determine where the money is going and what if anything is being done in return. Only about 12 percent of the senator-group dyads contain any contributions. Thus, contributions are rare – and contributors are special. Relative to the countless lobbyists who make legislative requests, the group that contributes is unusual in that it shows some appreciation for the effort the senator puts forth on the group's behalf. Viewed from the eyes of the legislator, a group that contributes to a senator might be at least a little more deserving than other groups of the senator's legislative effort.

Table 5.2 shows the model estimates for the dyadic analysis and Figure 5.3 presents the corresponding coefficient plot. We see first that the variable *group contributes to the senator* is the strongest predictor in the model. Controlling for the other variables listed, the odds that the senator in the dyad offers an amendment requested by the group in the dyad are nearly four times (3.67, exponentiating 1.30) as large when a contribution occurs.

The next-largest coefficient in the dyadic analysis – *group is from the senator's home state* – also predicts a higher probability of securing the requested amendment, but the effect is notably smaller than the effect of contributing: groups in the senator's home state have a predicted *success in getting an amendment offered* of 0.024, while groups outside of the senator's state have a predicted *success in getting an amendment offered* of 0.010.

Three of the four variables capturing lobbying intensity are significant. Having an *office in the Washington area* moves predicted success in this model from 0.008 to 0.014. Hiring a greater *number of health lobbying firms* also seems to enhance the group's amendment success: Groups that hire no firms can expect a 0.009 probability of securing a desired amendment, while hiring three firms boosts success to 0.012 and hiring seven firms predicts a 0.080 probability of success. The *total number of requests made* matters somewhat, with the predicted probability of success moving from 0.005 to 0.007 as the number of requests increases from the 25th to the 75th percentile. When controlling for these other measures of lobbying intensity, the *group's lobbying expenditures* is not significant. The significance of campaign contributions while also controlling for four indicators of lobbying intensity is further evidence that campaign contributions are related to senators' decisions to offer these amendments, and not just evidence of lobbyists' rhetorical persuasiveness.

TABLE 5.2 *Predicting whether a given senator offers an amendment requested by a given group*

	Senator offers an amendment requested by the group (logit)
Group contributes to the senator	**1.30**
	(0.25)
Group is from senator's home state	0.99
	(0.48)
Group's annual revenue (ln)	0.01
	(0.04)
Group's lobbying expenditures ($ millions)	−0.01
	(0.00)
Number of health lobbying firms the group has hired	**0.16**
	(0.03)
Group has an office in Washington area	**0.63**
	(0.25)
Total number of requests made	**0.04**
	(0.00)
Constant	**−25.48**
	(0.71)
N	18,186
Clusters	866
Pseudo-R2	0.18

Notes: Cells contain logit coefficients with standard errors below in parentheses. Errors are clustered on the 866 groups in the data. Bolded coefficients are significant at $p < 0.05$.

The use here of fixed effects also means that it is not just that some senators are more likely than others to offer group-requested amendments. Rather, senators' decisions to offer or not offer amendments to particular groups are being compared to those same senators' propensity to offer amendments to other groups, some of which contribute and some of which do not. The dyadic analysis shows that when a given lobby group makes a contribution to a given senator, that senator is significantly more likely to offer an amendment requested by the group. This is a stronger conclusion than our inferences from the group-level analysis that groups that tend to contribute to senators' campaigns also tend to be good at securing preferred legislation.

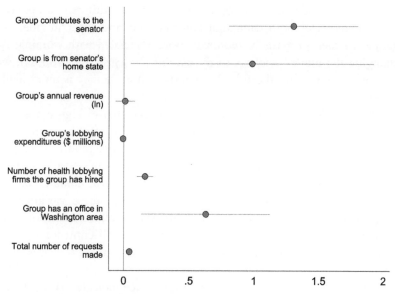

FIGURE 5.3 Factors that predict whether the senator offers in committee an amendment requested by the lobby group
Notes. *Markers show logit coefficients surrounded by 95 percent confidence intervals. N = 19,052 senator-lobby group dyads.*

We see in the dyadic analysis that, consistent with the findings of Chapter 3, lobby groups typically do not use a fire hose approach and give contributions to everyone in the Senate or every senator on the Finance committee. The average group in these data gives to fewer than three senators on the Finance committee. Even for groups that make some contributions, the average group donates to only about eight committee members, though there are twenty-three senators on the committee to whom they could give. Just 7 of the 866 organizations that submit comments to members of the Finance committee contribute to every member of the committee.

5.6.3 Results for the Null Effects Hypothesis (III): Success for the Legislative Provision

One of the hypothesized reasons that scholars have had such difficulty in identifying the effects of money in politics is that by studying individual groups as the unit of analysis, we are bound to find both winners and losers (Baumgartner et al. 2009; Lowery 2013). As such, it makes sense to evaluate each side of a proposal and identify net differences between them in terms of both campaign contributions and sheer numbers to gauge whether *lobbyists* or *money* is more associated with winning. By changing the unit of analysis to the *side* of the legislative proposal, we can evaluate whether the side that controls more money is more likely to win.

The models presented in Table 5.3 and depicted in Figure 5.4 estimate the probability that a provision in the bill makes it into the Chairman's Mark (as 48 percent do) or the committee report (as 52 percent do), using three kinds of advantages for the "pro" side of a provision defined earlier – *contributions advantage, numeric advantage*, and *lobbying expenditures advantage*. Since these variables all range from –1 (in which case all lobbyists or all contributions are from the anti side) to +1 (when all lobbyists or all contributions are from the pro side), we can compare them directly to see which is most important.

Despite the findings of Analysis I and II, which indicate that contributions increase lobbyists' success in securing preferred policy objectives, the null effects hypothesis predicts that in Analysis III, when considering the

TABLE 5.3 *Predicting success for a provision as a function of lobbying expenditures, lobbyists' contributions, and the number of lobbyists on each side*

	Success in the mark	Success in the report
Contributions advantage of supporters	–0.63	–0.69
	(0.44)	(0.44)
Numeric advantage of supporters	**3.13**	**3.09**
	(0.49)	(0.47)
Lobbying expenditures advantage of supporters	–0.37	–0.12
	(0.40)	(0.39)
Constant	**–1.10**	**–0.91**
	(0.24)	(0.23)
N	254	254
Pseudo-R2	0.23	0.25

Notes: Cells contain logit coefficients with standard errors below in parentheses. Bolded coefficients are significant at $p < 0.05$.

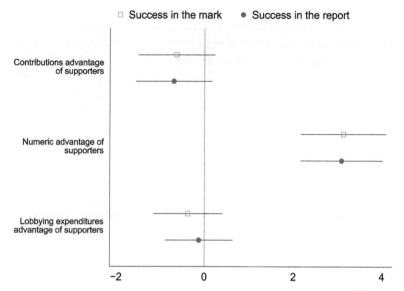

FIGURE 5.4 Factors that predict the success of legislative provisions at the Chairman's Mark and committee report stages of bill consideration
Notes. *Markers show OLS coefficients surrounded by 95 percent confidence intervals. Contributions include those from the group's in-house lobbyists, contract lobbyist, and PAC. N = 254 legislative proposals.*

lobbying activity surrounding a policy proposal in toto, we should not see an effect of money over policy outcomes. Indeed, a null effect is what we see here. At both the mark and report stages, as seen in Table 5.3 and illustrated in Figure 5.4, the net contributions advantage of proponents is not a significant predictor of whether the provision appears in the mark when also controlling for the numeric and lobbying expenditure advantages.

This null effect is due in large part to the fact that in 76 percent of cases, the side with more lobbyists is also the side with more campaign contributions. However, when the side that contributes more is not the side that has more lobbyists, *numeric advantage* wins four out of five times. So while the majority wins the majority of the time, in a nontrivial number of cases (twelve in the mark and ten in the report), money has a stronger effect on outcomes than the level of support.

While the level of numeric support for a measure dominates over the level of contributions most of the time, we see here that sometimes it does not, and those cases are worth examining more closely. Figure 5.5

presents marginal predictions from two bivariate regression models, each of which predicts the probability that the proposal is adopted in the mark. (A graph for the report, which looks very similar, is not included.) We saw in Table 5.3 that the effect of *contributions advantage* is not significant when controlling for the other two variables in the models. But now, when we instead separate *numeric advantage* from *contributions advantage* by modeling them individually, each has a positive and significant relationship with success for the legislative provision.

Figure 5.5 illustrates that when either the majority of lobbyists or the majority of contributions opposes the proposal (i.e., X < 0), the proposal fails, and the downward pull of numeric opposition on provision adoption (shown by the dotted line) is greater than the downward pull of contributors' opposition on provision adoption (shown by the solid line). Likewise, when 50 percent more lobbyists or 50 percent more contribution dollars favor the proposal (i.e., X > 0.5), the provision is likely to be adopted, and the positive pressure of the *numeric advantage* dominates over the positive pressure of *contributions advantage* at the

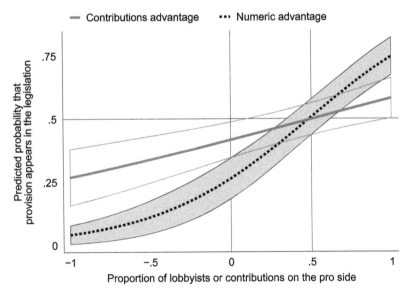

FIGURE 5.5 Comparing numeric to contributions advantages in predicting legislative proposal success
Notes. *Graph gives the predicted probabilities of provision success at different levels of either contributions or numeric advantage, surrounded by 95 percent confidence intervals. N = 254 legislative provisions.*

same level. So when there is a clear majority of lobbyists on the same side of a provision, that side tends to win. The fact that opposition to a proposal (whether from the majority of lobbyists or the majority of contributions) tends to depress the proposal's chances more strongly than support for the proposal enhances the proposal's chances shows the power of negative lobbying.

More to the point, though, we see in Figure 5.5 that when the proportion of supporters or of supporters' contributions is above 0 but less than about 0.45, for a given level of X, supportive contributions predict a higher probability of adoption than supportive lobbying does. Here we have yet another example of stealth lobbying. When lobbying for and against a proposal is roughly evenly split, and controlling for the disproportionate power of negative lobbying, the predicted probabilities suggest that the side that makes more campaign contributions to key committee members has an advantage over the side that merely has more lobbyists. This conclusion is wholly consistent with the arguments and the findings put forth in this book that in the absence of a single, majority opinion, campaign donors can nudge policy in their preferred direction.

5.7 DISCUSSION AND CONCLUSIONS

This chapter has examined and compared highly specific, and usually unavailable, information about the preferences of interest groups and senators during successive phases of committee consideration of a major piece of legislation. Analyses of these data suggest that groups that give contributions to committee members are more likely to achieve legislative success than groups that do not contribute. The effect of contributions is clear in both the group's aggregate contributions to all committee members (Analysis I) and in contributions to specific senators (Analysis II), and it is hinted at in the ability of contributors to be favored over supporters in the adoption of a provision of the larger bill (Analysis III).

In contrast to the first stage of committee consideration when the Chairman's Mark is being written, and the last stage of committee consideration when senators vote on the legislation, the amendment-offering stage is the point at which the data show that interest groups' campaign contributions are most effective. During the amendment stage, few outsider observers – and few putative insiders too – can see what is happening, and a single legislator can offer a narrow benefit to an interest group outside of public view – making it the quintessential example of stealth lobbying. At this middle stage, the expected probability of getting a desired amendment offered is four times as great for groups that contribute to any number of Finance members as for groups that lobby the same legislators on the same issue at the same time but do not contribute to them. Even more compellingly, the dyadic analysis (Analysis II) shows that when a group contributes to a committee member, the odds that the *specific* senator offers an amendment desired by the *specific* contributing group are about four times as great as when the group in the dyad does not contribute to the senator in the dyad.

As mentioned in Chapter 4, group-requested amendments are more than twice as likely to be accepted into the bill relative to amendments not linked to a specific group. Since the committee's reported version of the legislation is very similar to the language of the adopted Affordable Care Act as modified by the Health Care and Education Reconciliation Act, this means that group-requested amendments were twice as likely as other amendments to become law. Of the fifty-six amendments requested by one or more groups, 41 percent were accepted into the bill in committee; of the 508 amendments not clearly linked to any interest group, 18 percent were accepted. Thus, the probability that a senator's amendment is accepted into the legislation is much greater when the amendment is requested by an identifiable interest group. It is probably the case that more of the amendments offered by senators were initiated by interest groups' requests than I could detect based on language similarity alone – so the true number may be much higher. This possibility is supported by the finding in Chapter 2 that lobbyists working on a bill are more likely to meet with the Member who introduces it before the bill is introduced than only afterward.

While the link found here between interest groups' contributions and amendment success has not been identified by previous researchers, it is important, as it presents a somewhat worrisome empirical finding about the influence of interest groups in lawmaking. Beyond securing greater *access* to Members of Congress, which we documented in Chapter 2 (as did Kalla and Broockman 2016), this chapter shows that groups' campaign contributions are associated with legislative *action* on behalf of contributing groups. Lobbyists know that securing a commitment to *act* is far more desirable than merely securing a meeting with the Member or even securing the Member's support on the issue. The link provides the strongest evidence we have seen in this book of the Third Circuit court's standard for bribery, in which "the payor provided a benefit to a public official intending that he will thereby take favorable official acts that he would not otherwise take" (*United States* v. *Wright*, 2012).

In addition to amendment-offering, the effect of contributions appears at other stages in the development of legislation as well. Groups that contribute increase their success in the mark by 63 percent and also increase their success in the report by 63 percent relative to groups that do not contribute. These differences are notably smaller than the four-times-greater odds of success for contributing groups in the stealthier amendment-offering stage.

In the provision-level analysis, we find support for both the null effects and the salience hypotheses. When all lobbying for and against a proposal is added up separately, the data suggest that lobbying works, and that contributions may act as an additional incentive, especially when support for a proposal is divided. We saw that when a proposal has many more supporters than opponents, it is very likely to be adopted, and when it has more opponents than supporters, it is quite unlikely to be adopted. (It is also likely the case that when the majority of lobbyists oppose a proposal, its supporters supply more campaign contributions than normal to counteract the effects of negative lobbying.) But when the number of supporters is just a bit higher than the number of opponents (i.e., the proportion of support is between 0 and 0.45), the campaign contributions of supporters are more strongly associated with the outcome than are the sheer number of supporters. This finding supports the notion that when it is not very clear which side has more supporters, and lawmakers can avoid the appearance of giving in to the preferences of contributors, they are more likely to do just that.

The significance of groups' contributions in determining their legislative success is present while also controlling for important alternative explanations, including groups' lobbying intensity, annual revenue, and ties to committee members' constituencies. Members appear to be more willing to provide microlegislation for contributors than for noncontributing constituents, and this may be troubling for citizens who make their preferences known through letters and conversations but do not make campaign contributions, or for those who are concerned generally about achieving fair representation in legislative outcomes.

As recommended by David Lowery (2013), to really gauge the effects of interest groups' attempts to influence policy requires the kind of before–after research design employed here. Because of the strong incentives facing legislators as well as lobbyists to conceal any activity that may be construed as an exchange of money for favors, future studies of interest groups and lobbying will require sophisticated and creative techniques of data-gathering and analysis to demonstrate what lawmakers and lobbyists try to do in stealth.

6

Conclusions about Money in Politics

In the preceding chapters we have seen a variety of original datasets built, merged, statistically analyzed, and interpreted. These data reveal how lobbyists' efforts – including any campaign assistance they provide – are significantly linked to observable legislative actions by Members of Congress. Using lobbyists' personal and PAC contributions, which I linked to their clients and employers; Members' daily schedules; information about fundraising events; the written preferences of 866 groups regarding proposed health reform provisions; and the details of 564 amendments offered by senators in committee, we have seen the influence of lobbyists' campaign assistance on their access to Members, on groups' propensity to realize their policy objectives, and on lobbyists' ability to secure microlegislation. In this final chapter, we draw together and evaluate the three themes of the book, noting some lessons for future researchers about where to look for possible influences of lobbying and campaign donations on politicians and the laws they produce. And we conclude the story of health reform legislation in 2009–10 – though the issues surrounding health care policy in the United States continue to this day.

6.1 THE IMPORTANCE OF SALIENCE

The first of the major themes of this book has been that lobbying influence is most likely to be observed when salience is low. Salience – the degree of attention and importance that the general public gives to an issue or policy debate – can have a profound effect on how interest groups lobby and how legislators react. Yet as Baumgartner and Leech noted, before their 1998 book *Basic Interests*, studies of the influence of interest groups were noncumulative, evaluating just one or a few issues, votes, or groups at a time (Baumgartner and Leech 1998) – so they varied little in salience. Subsequently, a small but growing number of studies have examined issues that intentionally vary salience in order to gauge the effect of lobbyists and money over policy outcomes (Fellowes and Wolf 2004; Baumgartner et al. 2009; McKay 2011; Grose et al. 2019). But more than a decade later, Hojnacki and colleagues argued that the literature as a whole was still doing a poor job evaluating how variation in salience conditions the effects of money on policymaking (Hojnacki et al. 2012, 387).

This book has addressed this critique in two ways. By evaluating lobbyists' influence in very low-salience conditions, we have seen tangible evidence that lobbyists do have an influence over legislation when salience is low. And by measuring lobbyists' influence over legislation when the public might be paying attention, as well as when it is impossible for it to pay attention, we have demonstrated that influence is greater when salience is lower. These contributions advance the literature by illustrating, in a variety of contexts and methods of measurement, that salience has a significant and measurable influence on lobbyists' legislative success.

Examples of the effects of salience are found in every one of the preceding chapters. Contributions are more closely linked to policy outcomes in the relatively dark amendment stage than in the more public stages of votes and floor debate (Chapter 5). Contributions have a greater effect on the probability that a proposal is adopted when the majority of lobbyists involved do not exhibit a clear preference (Chapter 5). Apparently innocuous phrases in amendments to committee legislation, most of which do not even find their way into the bill, are more likely to be accompanied by special interest money (Chapters 4 and 5). Groups that are willing to fundraise for senators – an activity that is very common but not publicly disclosed – are significantly more likely to be rewarded by the benefitting senators relative to groups that did not fundraise for those senators (Chapter 4). Contribution solicitations are more explicit in non-public situations, such as a private voice mail message (Chapter 4). Individual lobbyists' contributions are more closely linked to the timing of legislation than PAC contributions are (Chapter 3). Lobbyist-controlled PACs seem to shift their contributions away from the high-salience domain of official campaign committees to the murky world of SuperPACs (Chapter 3). Campaign donors are more likely to secure repeat meetings with Members than are non-donors (Chapter 2). Lobbyists are more likely to secure more meetings with members of less powerful (and less observable) congressional committees (Chapter 2). Leading health care interest groups meet quietly with senators and their staff to form deals (Chapter 1). And in all of these cases, the public is none the wiser. Just as Mayhew (1974) argued that *if* Members of Congress were single-minded seekers of reelection, they would behave as they do, I argue that *if* Members of Congress and the lobby groups that subsidize them wanted to exchange favors for funds, they would do so in the ways we observe here.

6.2 THE USEFULNESS OF MONEY

The second major theme of the book has been that legislators are more likely to provide benefits to those lobbyists who are useful to them. The data are fully compatible with the possibility that lobbying is primarily the transmission of useful information, as lobbyists provide legislators with an understanding of the points of view of (particular) stakeholders. Yet some of the things that lobbyists provide – especially campaign assistance in the forms of fundraising and contributions from the lobbyists and their organizations – are in the interest of the particular Member, and not the public at large.

6.2.1 Increasing Access

Chapter 3 presents data about lobbyists' contributions patterns that support the notion that lobbyists use money to enhance their access. As health reform legislation is being written, contributions from individual health lobbyists suddenly and dramatically exceed the contributions of lobbyists not working on health care issues. This increase is seen in both the number of lobbyists who contribute and the amounts of money that health lobbyists – often the very same lobbyists – are giving over time. Health lobbyists focus on key committee members at key times. Lobbyist-controlled health PACs also give out of proportion to their number relative to nonhealth lobbyists' PACs. During consideration of health reform legislation, individual health lobbyists and the PACs they control both contribute more than all of their nonhealth counterparts combined. Moreover, health lobbyists single out the two Senate committees with jurisdiction over health reform. This is in remarkable contrast to the oft-studied PACs, whose contributions, timing, targets, and amounts are less influenced by the timing of health reform legislation.

Further, in Chapter 2 we saw that Members seem to reward donors and fundraisers with additional access. Given the scarcity of attention in Washington discussed in Chapter 2, combined with the fact that access is a necessary precursor to influencing the content of legislation, we can infer that lobbyists' contributions do significantly increase lobbyists' access to politicians.

6.2.2 Maximizing Policy Success

Chapters 2, 4, and 5 present the strongest statistical evidence I have ever seen of lobbyists' having an effect on legislative policy. The data used in this book make possible a rare but important mechanism through which we can approach an explanation that is not just correlational but, most likely, *causal.* The research design I use compares two versions of a policy proposal, one before and one after interest groups got their fingerprints on it, as recommended by senior interest groups scholar David Lowery (2013). Short of a field experiment in which a random set of proposals or legislators are subject to lobbying while a control group is not lobbied, it may be impossible to know for sure the extent to which lobbyists are responsible for changes in legislation between versions. But the before –after research design, the observations I made from inside the congressional committee process, and most compellingly, the virtually identical language between amendments and interest group requests jointly make it probable that the groups influenced the content of the bill and its proposed amendments.

In addition to demonstrating the influence of lobbyists over the content of public laws, Chapters 4 and 5 find that such influence is more likely when the lobbyist contributes to or holds a fundraiser for the senator who proposes the legislation. Lobbyists who provide campaign contributions to members of the committee around the time its members are deciding what provisions to put in health reform legislation are more likely to be successful in securing preferred policies than those who lobby the same people at the same time but do not contribute to them. The models predict that groups that contribute to members of the key committee have about 41 percent of their preferences met in the Chairman's Mark, compared to 22 percent for groups that do not contribute to those senators. And groups improve their proportion of requests realized in the committee report from 26 percent to 43 percent if they contribute to committee members.

Moreover, senators who receive campaign donations from a lobbyist or the organization they represent are four times as likely to offer an amendment requested by the group in the form of committee microlegislation. Contributions increase the predicted probability that a group "gets" an amendment it wants from 7 to 26 percent, and fundraising for a senator increases the odds of securing a requested piece of microlegislation by a factor of almost 4 (Chapter 5). This is stunning evidence of the influence of lobbyists – amplified by campaign assistance – over adopted legislation, which senior interest groups scholar Beth Leech has called "the closest thing to a smoking gun we are ever likely to see in interest group research."[1]

6.3 THE PERVASIVENESS OF NULL EFFECTS

Writing about the failure of so many studies to produce significant findings of the influence of lobbying over public policy (e.g., Smith 1995; Baumgartner and Leech 2001; Baumgartner et al. 2009), Lowery (2013) details an "inventory of null hypotheses" – a dozen or so reasons that we so often see no effect of interest group lobbying in our statistical models. The present book shows, similarly, that most of the time lobbyists have minimal observable effect on policy outcomes. But that does not mean the effects are not there. The analysis here demonstrates several reasons for the persistence of null effects in research on lobbying influence, including the inverse pull of power and access, the phenomenon of negative lobbying, and the narrow scope of microlegislation.

6.3.1 The Inverse Pull of Power and Access

As explained and tested in Chapter 2, the phenomenon that I call the inverse pull of legislative power and lobbyists' access describes the tendency that the Members of Congress with the most power also have the least time and attention to focus on various interest groups' narrow priorities. Conversely, the Members who are the most accessible to lobbyists have the least power to carry out their requests. The data show that Members of Congress who are on more prestigious committees, and who have greater seniority on these committees, spend less time overall with lobbyists. Even Members of the same party and in the same chamber spend radically different levels of time with lobbyists of different national importance: Witness Montana-focused Senator Jon Tester and locally focused Representative Kathy Castor, versus the nationally focused Senator Max Baucus and Representative Suzanne Kosmas.

Given that legislative power is not equally distributed among Members of Congress, it follows that for lobbyists to influence the content of legislation, they must compete successfully against many other interests both for access and for the influence access is aimed at achieving. Recall

---

[1] This was written in an anonymous peer review that Professor Leech later emailed to me.

the way that four minority-party Members, Senators Kyl, Roberts, Crapo, and Cornyn, were unable to stifle comparative effectiveness research because of the dominating power of Chairman Baucus, who had co-authored a bill establishing a comparative effectiveness institute. While lobbyists for the Alliance for Comparative Effectiveness Stakeholders were successful in getting four senators to take up their cause, they were not able to overcome the force of the chairman's will.

6.3.2 Negative Lobbying

Chapter 1 describes the concept of negative lobbying as it occurred quite successfully in 1994, bringing down the health reform efforts of Bill and Hillary Clinton, suggesting negative lobbying could easily have sunk the Affordable Care Act as well. Politicians' asymmetric preference for avoiding blame over receiving praise – or over even creating good public policy – makes legislators fearful of writing bills that may engender backlash from powerful interest groups. Risk-averse politicians are reluctant to make a change if they do not think it has broad support, while leaving the status quo alone is much easier to defend, even if it is not the better alternative. Politicians frequently "kick the can down the road," postponing a decision until a later congress or date. They agree to do nothing rather than to legislate. For Chairman Baucus, the possibility of failing to get a law passed – as happened in 1994 – was worse than the trade-offs the committee chair made with the most powerful national health lobby groups. The dominant strategy was to avoid setting off a massive backlash from the major "stakeholders" – read interest groups.

We also saw the power of negative lobbying in Chapter 5's third unit of analysis. When competition among interest organizations is as fierce as we observed it to be during consideration of health reform, as witnessed in Chapter 3, no single lobbyist or group is likely to "win" over the others. Indeed, for 193 of 254 policy proposals in the Finance committee's draft of the Affordable Care Act, the side of the debate with more lobby groups is also the side of the debate that makes more campaign contributions – thus making it very difficult to detect the influence of campaign contributions as separate from the power of successful information-oriented lobbying. As we saw, the power of negative lobbying means that if more lobbyists oppose a measure than support it, it is very unlikely to be adopted. Similarly, when an overwhelming number of lobbyists support the measure, it is very likely to be adopted. But when the number of lobbyists on the two sides is roughly even, or when supporters only

slightly outweigh opponents, campaign contributions offered by supporters can pull the policy outcome over the line to adoption more easily
than a few more supporters can.

6.3.3 Microlegislation

A third reason for the pervasiveness of null effects in this literature is that,
contrary to popular imagination, lobby groups very often are not trying to
push proposed legislation toward or away from passage. Much, if not
most, of the time, lobbyists, acting in stealth, seek small changes in the law
that would benefit their profession, industry, company, or organization.
These requests are what I call microlegislation. (Similar concepts using
different words are found in Alexander et al. 2009; Richter et al. 2009;
Godwin et al. 2012; and LaPira and Thomas 2017).

In addition to the low salience of microlegislation, requests for microlegislation encounter little resistance. This fact distinguishes them from
"pro/anti" lobbying, which is a much rarer phenomenon than the large
number of studies of it would suggest (e.g., Langbein and Lotwis 1990;
Austen-Smith and Wright 1994; Brooks et al. 1998; McGarrity and Sutter
2000; Wawro 2001; Stratmann 2002; Roscoe and Jenkins 2005; Mian
et al. 2010; Dorsch 2013). As we saw in Chapters 4 and 5, lobbyists
seeking narrow benefits for their organizations do not encounter much
opposition, because other lobbyists see little reason to use their scarce time
with congressional Members and staff to oppose the benefits other groups
might be seeking for themselves. In particular, when the opposing "side"
is not other groups but the government itself, and more to the point the
United States Treasury, legislators take advantage of the collective action
problem (especially Democrats) or use anti-government rhetoric (especially Republicans) to justify providing the requested microlegislation
despite the cost to the government. By stealthily pursuing concentrated
benefits with diffuse costs, successful lobbying organizations extract rents
from legislators without anyone objecting or, most of the time, even
noticing.

6.4 LOOKING FOR INFLUENCE IN ALL THE WRONG PLACES

This book makes advances in the literature about the influence of lobby
groups over public policy by looking in unusual places, using novel
techniques, and lowering the evidence threshold. Having summarized
earlier the evidence for the three and a half hypotheses presented in this

book, I will now conclude by urging future researchers to search for the evidence where it is likely to be.

Over the last thirty years, many studies have presented compelling empirical evidence of the influence of lobbying and money over legislators (Hall and Wayman 1990; Neustadtl 1990; Quinn and Shapiro 1991; Stratmann 1991, 1995, 1998, 2002; Fleisher 1993; Nollen and Quinn 1994; Steagall and Jennings 1996; Brooks et al. 1998; Calcagno and Jackson 1998; McGarrity and Sutter 2000; Gordon 2001; Cohen and Hamman 2003; Fellowes and Wolf 2004; Kroszner and Stratmann 2005; Roscoe and Jenkins 2005; Miler 2007; Alexander et al. 2009; Richter et al. 2009; Mian et al. 2010; Dorsch 2011; Grasse and Heidbreder 2011; Witko 2011; Lazarus and McKay 2012; Rocca and Gordon 2013; Igan and Mishra 2014; Choi 2015; Kalla and Broockman 2016; Kang 2016). Yet the common refrain in the literature is that we cannot prove the influence of lobbying and contributions over public policy (e.g., Mahoney 2007; Lewis 2013; Kalla and Broockman 2016; Powell and Grimmer 2016), because, for example, the amounts of money are too small (Milyo et al. 2000), the vast majority of corporations do not contribute at all (Fouirnaies and Hall 2018), or the standard for proving influence is too high (Lowery 2013).

It will never be the case that legislators say, in captured audio recordings, "Just so we're clear, I'm doing this specific legislative favor for you solely because you gave me a campaign contribution, and not for any other reason." Yet this is the standard a federal court set for bribery in *United States* v. *Wright* (2012): "the payor provided a benefit to a public official intending that he will thereby take favorable official acts that he would not otherwise take." We need to be able to make some inferences short of demonstrating actual bribery.

If researchers are interested in identifying the influence of lobbying and campaign assistance over public policy, they should bear in mind the following ways in which lobbying influence is more likely to be found.

6.4.1 Access, Rather Than Votes

While I am not the first or the last to observe that money may buy access more than it buys influence (e.g., Milbrath 1963; Langbein 1986; Hansen 1991; Austen-Smith 1995; Chin 2005; Apollonio et al. 2008; Cotton 2012; Powell and Grimmer 2016; Binderkrantz et al. 2017; Fouirnaies and Hall 2018), I am the first to use the data from actual meetings between Members of Congress and lobby groups, combined with data about their contributions, the bills they lobbied on, and any fundraising they did for the member they visited, to draw clear connections between money and the disproportionate access it is associated with.

Access is the opportunity to influence. In Congress, access means face time with the politician. Researchers are hard-pressed to demonstrate that a particular meeting led to a specific behavior. It is much easier, however, to document that the opportunity to influence took place. In the first empirical chapter of the book, Chapter 2, I used Members' daily schedules to evaluate who gets meetings with whom. Only the people "in the room where it happens" (to make a *Hamilton* reference) know exactly what transpires in these meetings. What we know is that lobbyists are more likely to get repeat meetings with Members when they financially assist the member's reelection campaign. If money buys access, and access is the opportunity to influence, then money buys greater opportunities to influence.

But we do have some idea of what is discussed in these meetings. As we learned in the data for Chapter 2, bills introduced by Members of Congress frequently follow meetings with lobbyists who later report lobbying specifically on those same bills. And in 59 percent of those cases, the first meeting preceded the introduction of the bill. This fact is hard evidence that lobbyists who successfully achieve access are using their meetings with legislators to shape the content of legislation that has not yet been formally introduced.

Studying access is a promising route for scholars interested in detecting influence. A growing number of studies are using transparency initiatives (Dommett et al. 2017; McKay and Wozniak 2020) or field experiments (Kalla and Broockman 2016; Grose et al. 2019) to develop reliable data on meetings between legislators and lobbyists. Others use public comments (e.g., Golden 1998; Yackee and Yackee 2006) or, as they are called in Europe, consultation (Klüver 2011; Bunea 2015; Bunea and Thomson 2015; Braun and Arras 2018) to measure influence efforts by lobby groups (known as "stakeholders" in the bureaucracy literature). For their part, Members of Congress could easily release their daily schedules and even archive them for public use. Future researchers should continue to search for calendars, visitor logs, meeting minutes, and similar sources in order to understand who is being lobbied by whom, when, and why.

6.4.2 Narrow Provisions, Rather Than Bill Passage

A central argument of this book is that influence in Congress lies in the favors that Members quietly perform for lobbyists, in contrast to high-volume influence by many lobbyists working on an issue. This argument is most directly tested in Chapter 5, in which we saw that health care lobbyists are more likely to achieve policy goals when they donate to senators on the Finance committee, or at least to those senators who introduce low-salience amendments requested by the donating group. I identified 187 examples of language from amendments offered by senators that matches the language submitted in an interest group's letter. That this happens at all is important. It exposes a rare, indisputable connection between lobbyists' requests and Members' willingness to entertain them. It is even more significant that these favors are more likely when the group makes one or more campaign contributions to the senator around the same time.

This connection between campaign assistance and microlegislation is consistent with a small but compelling set of studies showing that lobbyists' influence is more readily seen in narrow provisions of legislation rather than the ultimate outcome of large bills. These quietly lobbied-on provisions include congressionally appropriated funds earmarked for specific projects (Lazarus and McKay 2012; Rocca and Gordon 2013), signing statements that accompany legislation (Evans 2004), federal government contracts (Witko 2011; Dusso et al. 2019), and firm-specific tax breaks (Fellowes and Wolf 2004; Alexander et al. 2009; Richter et al. 2009).

Previous work has shown that the US system of checks and balances and its many veto points make it extremely hard for interest groups to change existing policies (Baumgartner et al. 2009). The atypical case of amendment-offering, which involves just one veto point and little or no countervailing pressure, makes influence more likely than in just about any other situation. Amendments offered in committee are a perfect storm of senators unilaterally providing low-salience, private-benefit legislation to lobby groups. We saw in Chapter 5 that the effect of contributions on a senator's decision to offer a requested amendment is stronger than it is in influencing the portion of a group's requests that is realized in complete drafts of legislation. In the case of health reform legislation in 2009 as drafted by the Senate Finance Committee, which had never before published the full set of amendments to a draft bill, the low visibility of amendment-offering, combined with the newness of the requirement that lobbyists report their personal contributions as well as the rare availability of lobby groups' specific preferences on pending legislation, coalesced to allow significant links to be made between amendment-offering and campaign contributions or fundraising.

This book provides evidence that lobbyists frequently ask for, and senators often grant, short pieces of legislation that benefit only a relatively small number of lobby organizations, and that Members are more likely to grant these favors when they are accompanied by campaign assistance. Chapter 4 demonstrates that microlegislation is more than three times as likely to occur when the group or its lobbyists host a fundraiser for the senator, and Chapter 5 shows that the effect of contributions on amendment-offering is stronger than it is in influencing how many of a group's requests are realized in the full drafts of legislation. Future scholars should continue to look for evidence of lobbyists' influence in places where politicians and their staff, as well as the lobbyists who want to help politicians in any way they can, believe their interactions will go unnoticed: not major legislation being considered on the world stage, but in narrow provisions, tax breaks, earmarks, and microlegislation.

6.4.3 Fundraising and Personal Contributions, Rather Than (Just) PAC Contributions

After the HLOGA of 2007, and before the invention of SuperPACs in 2010, Members of Congress and lobbyists operated in a brief period of peak scrutiny. Lobbyists were no longer able to provide gifts, travel, or meals to Members and their staff. That left two legal means of using money to attract legislators' attention and assistance: campaign contributions and fundraising.

Previous scholars focused on the data available to them: PAC contributions. But we saw in Chapter 3 that PACs – even those that are controlled by registered lobbyists – behave differently from individuals. Before HLOGA, lobbyists could make contributions just like other citizens without having to report them (the campaigns did and do report such contributions if they are over $200, but campaigns do not have to specify that the donor is a registered lobbyist). As HLOGA was first taking effect in 2008–09, lobbyists continued to make contributions, perhaps without fully recognizing that these would now be traceable to their lobbying disclosure reports, since the systems for reporting them are not linked, and they are not reported to the same government agency. And it turns out, as we saw in Chapter 3, when lobbyists make contributions independently of a PAC, they behave more strategically than PACs do, targeting key legislators at key times. While the contributions of lobbyist-controlled health PACs also increase during the health reform debate, PACs demonstrate less sensitivity to political factors such as the timing of health reform legislation and who the key players are.

In addition to being newly required to report their campaign donations, registered lobbyists were also required to report any so-called bundled contributions they made to candidates – but due to loopholes, such as that the threshold amount could be divided over an unlimited number of hosts, the bundling requirement did not increase transparency, let alone tamp down on lobbyists' fundraising activities. Thus, in spite of the intentions of reformers, fundraising became an increasingly attractive method lobbyists could use to engender lawmakers' support. Since no public disclosure of fundraising events is required, we have no official, comprehensive source of data about fundraising events. Yet even with the incomplete picture provided by the sample of fundraising invitations published by the Sunlight Foundation (now a part of the Center for Responsive Politics), Chapter 4 provides evidence of a significant connection between fundraising events hosted by lobbyists and the success of their clients in getting requested amendments into the law.

The data used in this book have thus far combined contributions from different sources into a single variable, whether these contributions come from individual lobbyists on contract, in-house lobbyists, or PACs. But the contributions of these three sets of actors may have differential effects on Members' behavior. Especially since contract lobbyists have many clients, while in-house lobbyists have only one client (their employer), we might expect lower effects of contract lobbyists' contributions relative to in-house lobbyists' contributions.

Figure 6.1 presents marginal predictions using the data from Chapter 5 to show that increasing contributions from in-house individual lobbyists are associated with a sharply increasing probability that the senator offers an amendment requested by the group. For firm lobbyists, who represent many clients, giving greater contributions seems to be associated with somewhat lower probability of success. And greater PAC contributions have an effect that appears to be greater than the effect of firm lobbyists' contributions but lower than the effect of in-house lobbyists' contributions. Figure 6.1 is evidence that future scholars should not limit themselves to PAC contributions when they search for evidence of the influence of special interest money over politicians, notwithstanding the time-consuming challenges of linking individual donations to clients and organizations.

6.4.4 The Committee, Rather Than the Floor

A significant number of studies of lobbyists' influence have focused on what happens in committee, rather than on the floor (e.g., Schroedel 1986;

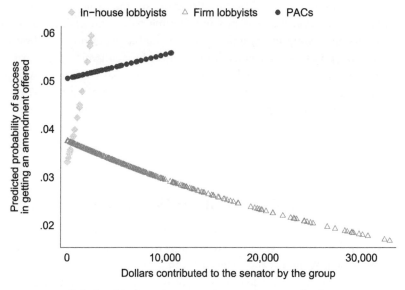

FIGURE 6.1 Relationship between groups' campaign contributions to a senator and the predicted probability that the senator sponsors an amendment requested by the group, by source of contribution

Hall 1987; Heitshusen 2000; Hojnacki and Kimball 2001; Powell and Grimmer 2016). Still, data about floor votes is much easier to come by. As just two examples, the website voteview.org, first created by Keith Poole and Howard Rosenthal, allows users to download congressional floor votes with a few clicks, all the way back to the first Congress in 1789; the Congressional Bills Project (Adler and Wilkerson 2013) provides similar data.

Congressional committees, however, choose what information they release to the public, and researchers must typically search transcripts of executive sessions (markups) to find out who supported or objected to what provisions. And as discussed in Chapters 4 and 5, much of what goes on in committee – especially individual Members' efforts to quietly influence the content of legislation through amendments and behind-the-scenes negotiation – is usually totally invisible to researchers. Some congressional committees, including the Senate Finance Committee, make considerable data available on their website that goes back many years. I hope this and all congressional committees continue to look for ways to make data about votes, amendments, bill drafts, submitted public comments, witness testimony, transcripts, and calendars available to the public for download.

The Congressional Fellowship Program of the American Political Science Association made it possible for me to get an insider view of what was happening in committee. This valuable program – the first of its kind, since 1953 – is a tremendous resource for academics and journalists to gain more insight into the congressional process. Decades' worth of scholars have benefitted from the personal experience of having worked directly for a Member of Congress or congressional committee (American Political Science Association 2003). Future scholars should continue in this vein by "soaking and poking" (Fenno 1978) among the decision-makers we study.

6.4.5 The Senate, Rather Than the House

Relative to the large number of studies of the influence of lobbying in the House of Representatives (e.g., Jones and Keiser 1987; Saltzman 1987; Snyder 1990; Wright 1990; Fleisher 1993; Bennett and Loucks 1994; Evans 1996; Steagall and Jennings 1996; Rudolph 1999; McGarrity and Sutter 2000; Fellowes and Wolf 2004; Miler 2007; Lazarus 2010; Loucks and Bennett 2011; Rocca and Gordon 2013; Curry 2015; Peoples and Sutton 2015), few researchers have studied the influence of lobbyists in the Senate in its own right (e.g., Grier et al. 1990 and Calcagno and Jackson 1998 are exceptions). A smaller number of studies simultaneously investigate both chambers (Langbein and Lotwis 1990; Grier and Munger 1993; Cohen and Hamman 2003; de Figueiredo and Silverman 2006; Lazarus and Steigerwalt 2009; Bond et al. 2011). The two bodies are very different and the Senate deserves its own treatment.

By focusing on the Senate in this book, I have, I hope, shone needed light on what happens in the upper chamber. The Senate protects minority rights (Binder and Smith 2001) to a much larger extent than the House, which is controlled entirely by the majority party (Marshall 2003). Each senator has the ability to filibuster or to put a "hold" – an anonymous filibuster – on pending legislation, regardless of their party, seniority, or committee assignments. This privilege gives senators amazing additional power relative to the House. It also forces them to work together to move policies forward. The necessary deal-making in the Senate creates opportunities for lobbyists that are not as evident in the House, allowing lobbyists to play senators off each other, for example, and to be more vocal in their objections to proposed legislation (Mann and Ornstein 2006).

The version of health reform legislation adopted by the Democratic House was significantly more liberal than the Senate Finance Committee's version.

House Speaker Nancy Pelosi and the Democratic majority did not have to compromise with Republicans at all, in stark contrast to the Democrats' fragile sixty-person majority (McKay and Clark 2009). Even one absence could threaten passage of the bill, and Senator Kennedy was in ill-health. As a result of their narrow advantage, and under pressure from the insurance industry, Senate Democrats declined to include in their bill the House Democrats' wish for a public option that would have created a federal health insurance plan to compete with private plans on the Exchange. In essence, the Senate's differing rules gave lobby groups critical leverage that they lacked in the House.

While the Senate is in general more opaque, more elite, and less accessible than the House, the unique institutions that govern it have consequences for the lobbyists who pressure senators – and for the laws that result. Future scholars should seek to continue to pry open the Senate in their studies of the influence of lobby groups over congressional legislation.

6.4.6 State Data, Rather Than Federal Data

In addition to insider knowledge of Congress, state legislatures provide a wealth of resources that scholars are increasingly recognizing (Hogan 2005; Primo and Milyo 2006; Lowery et al. 2009; Grasse and Heidbreder 2011; Powell 2012; Lewis 2013; Flavin 2015; Strickland 2020; see Ramsden 2002 for a review of state campaign finance research). There are fewer practical barriers to field experiments on state legislators, as demonstrated by, for example, Nyhan and Reifler (2015), Grose et al. (2019), and Wiener (2021) (and see Costa 2017 for a review of research that uses field experiments to test the responsiveness of public officials). All fifty states already have lobbying disclosure laws (Chari et al. 2019), and researchers should continue to take advantage of this wellspring of potential data.

6.4.7 Anticipating Opposition, Rather Than Yielding to Pressure

Members of Congress, on average, are extremely risk-averse. We saw in Chapter 1 that Democrats, fearful of repeating the failure of major health reform legislation in 1994, committed to securing the support of the most powerful lobby groups in the health care policy domain in an effort to avoid "Harry and Louise"-style negative lobbying. A small literature has shown negative lobbying, or status quo bias, to be effective in preventing new laws from passing (Baumgartner et al. 2009; McKay 2012a; Lewis 2013).

We have seen in the Obamacare effort that the threat of lobbying can be even more effective than actually carrying it out. Democrats who anticipated their opposition made deals with the peak health care associations, which therefore never had to carry out their implicit threat to conduct a negative lobbying campaign against the bill.

6.4.8 Inferring Intent, Rather Than Proving Effects

I do not claim to have met the Third Circuit's (*United States* v. *Wright*, 2012) standard and proven that Members are influenced by campaign assistance to do things they would not otherwise do. Scholars must be allowed to make informed, reasonable inferences about Members' intentions, rather than demonstrating that they were bought. Chapter 2 shows that, even when controlling for Members' legislative and jurisdictional interests, as well as their position of seniority or power in the legislature, lobbyists who contribute are more likely to be able to secure repeat meetings with Members than lobbyists who do not make campaign contributions. We cannot necessarily conclude that the money influenced the decision to take the meeting; we can only infer. In Chapter 3 we saw that when health reform moved to the top of the congressional agenda, individual health lobbyists gave disproportionately more money than before health reform was being written and relative to nonhealth lobbyists, and health lobbyists were significantly more likely to direct their funds to the key decision-makers rather than to other legislators. We can infer, even if we cannot prove, that individual lobbyists interested in a piece of legislation are motivated to donate to the most important legislators at the very time they are drafting details of the legislation.

Lobbyist-controlled PACs sharply curtail their publicly reportable direct campaign contributions as soon as they are able to donate instead to SuperPACs, which are under far less scrutiny, as we saw in Chapter 3. Evidence of intent is also seen in Chapter 4, in which we see lobbyists hosting fundraising events for senators, only some of whom offer amendments requested by those hosts. And in Chapter 5, lobbyists' contributions are more closely associated with legislative actions when neither side thinks they are being watched. In all of these examples, the evidence that money has some association with legislative actions is suggestive, not definitive.

In particular, we cannot rule out the realistic possibility that a donation is not an effort to influence but a reward or thank-you to legislators who also happen to do what the lobbyist's organization wanted. Whether contributions are intended to serve as bribes, as relationship builders, or as thank-yous is not important to my argument – especially if the objective is to reasonably infer lobbyists' intent, rather than to prove the effects of their contributions. The point is not to prove a quid pro quo: such an attempt will never be successful. Rather, I have revealed statistically improbable associations between campaign money and legislators' decision-making. It is left to the reader to decide just how compelling these associations are.

6.5 THE DEALS

Health reform legislation in 2010 did not suffer the same fate that similar legislation suffered in 1994. Senator Baucus, President Obama, and the other Democrats in charge committed themselves to avoiding the downfall of imperfect legislation as a casualty of negative lobbying. But this outcome would take some fairly explicit quid pro quo exchanges with powerful lobby groups.

In the summer of 2009, the Finance chairman and the White House held a series of meetings with lobbyists for the top health industries. In exchange for the lobby groups' support, Baucus and Obama would make certain concessions in the legislation.

The doctors. Physicians, represented principally by the American Medical Association (AMA), were most interested in replacing the sustainable growth rate (SGR) with a more favorable system for determining the growth rate of Medicare reimbursements. In the end, the SGR was not replaced, because to do so would have cost $210 billion according to the Congressional Budget Office. Yet, physicians were eventually the only major group that did not have to agree to cuts or fees in order to pay for the bill. In addition, the AMA was able to secure two other important asks: universal coverage and no public option. Universal coverage meant that more Americans would be seeking the services of doctors, and that services would be paid for by insurance companies or the government. A public option – a government-run alternative to private insurance that was heavily advocated by House Democrats – threatened to institute government-controlled reimbursement rates for all providers. Doctors did not want to increase the number of patients on these lower, government-set rates. So physicians were net winners.

The hospitals. The three peak hospital associations – the American Hospital Association, the Catholic Health Association, and the Federation of American Hospitals – agreed to collective Medicare and

Medicaid cuts of $150 billion. In exchange, the government pledged not to adopt a public option, which was commonly thought would have the effect of reducing hospitals' revenue.

The insurance industry. Baucus Senate staff wanted the insurance companies, represented principally by America's Health Insurance Plans (AHIP), to match the savings that the hospitals were promising. But the changes AHIP offered would not have saved money, according to the official estimator Congressional Budget Office, such as moving toward electronic health records (McDonough 2011, 169). AHIP also objected to the creation of an independent commission to set Medicare rates (now the Independent Payment Advisory Board or IPAB), fearing – accurately – that IPAB's independence would make it harder for the industry to lobby against payment cuts (because its recommendations would be adopted if Congress did not act). So no deal was struck between Democrats and the insurers.

Medical device makers. The peak association of medical device makers, the Advanced Medical Technology Association (AdvaMed), was invited to the deal meetings but did not agree to a deal. The two senators from Minnesota – a state that employed 50,000 people in the industry and housed major manufacturers including Boston Scientific, Medtronic, and St. Jude Medical Inc. (Moore 2009) – were not on the Finance committee as it wrote health reform legislation. Neither were senators from California and Indiana, states in which device makers were disproportionately located (Chaddock 2009; Moore 2009). But the bill had to be paid for, and device makers were subject to a 2.3 percent excise tax on their products totaling an estimated $40 billion over ten years.

The drug companies. Because of the historically high and rising cost of prescription drugs, and in order to pay the costs of health reform, President Obama and Chairman Baucus decided to assess an annual fee on the whole of the drug industry. The amount of this fee was uncertain, as was the outcome of several other proposals made by other House and Senate Democrats to lower drug prices. These proposals included four in particular: allowing Medicare to negotiate the price of prescription drugs for its patients, facilitating reimportation of medicines from countries in which they were sold at lower prices (which is all other countries), restricting the length of patents for so-called follow-on biologics, and reimbursing home infusion of a drug as a drug rather than as a clinic visit. Each of these was a long-standing request of various Democrats in Congress, such as Florida's Senator Bill Nelson.

At a June meeting at the White House, attended by PhRMA and drug makers Abbott, Amgen, and Pfizer, the fee agreed to was $80 billion over ten years (Blumenthal 2010). Another meeting on July 7 between the White House and lobbyists for PhRMA, Abbott, Amgen, Pfizer, AstraZeneca, and Merck (Blumenthal 2010) added details to the deal, which were leaked in a memo made from notes taken by a lobbyist during the meeting (Grim 2009; see Figure 1.3). The deal specified four concessions by the drug industry totaling $80 billion that were explicitly "in exchange for" the government's opposition to four proposals many Democrats had favored – reimportation of drugs, negotiation, drug reimportation, home-infused drugs, and follow-on biologics.

A hiccup came in the form of Democratic Finance member Senator Nelson, who was not a part of this deal. Florida – Nelson's state – is heavily populated by seniors, and Nelson wanted to control what he saw as unnecessarily high prescription drug costs, which affect seniors more than any other age group. Nelson objected to cuts of $80 billion, proposing instead $186 billion in cuts to the pharmaceutical industry over ten years (Blumenthal 2010). Nelson's amendment, predictably, was defeated in the Finance committee, by a combination of the Republicans on the committee and three Democratic senators – Baucus, Menendez of New Jersey (home to Merck and Pfizer), and Tom Carper of Delaware (home to AstraZeneca) (Blumenthal 2010).

The $80 billion number stood, and this deal with drug makers – and similar ones with the doctors, hospitals, and insurance companies – was probably essential to securing passage of the bill. Democrats avoided the extreme negative lobbying that occurred in 1994 which spooked Members of Congress away from the Clinton legislation. We know this because in 2009, one unsatisfied group – the insurers – did attempt to thwart the bill as it neared a vote. When the Finance committee reduced the amount of the penalty that individuals would have to pay for not having health insurance, AHIP released a series of reports arguing that the health care bill would not, in fact, bend the cost curve, and would instead accelerate the rate of increasing prices (Starr 2011). AHIP also decided to secretly channel $104 million to the Chamber of Commerce to fund ads against the 2009 bill (Armstrong 2010). If the other key stakeholders had done the same, the ad campaign would likely have overwhelmed the Democrats' efforts and brought the bill to its end, just as in 1994.

And so, in 2009–10, Democrats in pursuit of meaningful health reform legislation chose to yield to the implicit threat of a massive negative lobbying campaign which could easily have sunk the Baucus-Obama bill, just as it had sunk the Clinton bill in 1994. Payment cuts to the peak organizations representing the hospital, doctor, insurance, drug, and device industries were limited, and as a direct result, these organizations allowed the bill to pass. Negative lobbying won – and it did not even have to occur.

6.6 GETTING TO PASSAGE

Just before the Finance committee was scheduled to mark up the bill that would become the Affordable Care Act, the August recess of 2009 intervened. Members of Congress went home to their states and districts, where many fell victim to attacks at town hall meetings by individuals, often not constituents, who protested against a "government take-over of health care." Worse, town hall meetings became boisterous protests against President Obama, whom some participants even likened to Hitler. We now know that the vocal protests in town hall meetings throughout the country were planned in advance by conservative activists, predecessors to SuperPACs, and Fox News (Starr 2011, ch. 7). Former vice presidential nominee Sarah Palin spread false rumors that the bill would create "death panels" of bureaucrats to determine who should be allowed to live – a claim that even Republican Senator Johnny Isakson called "nuts" (Klein 2009, quoted in Starr 2011). Yet the public was paying attention. Google Trends data show that searches of topics related to health reform reached a peak in the second week of August that was exceeded only in March when the bill became law.[2]

At the height of public protests against the health care bill, in August of 2009, Senator Ted Kennedy, who called health reform "the cause of my life," died of a brain tumor. His role as chairman of the Senate HELP committee and as the longest-serving advocate of health reform made his death especially untimely. While some liberals and Democrats used Kennedy's death as a rallying cry to adopt comprehensive health reform, conservatives and Republicans saw Kennedy's absence as an opportunity to defeat the bill. Senate Finance Committee ranking member Chuck Grassley returned from Iowa to Washington, having criticized the bill for allowing the government to "pull the plug on Grandma" (McDonough 2011, 223). From that point forward, virtually no Republican would

---

[2] "Patient Protection and Affordable Care Act." Google Trends, January 6, 2009–January 5, 2010. https://trends.google.com/trends/explore?q=percent2Fmpercent2Fo9g7pqs& date=2009–06–01percent202010-05–01&geo=U.S.

support health reform legislation in any way, shape, or form. Inside the White House, even Obama's closest advisors were urging him to give up. Jonathan Cohn of the *New Republic* (Cohn 2010) paints this picture:

Counselor David Axelrod, who viewed health care as a political graveyard, presented a stark view of the president's falling poll numbers. Axelrod didn't argue that it was time to abandon comprehensive reform, but Vice President Joe Biden and chief of staff Rahm Emanuel did. Make a quick deal that would extend insurance coverage to parents and children, they urged, and put off broader action until later. Neither man had substantive qualms with comprehensive reform. They simply saw it sucking the political life out of the new presidency, just like it did to Bill Clinton more than a decade ago.

On Christmas Eve, the Senate, including Kennedy's Democrat-appointed temporary replacement senator, voted for cloture on the bill and then passed it 60–39. These sixty votes included every Democrat and no Republicans. It was a momentous occasion. On a hot mic, Vice President Biden called it "a big f– ing deal."

Less than a month later, on January 19, 2010, a special election was held in Massachusetts to fill Kennedy's unexpired term. Republican state senator Scott Brown defeated Democratic nominee and state attorney general Martha Coakley. The surprise outcome was notable both for its seeming repudiation of Kennedy and for what it meant for health reform – death. Though the Senate had already passed the bill, the normal proced-ure would be for the House to vote on its own version of the bill, for a conference committee to iron out chamber differences, and for identical versions of the bill to be voted on by both chambers. Everyone knew, though, that with Scott Brown as a new Republican, the Republican minority had forty-one votes, while the Democrats had only fifty-nine. Modern application of the nearly 100-year-old cloture rule meant that all controversial bills required the support of three-fifths of the Senate, or sixty votes – one more than the Democrats had.

What to do? The House had carefully developed its own version of health reform legislation for as long as the Senate had. The House bill was considerably more liberal than the Senate's, given the absence of a supermajority requirement in the House. As when Members of Congress bristled at having a completed health reform bill written for them by the new President Clinton, House Members did not welcome having their prerogatives usurped by the seemingly uppity Senate – espe-cially when the House had approved its version six weeks prior, on November 7. House Democrats were also ideologically committed to health reform elements that were absent from the Senate bill –

a government-supported public option for health insurance; a larger Medicaid expansion that would cover all Americans up to 150 percent of the poverty level (versus 133 percent in the Senate); greater premium credits for Americans under 400 percent of the poverty level; more generous benefits at each level in the exchange; a national health exchange instead of the Senate's fifty state exchanges; and using as its principal "pay-for" a 5.4 percent surcharge on individuals with incomes over $500,000 per year or families with annual incomes over $1 million. Thus, accepting the Senate bill as-is was a hard pill for House Democrats to swallow.

This necessity led to a remarkable compromise: The House would pass the Senate-passed bill without changes. This way the Senate would not have to vote on it again. Changes that the House wanted to make would be put into a separate bill that would be passed at the same time. How could Democrats be sure this "sidecar" bill would pass, given that Senate Democrats were only fifty-nine? Simple: the sidecar bill would be passed under a unique procedure known as reconciliation.

Reconciliation is a process designed to reconcile outlays and revenue in the budget. Every year separate committees create a set of appropriations and a set of financing bills. The reconciliation process, which is governed by the Budget committees in each chamber, provides for changes that enable the two sides of the ledger to balance. Because reconciliation is supposed to pertain only to the budget, Senate rules limit debate to twenty hours, which is shorter than the twenty-four hours required for a cloture vote to be allowed. Thus the reconciliation procedure eliminated the possibility of a filibuster – and that meant the outcome was decided by a simple majority of fifty-one votes rather than the supermajority threshold of sixty. The House passed the Senate-passed Patient Protection and Affordable Care Act on March 21, 2010, and the President signed it on March 23. Two days later, the Senate passed the House reconciliation bill. With President Obama's signature on the reconciliation bill on March 30, 2010, health reform legislation became the law of the land.

6.7 THE AFTERMATH OF HEALTH REFORM

Republicans in Congress voted to repeal the law nearly fifty times before the federal marketplace became operational at the beginning of 2014. The Health and Human Services Administration so botched the rollout of the federal exchange that Secretary Kathleen Sibelius publicly apologized and then resigned. Nineteen states opted out of the Medicaid expansion entirely, citing the 5–10 percent of new costs the state would have to pay starting in 2017. As a result, fourteen states – including populous states like Texas, Florida, and Georgia – left a combined 4.4 million people ineligible for coverage despite earning annual income below the poverty line. In Texas, for example, the nation's second-most populous state, the only people eligible for Medicaid coverage are children (up to 133–200 percent of poverty, depending on age), pregnant women (up to 200 percent of the federal poverty line), and parents of dependent children whose income is below 15 percent of the federal poverty line.

But the law survived. In 2012, the Supreme Court upheld the individual mandate, a major victory for the law's supporters. Chief Justice John Roberts, a George W. Bush appointee, cast the deciding vote. The court ruled that constitutionally it could not eliminate the individual mandate without fundamentally undermining the work of the US Congress to put together a workable bill. He was right: the mandate was essential to keeping insurance companies from cherry-picking healthy clients. While the government might have been able to regulate the insurance companies without an individual mandate, the insurance companies would never have agreed to this. They would have resorted to the Harry and Louise model of negative lobbying. Premiums would have increased immensely as only ill people purchased insurance. In essence, the agreement was necessary from both a pragmatic and a policy point of view.

The open and public consideration of the Affordable Care Act over more than a year helped legitimize the law. In particular, by making somewhat unsavory – but publicly announced – deals with doctors, hospitals, PhRMA, and others, Senator Baucus and President Obama secured the buy-in of these essential supporters of the law. As James Madison wrote in the Federalist Papers, government's role is to mediate and synthesize among factions, not to ignore them and do whatever it wants. To do so might bring short-term victories, but it is probable that the Affordable Care Act would not have survived to today if Baucus and his colleagues had failed to secure the support they got from the major stakeholder interest groups.

Tellingly, none of the organizations with whom the Democrats made deals ever campaigned openly to repeal and replace the law, as Senator Mitch McConnell (R-KY) and others in Congress tried repeatedly to do. Insurers, for one, who mostly gained from the Affordable Care Act, were not present because fissures within AHIP over whether or not to go along with the Baucus bill led several major insurers to leave the organization, and the remainder were not interested in revisiting their support for the bill (Demko 2017). As Medicaid plans became more profitable for insurance companies, one insurer (UnitedHealth) even advocated to preserve the Medicaid expansion (Demko 2017). AdvaMed, the peak association for medical device makers, which had not gotten a deal from the Finance committee in 2009, did lobby to try to end the 2.3 percent excise tax on its products, but there was little appetite for rescinding this small tax on medical devices, and the tax revenue was needed to pay for the insurance subsidies. Doctors and hospitals did not want to lose the individual mandate that kept patients covered and able to pay for treatment. Patient groups did not want people to lose coverage. Senate minority leader McConnell wanted to end a tax on tanning beds that was introduced toward the end of negotiations, but there was no tanning bed lobby to support this change. The pharmaceutical lobby, which had been criticized vehemently for prices that had recently sometimes increased exponentially overnight, chose to keep quiet and avoid publicity. Even years later, the major health care groups were notably absent from discussions of "repeal and replace." Not only had the unsavory deals worked – they had staying power.

Today, many of the bill's original authors have moved on. Health reform's chief architect, Max Baucus, left the Senate to become the US ambassador to China under the Obama administration. Chris Dodd, the interim chairman of the HELP committee, left Congress and became a lobbyist for the motion picture industry (the MPAA). Moderate Senator Olympia Snowe, the only Republican to vote for health reform (albeit in committee only), retired. Blanche Lincoln, a Democrat running for reelection in a conservative state, whose support of health reform dwindled as did her poll numbers, voted for the bill and was defeated for reelection. Senator John Kerry became Secretary of State in 2012. Finance committee members Conrad, Bingaman, Kyl, Bunning, and Ensign retired. The Finance committee chairmanship circulated among Senators Wyden, Grassley, and Hatch.

President Obama's legacy will be determined by long-term appraisals of his signature law. *Newsweek* counted seventy failed attempts by Republicans to repeal, modify, or replace the law between 2010 and 2017 (Riotta 2017); the dispute even led to a federal government shutdown in 2013 (Weisman and Peters 2013). As of this writing, it seems unlikely that the law's detractors will have another opportunity to repeal it. Such a change would be protested against by the millions of people who

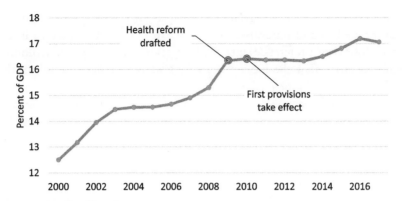

FIGURE 6.2 Bending the cost curve

Notes. *US health expenditures as a share of gross domestic product. Source: World Health Organization*

have coverage as a result of the law. The law also is likely to stay because of the agreements waged by Senator Baucus and the White House to secure the endorsements of the key interest groups. It shows the power groups sometimes have to influence public policy outcomes.

In the year in which the law went into effect, the number of uninsured Americans dropped by an estimated 3.4 percent. About 0.85 percent was due to the subsidies incorporated in the exchange plans, and another 0.4 percent gained health coverage through the Medicaid expansion (Frean et al. 2016). Data from the World Health Organization show that health reformers succeeded in bending the cost curve, slowing the acceleration of medical inflation in the United States. As illustrated in Figure 6.2, in 2008, health expenditures as a portion of the economy had grown nearly 4 GDP percentage points in just eight years. During the following eight years, while and after health reform legislation was being adopted, health spending grew by less than 1 GDP percentage point. The timing of this plateau, and the intention of health reformers to achieve this very phenomenon, suggests that it was induced by the adopted Affordable Care Act. Figure 6.2 suggests that Democrats were successful in bending the cost curve.

6.8 THE EFFECTS OF MONEY OVER PUBLIC POLICY

It is indisputable that lobbyists influenced the content of health reform legislation in 2009–10, and we know they used their money to try to achieve that end. The overlapping language of the law and the letters proves that influence occurrèd, and we also know that health lobbyists contributed to and fundraised for the senators who attempted to insert those lobbyists' preferences into the legislation. Yet, it is virtually impossible to prove that the money *caused* legislators to alter the bill in the helpful lobbyists' preferred way.

In a 2014 academic book on lobbying, scholars Holly Brasher and Jason Britt lament the difficulty of linking lobbyists' actions to legislative outcomes, calling bills and bill content "the last piece of the puzzle":

A perfect model in an ideal world would include a detailed measure of the content of congressional bills and would provide some way to connect the lobbying effort with the specific provisions. With the general listing of bills by the lobbying organizations unaccompanied by information about the specific provisions that matter to the organization, both of these things are lacking. Many are omnibus bills of staggering complexity and it is difficult to discern with multiple provisions what is of interest to any individual lobbying organization. With new methodologies for analyzing digitized text, perhaps a future project will undertake the mammoth task of coding bill content at a detailed level, for this is an important missing piece of the puzzle. And perhaps new data or innovative data gathering strategies will reveal organizations' interests in the specific components of a bill. (Brasher and Britt 2014, 200)

This book comes close to fulfilling this wish. By focusing in on the details of legislation at the committee stage, and matching lobbyists' requests to specific portions of legislation, we can tell that certain groups had an influence over the bill. Lobbyists' success is evident in introduced amendments (Chapters 4 and 5), in the degree to which their preferences are met in the bill (Chapter 5), and in the access they are granted (Chapter 2). And this success is significantly associated with their personal and PAC-funded campaign contributions and their fundraising activities (Chapters 3 and 4).

I do not claim – and I do not even think – that senators were bought. If the senators on the Finance committee had said no to the health lobbyists' requests, the senators still could probably recoup the campaign money from some other source. If the lobbyists tried to punish legislators who did not cooperate, the lobbyists would likely find themselves unable to secure meetings with those legislators or their friends for months or years to come. Moreover, when senators' objectives are aligned with lobbyists' objectives, no contribution is necessary to cement the relationship.

Lobbyists' own words help illustrate how a connection may be present and substantively important but fall short of the definition of causation.

One lobbyist described to political scientist Beth Leech how he approaches contributions: "I can't come up with $1000 ... For it to mean something, I would have to put together one fundraiser after another." But occasionally he makes an exception: "When I do give, to me what it means is, 'Here. This is a token of appreciation'" (Howard Marlowe, quoted in Leech 2013, 8).

Another lobbyist, former Congressman Robert Walker, remarks about fundraising events: "Every once in a while, if you have a direct issue and so on, you actually get a chance to say, 'I'd like to come in and see you about such-and-such and so on,' and the answer will usually be, 'Sure, stop by and see me sometime'" (Leech 2013, 22). "Stop by and see me some time" is hardly evidence of quid pro quo behavior. But it is consistent with the view that fundraising by lobbyists for legislators is a form of favor provision that may tend to increase the probability of reciprocal favor provision by legislator to lobbyist. Before I began the research that produced this book, I tended to give lobbyists and legislators the benefit of the doubt, relying on a number of alternative explanations for what might look like exchanges of lobbyists' money for legislative favors. These include ideological commonality, the endogeneity problem described in Chapter 1, constituent influence, and the low maximum of individual contributions. But now having conducted this research and having witnessed lobbying and its effects in person, I have no doubt that some large portion of the time, lobbyists are using money to influence policy outcomes. This leaves constituents, members of the public, and the people who are affected by public laws for generations with limited ability to overcome the power of stealth lobbying.

References

Adler, E. Scott, and John D. Wilkerson. 2013. *Congress and the Politics of Problem Solving*. Cambridge: Cambridge University Press.

Alexander, Raquel Meyer, Stephen W. Mazza, and Susan Scholz. 2009. "Measuring Rates of Return for Lobbying Expenditures: An Empirical Case Study of Tax Breaks for Multinational Corporations." *Journal of Law and Politics* 25 (4): 401–58.

American Political Science Association. 2003. "Congressional Fellowship Program Celebrates 50 Years." *PS: Political Science & Politics* 36 (4): 856–58.

Anderson, William D., Janet M. Box-Steffensmeier, and Valeria Sinclair-Chapman. 2003. "The Keys to Legislative Success in the U.S. House of Representatives." *Legislative Studies Quarterly* 28 (3): 357–86.

Ansolabehere, Stephen, John M. de Figueiredo, and James M. Snyder. 2003. "Why Is There So Little Money in U.S. Politics?" *The Journal of Economic Perspectives* 17 (1): 105–30.

Apollonio, Dorie, Bruce E. Cain, and Lee Drutman. 2008. "Access and Lobbying: Looking Beyond the Corruption Paradigm." *Hastings Constitutional Law Quarterly* 36: 13–50.

Apollonio, Dorie, and Raymond J. La Raja. 2004. "Who Gave Soft Money? The Effect of Interest Group Resources on Political Contributions." *Journal of Politics* 66 (4): 1134–54.

Armstrong, Drew. 2010. "Health Insurers Gave $86 Million to Fight Health Law." Bloomberg, November 17.

Arnold, R. Douglas. 1990. *The Logic of Congressional Action*. New Haven: Yale University Press.

Austen-Smith, David. 1995. "Campaign Contributions and Access." *American Political Science Review* 89 (3): 566–81.

Austen-Smith, David, and John R. Wright. 1994. "Counteractive Lobbying." *American Journal of Political Science* 38 (1): 25–44.

Baldwin, Robert E., and Christopher S. Magee. 2000. "Is Trade Policy for Sale? Congressional Voting on Recent Trade Bills." *Public Choice* 105 (1): 79–101.

Barber, Michael J. 2016. "Ideological Donors, Contribution Limits, and the Polarization of American Legislatures." *The Journal of Politics* 78 (1): 296–310.

Bartlett, Donald L., and James B. Steele. 1988. "The Great Tax Give-away." *Special Section of the Philadelphia Inquirer*, April 10–16 and September 25–26.

Baum, Christopher F. 2008. "Stata Tip 63: Modeling Proportions." *The Stata Journal* 8 (2): 299–303.

Baumgartner, Frank R., and Beth L. Leech. 1998. *Basic Interests: The Importance of Groups in Politics and in Political Science*. Princeton: Princeton University Press.

Baumgartner, Frank R., and Beth L. Leech. 2001. "Interest Niches and Policy Bandwagons: Patterns of Interest Group Involvement in National Politics." *The Journal of Politics* 63 (4): 1191–213.

Baumgartner, Frank R., Jeffrey M. Berry, Marie Hojnacki, David C. Kimball, and Beth L. Leech. 2009. *Lobbying and Policy Change: Who Wins, Who Loses, and Why*. Chicago: University of Chicago Press.

Bennett, Randall W., and Christine Loucks. 1994. "Savings and Loan and Finance Industry PAC Contributions to Incumbent Members of the House Banking Committee." *Public Choice* 79 (1/2): 83–104.

Binder, Sarah A., and Steven S. Smith. 2001. *Politics or Principle? Filibustering in the United States Senate*. Washington, DC: Brookings Institution Press.

Binderkrantz, Anne S., Helene H. Pedersen, and Jan Beyers. 2017. "What Is Access? A Discussion of the Definition and Measurement of Interest Group Access." *European Political Science* 16: 306–21.

Blumenthal, Paul. 2010. "The Legacy of Billy Tauzin: The White House-PhRMA Deal." Sunlight Foundation, February 12.

Bond, Craig A., Dana L. Hoag, and Jennifer Freeborn. 2011. "Are Agricultural PACs Monolithic? An Empirical Investigation of Political Contributions from Agricultural Subsectors." *American Journal of Economics and Sociology* 70 (1): 210–37.

Bonica, Adam. 2016. "Avenues of Influence: On the Political Expenditures of Corporations and Their Directors and Executives." *Business and Politics* 18 (4): 367–94.

Box-Steffensmeier, Janet M., Peter M. Radcliffe, and Brandon L. Bartels. 2005. "The Incidence and Timing of PAC Contributions to Incumbent U.S. House Members, 1993–94." *Legislative Studies Quarterly* 30 (4): 549–79.

Brady, Henry E., Lee Drutman, Kay Lehman Schlozman, and Sidney Verba. 2007. "Corporate Lobbying Activities in American Politics." In Annual Meeting of the American Political Science Association. Chicago.

Brambor, Thomas, William Roberts Clark, and Matt Golder. 2006. "Understanding Interaction Models: Improving Empirical Analyses." *Political Analysis* 14 (1): 63–82.

Brasher, Holly, and Jason Britt. 2014. "Understanding the Influence of Lobbying in the U.S. Congress: Preferences, Networks, Money, and Bills." In *New Directions in Interest Group Politics*, ed. Matt Grossmann. New York: Routlege.

Bratton, Kathleen A., and Kerry L. Haynie. 1999. "Agenda Setting and Legislative Success in State Legislatures: The Effects of Gender and Race." *The Journal of Politics* 61 (3): 658–79.

Braun, Caelesta, and Sarah Arras. 2018. "Stakeholders Wanted! Why and How European Union Agencies Involve Non-State Stakeholders." *Journal of European Public Policy* 25 (9): 1257–75.

Bronars, Stephen G., and Jr. John R. Lott. 1997. "Do Campaign Donations Alter How a Politician Votes? Or, Do Donors Support Candidates Who Value the Same Things That They Do?" *The Journal of Law & Economics* 40 (2): 317–50.

Brooks, Jonathan C., A. Colin Cameron, and Colin A. Carter. 1998. "Political Action Committee Contributions and U.S. Congressional Voting on Sugar Legislation." *American Journal of Agricultural Economics* 80 (3): 441–54.

Bullock, Charles S. 1973. "Committee Transfers in the United States House of Representatives." *The Journal of Politics* 35 (1): 85–120.

Bunea, Adriana. 2015. "Sharing Ties and Preferences: Stakeholders' Position Alignments in the European Commission's Open Consultations." *European Union Politics* 16 (2): 281–99.

Bunea, Adriana, and Robert Thomson. 2015. "Consultations with Interest Groups and the Empowerment of Executives: Evidence from the European Union." *Governance* 28 (4): 517–31.

Burstein, Paul. 2014. *American Public Opinion, Advocacy, and Policy in Congress: What the Public Wants and What It Gets*. Cambridge: Cambridge University Press.

Burstein, Paul, and April Linton. 2002. "The Impact of Political Parties, Interest Groups, and Social Movement Organizations on Public Policy: Some Recent Evidence and Theoretical Concerns." *Social Forces* 81 (2): 381–408.

Calcagno, Peter T., and John D. Jackson. 1998. "Political Action Committee Spending and Senate Roll Call Voting." *Public Choice* 97 (4): 569–85.

Callahan, Scott. 2019. "Do Campaign Contributions from Farmers Influence Agricultural Policy? Evidence from a 2008 Farm Bill Amendment Vote to Curtail Cotton Subsidies." *Journal of Agricultural and Applied Economics* 51 (3): 417–33.

Cameron, A. Colin, Jonah B. Gelbach, and Douglas L. Miller. 2011. "Robust Inference with Multiway Clustering." *Journal of Business & Economic Statistics* 29 (2): 238–49.

Cassata, Donna. 1996. "Steadfast Republican Trooper to Battle Again for Finance Overhaul." *All Politics CNN Time*, November 21.

Chaddock, Gail Russell. 2009. "Healthcare Reform: Obama Cut Private Deals with Likely Foes." The Christian Science Monitor, November 6.

Chari, Raj, John Hogan, Gary Murphy, and Michele Crepaz. 2019. *Regulating Lobbying: A Global Comparison*, 2nd ed. Manchester: Manchester University Press.

Chin, Michelle L. 2005. "Constituents versus Fat Cats: Testing Assumptions About Congressional Access Decisions." *American Politics Research* 33 (6): 751–86.

Chin, Michelle L., Jon R. Bond, and Nehemia Geva. 2000. "A Foot in the Door: An Experimental Study of PAC and Constituency Effects on Access." *Journal of Politics* 62 (2): 534–49.

Choi, Youngmi. 2015. "Constituency, Ideology, and Economic Interests in U.S. Congressional Voting: The Case of the U.S.–Korea Free Trade Agreement." *Political Research Quarterly* 68 (2): 266–79.

Clawson, Dan, Alan Neustadtl, and Mark Weller. 1998. *Dollars and Votes: How Business Campaign Contributions Subvert Democracy.* Philadelphia: Temple University Press.

Clymer, Adam, Robert Pear, and Robin Toner. 1994. "For Health Care, Time Was a Killer." *The New York Times*, August 29, A1, A8–9.

Cohen, Jeffrey E., and John A. Hamman. 2003. "Interest Group PAC Contributions and the 1992 Regulation of Cable Television." *The Social Science Journal* 40 (3): 357–69.

Cohn, Jonathan. 2010. "How They Did It: The inside Account of Health Care Reform's Triumph." *New Republic*, May 21, 14–25.

Corley, Pamela C. 2008. "The Supreme Court and Opinion Content: The Influence of Parties' Briefs." *Political Research Quarterly* 61 (3): 468–78.

Costa, Mia. 2017. "How Responsive Are Political Elites? A Meta-Analysis of Experiments on Public Officials." *Journal of Experimental Political Science* 4 (3): 241–54.

Cotton, Christopher. 2012. "Pay-to-Play Politics: Informational Lobbying and Contribution Limits When Money Buys Access." *Journal of Public Economics* 96 (3–4): 369–86.

Cox, Gary W., and Eric Magar. 1999. "How Much Is Majority Status in the U.S. Congress Worth?" *American Political Science Review* 93 (2): 299–309.

Croon, Marcel A., and Marc J. P. M. van Veldhoven. 2007. "Predicting Group-Level Outcome Variables from Variables Measured at the Individual Level: A Latent Variable Multilevel Model." *Psychological Methods* 12 (1): 45–57.

Curry, James M. 2015. *Legislating in the Dark: Information and Power in the House of Representatives.* Chicago: University of Chicago Press.

Curry, James M., and Frances E. Lee. 2020. "What Is Regular Order Worth? Partisan Lawmaking and Congressional Processes." *The Journal of Politics* 82 (2): 627–41.

Dabros, Matthew S. 2015. "Explaining Final Term Changes in US Congressional Foreign Travel." *The Journal of Legislative Studies* 21 (3): 428–46.

Davis, Sandra. 1988. "Goals & Strategies of Political Action Committees." *Polity* 21 (1): 167–82.

De Bruycker, Iskander. 2017. "Politicization and the Public Interest: When Do the Elites in Brussels Address Public Interests in EU Policy Debates?" *European Union Politics* 18 (4): 603–19.

de Figueiredo, John M., and Brian Kelleher Richter. 2014. "Advancing the Empirical Research on Lobbying." *Annual Review of Political Science* 17 (1): 163–85.

de Figueiredo, John M., and Brian S. Silverman. 2006. "Academic Earmarks and the Returns to Lobbying." *The Journal of Law and Economics* 49 (2): 597–625.

Deering, Christopher J., and Steven S. Smith. 1997. *Committees in Congress.* Washington, DC: CQ Press.

DeGregorio, Christine A. 1997. *Networks of Champions: Leadership, Access, and Advocacy in the U.S. House of Representatives*. Ann Arbor: University of Michigan Press.

Demko, Paul. 2017. "Insurance Companies Duck Obamacare Repeal Fight." Politico, June 3.

Denzau, Arthur T., and Michael C. Munger. 1986. "Legislators and Interest Groups: How Unorganized Interests Get Represented." *American Political Science Review* 80 (1): 89–106.

Dommett, Katharine, Andrew Hindmoor, and Matthew Wood. 2017. "Who Meets Whom: Access and Lobbying During the Coalition Years." *The British Journal of Politics and International Relations* 19 (2): 389–407.

Dorsch, Michael. 2013. "Bailout for Sale? The Vote to Save Wall Street." *Public Choice* 155 (3): 211–28.

Drope, Jeffrey M., and Wendy L. Hansen. 2004. "Purchasing Protection? The Effect of Political Spending on U.S. Trade Policy." *Political Research Quarterly* 57 (1): 27–37.

Durden, Garey C., Jason F. Shogren, and Jonathan I. Silberman. 1991. "The Effects of Interest Group Pressure on Coal Strip-Mining Legislation." *Social Science Quarterly* 72 (2): 239–50.

Dusso, Aaron, Thomas T. Holyoke, and Henrik Schatzinger. 2019. "The Influence of Corporate Lobbying on Federal Contracting." *Social Science Quarterly* 100 (5): 1793–809.

Egerod, Benjamin, and David Dryer Lassen. 2019. "Employing Legislators – Using Stock Market Reactions to Investigate Whether Legislators Reward Future Employers." In Annual Meeting of the Midwest Political Science Association. Chicago.

Eismeier, Theodore J., and Philip H. Pollock III. 1984. "Political Action Committees: Varieties of Organization and Strategy." In *Money and Politics in the United States: Financing Elections in the 1980s*, ed. Michael J. Malbin. Chatham: Chatham House.

Esterling, Kevin M. 2004. *The Political Economy of Expertise: Information and Efficiency in American National Politics*. Ann Arbor: University of Michigan Press.

Evans, Diana M. 1996. "Before the Roll Call: Interest Group Lobbying and Public Policy Outcomes in House Committees." *Political Research Quarterly* 49 (2): 287–304.

Evans, Diana M. 2004. *Greasing the Wheels: Using Pork Barrel Projects to Build Majority Coalitions in Congress*. Cambridge: Cambridge University Press.

Fellowes, Matthew C., and Patrick J. Wolf. 2004. "Funding Mechanisms and Policy Instruments: How Business Campaign Contributions Influence Congressional Votes." *Political Research Quarterly* 57 (2): 315–24.

Fenno, Richard F. 1973. *Congressmen in Committees*, 1st ed. Boston: Little, Brown.

Fenno, Richard F. 1978. *Home Style: House Members in Their Districts*. New York: HarperCollins.

Flavin, Patrick. 2015. "Campaign Finance Laws, Policy Outcomes, and Political Equality in the American States." *Political Research Quarterly* 68 (1): 77–88.

Fleisher, Richard. 1993. "PAC Contributions and Congressional Voting on National Defense." *Legislative Studies Quarterly* 18 (3): 391–409.

Fouirnaies, Alexander, and Andrew B. Hall. 2018. "How Do Interest Groups Seek Access to Committees?" *American Journal of Political Science* 62 (1): 132–47.

Fouirnaies, Alexander, and Anthony Fowler. 2022. "Do Campaign Contributions Buy Favorable Policies? Evidence from the Insurance Industry." *Political Science Research and Methods* 10 (1): 18–32.

Francia, Peter L., John C. Green, Paul S. Herrnson, Clyde Wilcox, and Lynda W Powell. 2003. *The Financiers of Congressional Elections: Investors, Ideologues, and Intimates*. New York: Columbia University Press.

Frean, Molly, Jonathan Gruber, and Benjamin D. Sommers. 2016. "Premium Subsidies, the Mandate, and Medicaid Expansion: Coverage Effects of the Affordable Care Act." *National Bureau of Economic Research Working Paper Series* No. 22213.

Gamble, Katrina L. 2007. "Black Political Representation: An Examination of Legislative Activity within US House Committees." *Legislative Studies Quarterly* 32 (3): 421–47.

Gerber, Alan S., Donald P. Green, and David Nickerson. 2001. "Testing for Publication Bias in Political Science." *Political Analysis* 9 (4): 385–92.

Giger, Nathalie, and Heike Klüver. 2016. "Voting against Your Constituents? How Lobbying Affects Representation." *American Journal of Political Science* 60 (1): 190–205.

Glass, Ira, Alex Blumberg, Andrea Seabrook, and Ben Calhoun. 2012. "Take the Money and Run for Office." In *This American Life*, ed. Ira Glass. Chicago: WBEZ Chicago and Public Radio International.

Godwin, Kenneth, Scott H. Ainsworth, and Erik Godwin. 2012. *Lobbying and Policymaking: The Public Pursuit of Private Interests*. Washington, DC: CQ Press.

Goldberg, Matthew H., Jennifer R. Marlon, Xinran Wang, Sander van der Linden, and Anthony Leiserowitz. 2020. "Oil and Gas Companies Invest in Legislators That Vote against the Environment." *Proceedings of the National Academy of Sciences* 117 (10): 5111–12.

Golden, Marissa Martino. 1998. "Interest Groups in the Rule-Making Process: Who Participates? Whose Voices Get Heard?" *Journal of Public Administration Research and Theory* 8 (2): 245–70.

Goldstein, Kenneth. 1999. *Interest Groups, Lobbying and Participation in America*. New York: Cambridge University Press.

Goodman-Bacon, Andrew. 2018. "Difference-in-Differences with Variation in Treatment Timing." *National Bureau of Economic Research Working Paper Series* No. 25018.

Gopoian, J. David. 1984. "What Makes PACs Tick? An Analysis of the Allocation Patterns of Economic Interest Groups." *American Journal of Political Science* 28 (2): 259–81.

Gordon, Stacy B. 2001. "All Votes Are Not Created Equal: Campaign Contributions and Critical Votes." *The Journal of Politics* 63 (1): 249–69.

Government Accountability Office. 2010. "2009 Lobbying Disclosure: Observations on Lobbyists' Compliance with Disclosure Requirements." GAO-10-499.

Government Accountability Office. 2021. "2020 Lobbying Disclosure: Observations on Lobbyists' Compliance with Disclosure Requirements." GAo-21-375.

Grasse, Nathan, and Brianne Heidbreder. 2011. "The Influence of Lobbying Activity in State Legislatures: Evidence from Wisconsin." *Legislative Studies Quarterly* 36 (4): 567–89.

Grenzke, Janet M. 1989. "Candidate Attributes and PAC Contributions." *The Western Political Quarterly* 42 (2): 245–64.

Grier, Kevin B., and Michael C. Munger. 1993. "Comparing Interest Group PAC Contributions to House and Senate Incumbents, 1980–1986." *Journal of Politics* 55 (3): 615–43.

Grier, Kevin B., Michael C. Munger, and Brian E. Roberts. 1994. "The Determinants of Industrial Political Activity, 1978–1986." *American Political Science Review* 88 (4): 911–26.

Grier, Kevin B., Michael C. Munger, and Gary M Torrent. 1990. "Allocation Patterns of PAC Monies: The US Senate." *Public Choice* 67 (2): 111–28.

Grim, Ryan. 2009. "Internal Memo Confirms Big Giveaways in White House Deal with Big Pharma." *HuffPost*, September 13.

Grose, Christian R., Pamela Lopez, Sara Sadhwani, and Antoine Yoshinaka. 2019. "Does Direct Lobbying Work? A Theory and Experiment." In Annual Meeting of the Midwest Political Science Association. Chicago.

Groseclose, Tim, and Charles Stewart III. 1998. "The Value of Committee Seats in the House, 1947–91." *American Journal of Political Science* 42 (2): 453–74.

Hall, Richard L. 1987. "Participation and Purpose in Committee Decision Making." *American Political Science Review* 81 (1): 105–27.

Hall, Richard L., and Alan V. Deardorff. 2006. "Lobbying as Legislative Subsidy." *American Political Science Review* 100 (1): 69–84.

Hall, Richard L., and Frank W. Wayman. 1990. "Buying Time: Moneyed Interests and the Mobilization of Bias in Congressional Committees." *American Political Science Review* 84 (3): 797–820.

Hamilton, James. 2004. *All the News That's Fit to Sell: How the Market Transforms Information into News*. Princeton: Princeton University Press.

Hansen, John Mark. 1991. *Gaining Access: Congress and the Farm Lobby, 1919–1981*. Chicago: University of Chicago Press.

Hart, David M. 2001. "Why Do Some Firms Give? Why Do Some Give a Lot? High-Tech PACs, 1977–1996." *Journal of Politics* 63 (4): 1230–49.

Heaney, Michael T. 2006. "Brokering Health Policy: Coalitions, Parties, and Interest Group Influence." *Journal of Health Politics, Policy and Law* 31 (5): 887.

Heinz, John P., Edward O. Laumann, Robert L. Nelson, and Robert H. Salisbury. 1993. *The Hollow Core: Private Interests in National Policy Making*. Cambridge, MA: Harvard University Press.

Heitshusen, Valerie. 2000. "Interest Group Lobbying and U.S. House Decentralization: Linking Informational Focus to Committee Hearing Appearances." *Political Research Quarterly* 53 (1): 151–76.

Hogan, Robert E. 2005. "State Campaign Finance Laws and Interest Group Electioneering Activities." *Journal of Politics* 67 (3): 887.

Hojnacki, Marie, and David C. Kimball. 1998. "Organized Interests and the Decision of Whom to Lobby in Congress." *American Political Science Review* 92 (4): 775–90.

Hojnacki, Marie, and David C. Kimball. 2001. "PAC Contributions and Lobbying Contacts in Congressional Committees." *Political Research Quarterly* 54 (1): 161–80.

Hojnacki, Marie, David C. Kimball, Frank R. Baumgartner, Jeffrey M. Berry, and Beth L. Leech. 2012. "Studying Organizational Advocacy and Influence: Reexamining Interest Group Research." *Annual Review of Political Science* 15 (1): 379–99.

Hurd, Richard, and Jeffrey Sohl. 1992. "Strategic Diversity in Labor PAC Contribution Patterns." *The Social Science Journal* 29 (1): 65–86.

Igan, Deniz, and Prachi Mishra. 2014. "Wall Street, Capitol Hill, and K Street: Political Influence and Financial Regulation." *The Journal of Law & Economics* 57 (4): 1063–84.

Jackson, David J., and Steven T. Engel. 2003. "Friends Don't Let Friends Vote for Free Trade: The Dynamics of the Labor PAC Punishment Strategy over PNTR." *Political Research Quarterly* 56 (4): 441–48.

Jansa, Joshua M., and Michele M. Hoyman. 2018. "Do Unions Punish Democrats? Free-Trade Votes and Labor PAC Contributions, 1999–2012." *Political Research Quarterly* 71 (2): 424–39.

Jeydel, Alana, and Andrew J. Taylor. 2003. "Are Women Legislators Less Effective? Evidence from the U.S. House in the 103rd–105th Congress." *Political Research Quarterly* 56 (1): 19–27.

Jones, Woodrow, and K. Robert Keiser. 1987. "Issue Visibility and the Effects of PAC Money." *Social Science Quarterly* 68 (1): 170–76.

Kahneman, Daniel, and Amos Tversky. 1979. "Prospect Theory: An Analysis of Decision under Risk." *Econometrica* 47 (2): 263–92.

Kalla, Joshua L., and David E. Broockman. 2016. "Campaign Contributions Facilitate Access to Congressional Officials: A Randomized Field Experiment." *American Journal of Political Science* 60 (3): 545–58.

Kang, Karam. 2016. "Policy Influence and Private Returns from Lobbying in the Energy Sector." *The Review of Economic Studies* 83 (1): 269–305.

Kaufman, Allen, Marvin Karson, and Jeffrey Sohl. 1988. "Corporate Political Action Committees' Strategies in the 1980 Congressional Elections." *Social Science Journal* 25 (3): 289–307.

Kessler, Daniel, and Keith Krehbiel. 1996. "Dynamics of Cosponsorship." *American Political Science Review* 90 (3): 555–66.

King, Gary, Robert O. Keohane, and Sidney Verba. 1994. *Designing Social Inquiry: Scientific Inference in Qualitative Research*. Princeton: Princeton University Press.

Kingdon, John W. 1984. *Agendas, Alternatives, and Public Policies.* Boston: Little, Brown.

Kingdon, John W. 1989. *Congressmen's Voting Decisions,* 3rd ed. Ann Arbor: University of Michigan Press.

Klein, Ezra. 2009. "Is the Government Going to Euthanize Your Grandmother? An Interview with Sen. Johnny Isakson." *The Washington Post,* August 11.

Klein, Ezra. 2010. "Sen. Evan Bayh: 'We've Got Good People Trapped in a Dysfunctional System'." *The* Washington Post, March 12.

Klüver, Heike. 2011. "The Contextual Nature of Lobbying: Explaining Lobbying Success in the European Union." *European Union Politics* 12 (4): 483–506.

Koerth, Maggie. 2019. "Everyone Knows Money Influences Politics … Except Scientists." FiveThirtyEight, June 4.

Kroszner, Randall, and Thomas Stratmann. 2005. "Corporate Campaign Contributions, Repeat Giving, and the Rewards to Legislator Reputation." *The Journal of Law & Economics* 48 (1): 41–71.

Langbein, Laura I. 1986. "Money and Access: Some Empirical Evidence." *Journal of Politics* 48 (4): 1052–62.

Langbein, Laura I. 1993. "PACs, Lobbies and Political Conflict: The Case of Gun Control." *Public Choice* 77 (3): 551–72.

Langbein, Laura I., and Mark A. Lotwis. 1990. "The Political Efficacy of Lobbying and Money: Gun Control in the U.S. House, 1986." *Legislative Studies Quarterly* 15 (3): 413–40.

LaPira, Timothy M., and Herschel F. Thomas. 2017. *Revolving Door Lobbying: Public Service, Private Influence, and the Unequal Representation of Interests.* Lawrence: University Press of Kansas.

Lazarus, Jeffrey. 2010. "Giving the People What They Want? The Distribution of Earmarks in the U.S. House of Representatives." *American Journal of Political Science* 54 (2): 338–53.

Lazarus, Jeffrey, and Amy McKay. 2012. "Consequences of the Revolving Door: Evaluating the Lobbying Success of Former Congressional Members and Staff." A Paper Prepared for Presentation at the Midwest Political Science Association Annual Meeting. Chicago, April.

Lazarus, Jeffrey, and Amy Steigerwalt. 2009. "Different Houses: The Distribution of Earmarks in the U.S. House and Senate." *Legislative Studies Quarterly* 34 (3): 347–73.

Leech, Beth L. 2006. "Funding Faction or Buying Silence? Grants, Contracts, and Interest Group Lobbying Behavior." *Policy Studies Journal* 34 (1): 17–35.

Leech, Beth L. 2013. *Lobbyists at Work.* New York: Apress.

Lewis, Daniel C. 2013. "Advocacy and Influence: Lobbying and Legislative Outcomes in Wisconsin." *Interest Groups & Advocacy* 2 (2): 206–26.

Loucks, Christine, and Randall Bennett. 2011. "The Importance of Committee Assignment: Health Care Industry Political Action Committee Contributions and the House of Representatives." *Contemporary Economic Policy* 29 (2): 163–77.

Lowery, David. 2007. "Why Do Organized Interests Lobby? A Multi-Goal, Multi-Context Theory of Lobbying." *Polity* 39 (1): 29–54.

Lowery, David. 2013. "Lobbying Influence: Meaning, Measurement and Missing." *Interest Groups & Advocacy* 2 (1): 1–26.

Lowery, David, Virginia Gray, Jennifer Benz et al. 2009. "Understanding the Relationship between Health PACs and Health Lobbying in the American States." *Publius* 39 (1): 70–94.

Luneburg, William V., and Thomas M. Susman. 2009. *The Lobbying Manual: A Complete Guide to Federal Lobbying Law and Practice*. Chicago: American Bar Association.

Magee, Christopher. 2002. "Do Political Action Committees Give Money to Candidates for Electoral or Influence Motives?" *Public Choice* 112 (3/4): 373–99.

Mahoney, Christine. 2007. "Lobbying Success in the United States and the European Union." *Journal of Public Policy* 27 (1): 35–56.

Mann, Thomas E., and Norman J. Ornstein. 2006. *The Broken Branch: How Congress Is Failing America and How to Get It Back on Track*. New York: Oxford University Press.

Marshall, Bryan W. 2003. "Controlling the Agenda with Special Rules: A House-Senate Comparison of Legislation in the Postreform Congress." *Politics & Policy* 31 (4): 672–93.

Marshall, David. 2010. "Who to Lobby and When: Institutional Determinants of Interest Group Strategies in European Parliament Committees." *European Union Politics* 11 (4): 553–75.

Masters, Marick F., and Gerald D. Keim. 1985. "Determinants of PAC Participation among Large Corporations." *The Journal of Politics* 47 (4): 1158–73.

Mayhew, David R. 1974. *Congress: The Electoral Connection*, vol. 26. New Haven: Yale University Press.

McCarty, Nolan, and Lawrence S. Rothenberg. 1996. "Commitment and the Campaign Contribution Contract." *American Journal of Political Science* 40 (3): 872–904.

McDonough, John E. 2011. *Inside National Health Reform*. Berkeley: University of California Press.

McGarrity, Joseph P., and Daniel Sutter. 2000. "A Test of the Structure of PAC Contracts: An Analysis of House Gun Control Votes in the 1980s." *Southern Economic Journal* 67 (1): 41–63.

McKay, Amy Melissa. 2010. "The Effects of Interest Groups' Ideology on Their PAC and Lobbying Expenditures." *Business and Politics* 12 (2): 1–21.

McKay, Amy Melissa. 2011. "The Decision to Lobby Bureaucrats." *Public Choice* 147 (1/2): 123–38.

McKay, Amy Melissa. 2012a. "Negative Lobbying and Policy Outcomes." *American Politics Research* 40 (1): 116–46.

McKay, Amy Melissa. 2012b. "Buying Policy? The Effects of Lobbyists' Resources on Their Policy Success." *Political Research Quarterly* 65 (4): 908–23.

McKay, Amy Melissa. 2018. "Fundraising for Favors? Linking Lobbyist-Hosted Fundraisers to Legislative Benefits." *Political Research Quarterly* 71 (4): 869–80.

McKay, Amy Melissa, and Antal Wozniak. 2020. "Opaque: An Empirical Evaluation of Lobbying Transparency in the UK." *Interest Groups & Advocacy* 9 (1): 102–18.

McKay, Amy Melissa, and Jennifer Hayes Clark. 2009. "The Politics of Health Reform: How Political Interests and Preferences Shape Political Strategy: Congressional Fellowship Report." *PS: Political Science & Politics* 42 (4): 808–11.

McKay, Amy Melissa, and Toni P. Miles. 2010. "The Politics of Health Reform: Whose Voices are Heard?" A Paper Presented at the Annual Meeting of the Southern Political Science Association. Atlanta.

Mian, Atif, Amir Sufi, and Francesco Trebbi. 2010. "The Political Economy of the US Mortgage Default Crisis." *American Economic Review* 100 (5): 1967–98.

Mian, Atif, Amir Sufi, and Francesco Trebbi. 2013. "The Political Economy of the Subprime Mortgage Credit Expansion." *Quarterly Journal of Political Science* 8 (4): 373–408.

Milbrath, Lester W. 1963. *The Washington Lobbyists.* Chicago: Rand McNally.

Miler, Kristina C. 2007. "The View from the Hill: Legislative Perceptions of the District." *Legislative Studies Quarterly* 32 (4): 597–628.

Miler, Kristina C. 2010. *Constituency Representation in Congress: The View from Capitol Hill.* Cambridge: Cambridge University Press.

Milyo, Jeffrey, David Primo, and Timothy Groseclose. 2000. "Corporate PAC Campaign Contributions in Perspective." *Business and Politics* 2 (1): 75–88.

Moore, Janet. 2009. "Health Bill Adds a Tax for Device Makers." *Minneapolis Star Tribune*, September 11.

Munger, Michael C. 1988. "Allocation of Desirable Committee Assignments: Extended Queues versus Committee Expansion." *American Journal of Political Science* 32 (2): 317–44.

Munger, Michael C., and Gary M. Torrent. 1993. "Committee Power and Value in the US Senate: Implications for Policy." *Journal of Public Administration Research and Theory* 3 (1): 46–65.

Neustadtl, Alan. 1990. "Interest-Group Pacsmanship: An Analysis of Campaign Contributions, Issue Visibility, and Legislative Impact." *Social Forces* 69 (2): 549–64.

Nollen, Stanley D., and Dennis P. Quinn. 1994. "Free Trade, Fair Trade, Strategic Trade, and Protectionism in the U.S. Congress, 1987–88." *International Organization* 48 (3): 491–525.

Nyhan, Brendan, and Jason Reifler. 2015. "The Effect of Fact-Checking on Elites: A Field Experiment on U.S. State Legislators." *American Journal of Political Science* 59 (3): 628–40.

Papke, Leslie E., and Jeffrey M. Wooldridge. 1996. "Econometric Methods for Fractional Response Variables with an Application to 401(K) Plan Participation Rates." *Journal of Applied Econometrics* 11 (6): 619–32.

Parker, Ashley. 2015. "In Era of Email, Some Senators Do Just Fine without It." *The New York Times*, March 11.

Peoples, Clayton D., and James E. Sutton. 2015. "Congressional Bribery as State-Corporate Crime: A Social Network Analysis." *Crime, Law and Social Change* 64 (2): 103–25.

Petersen, Mitchell A. 2009. "Estimating Standard Errors in Finance Panel Data Sets: Comparing Approaches." *The Review of Financial Studies* 22 (1): 435–80.

Poole, Keith T., and Howard Rosenthal. 2007. *Ideology and Congress: A Political Economic History of Roll Call Voting.* New York: Transaction.

Poole, Keith T., and Thomas Romer. 1985. "Patterns of Political Action Committee Contributions to the 1980 Campaigns for the United States House of Representatives." *Public Choice* 47 (1): 63–111.

Poole, Keith T., Thomas Romer, and Howard Rosenthal. 1987. "The Revealed Preferences of Political Action Committees." *The American Economic Review: Papers and Proceedings of the Ninety-Ninth Annual Meeting of the American Economic Association* 77 (2): 298–302.

Powell, Eleanor Neff, and Justin Grimmer. 2016. "Money in Exile: Campaign Contributions and Committee Access." *The Journal of Politics* 78 (4): 974–88.

Powell, Lynda W. 2012. *The Influence of Campaign Contributions in State Legislatures: The Effects of Institutions and Politics*: Ann Arbor: University of Michigan Press.

Primo, David M., and Jeffrey Milyo. 2006. "Campaign Finance Laws and Political Efficacy: Evidence from the States." *Election Law Journal* 5 (1): 23–39.

Quinn, Dennis P., and Robert Y. Shapiro. 1991. "Business Political Power: The Case of Taxation." *The American Political Science Review* 85 (3): 851–74.

Ramsden, Graham P. 2002. "State Legislative Campaign Finance Research: A Review Essay." *State Politics & Policy Quarterly* 2 (2): 176–78.

Rasmussen, Anne, Anne Skorkjær Binderkrantz, and Heike Klüver. 2021. "Organised Interests in the Media and Policy Congruence: The Contingent Impact of the Status Quo." *European Journal of Political Research* 60 (4): 975–93.

Rasmussen, Anne, Lars Kai Mäder, and Stefanie Reher. 2018. "With a Little Help from the People? The Role of Public Opinion in Advocacy Success." *Comparative Political Studies* 51 (2): 139–64.

Richter, Brian Kelleher, Krislert Samphantharak, and Jeffrey F. Timmons. 2009. "Lobbying and Taxes." *American Journal of Political Science* 53 (4): 893–909.

Riotta, Chris. 2017. "GOP Aims to Kill Obama Care yet Again after Failing 70 Times." *Newsweek*, July 29.

Rocca, Michael S., and Stacy B. Gordon. 2013. "Earmarks as a Means and an End: The Link between Earmarks and Campaign Contributions in the U.S. House of Representatives." *The Journal of Politics* 75 (1): 241–53.

Roscoe, Douglas D., and Shannon Jenkins. 2005. "A Meta-Analysis of Campaign Contributions' Impact on Roll Call Voting." *Social Science Quarterly* 86 (1): 52–68.

Rozell, Mark J., Clyde Wilcox, and David Madland. 2006. *Interest Groups in American Campaigns: The New Face of Electioneering.* Washington, DC: CQ Press.

Rudolph, Thomas J. 1999. "Corporate and Labor PAC Contributions in House Elections: Measuring the Effects of Majority Party Status." *Journal of Politics* 61 (1): 195–206.

Saltzman, Gregory M. 1987. "Congressional Voting on Labor Issues: The Role of PACs." *Industrial and Labor Relations Review* 40 (2): 163–79.

Schattschneider, Elmer Eric. 1960. *The Semisovereign People: A Realist's View of Democracy in America.* New York: Holt, Rinehart and Winston.

Schiller, Wendy J. 1995. "Senators as Political Entrepreneurs: Using Bill Sponsorship to Shape Legislative Agendas." *American Journal of Political Science* 39 (1): 186–203.

Schroedel, Jean Reith. 1986. "Campaign Contributions and Legislative Outcomes." *The Western Political Quarterly* 39 (3): 371–89.

Shepsle, Kenneth A. 1978. *The Giant Jigsaw Puzzle: Democratic Committee Assignments in the Modern House*. Chicago: University of Chicago Press.

Shevlin, Patricia, and Miles Doran. 2016. "Are Members of Congress Becoming Telemarketers?" *60 Minutes*, April 24.

Sinclair, Barbara. 2016. *Unorthodox Lawmaking: New Legislative Processes in the US Congress*. Washington, DC: CQ Press.

Skocpol, Theda, and Lawrence R. Jacobs. 2010. *Health Care Reform and American Politics: What Everyone Needs to Know*. New York: Oxford University Press.

Smith, Mark A. 2000. *American Business and Political Power: Public Opinion, Elections, and Democracy*. Chicago: University of Chicago Press.

Smith, Richard A. 1995. "Interest Group Influence in the U.S. Congress." *Legislative Studies Quarterly* 20 (1): 89–139.

Snyder, James M. Jr. 1990. "Campaign Contributions as Investments: The U.S. House of Representatives, 1980–1986." *Journal of Political Economy* 98 (6): 1195–227.

Sorauf, Frank J. 1988. *Money in American Elections*. Boston: Scott, Foresman.

Starr, Paul. 2011. *Remedy and Reaction: The Peculiar American Struggle over Health Care Reform*. New Haven: Yale University Press.

Steagall, Jeffrey W., and Ken Jennings. 1996. "Unions, PAC Contributions, and the NAFTA Vote." *Journal of Labor Research* 17 (3): 515–21.

Stewart, Charles, and Tim Groseclose. 1999. "The Value of Committee Seats in the United States Senate, 1947–91." *American Journal of Political Science* 43 (3): 963–73.

Stewart III, Charles, and Jonathan Woon. 2017. "Congressional Committee Assignments, 103rd to 114th Congresses, 1993–2017." https://web.mit.edu/17 .251/www/data_page.html#2

Stratmann, Thomas. 1991. "What Do Campaign Contributions Buy? Deciphering Causal Effects of Money and Votes." *Southern Economic Journal* 57 (3): 606–20.

Stratmann, Thomas. 1995. "Campaign Contributions and Congressional Voting: Does the Timing of Contributions Matter?" *The Review of Economics and Statistics* 77 (1): 127–36.

Stratmann, Thomas. 1998. "The Market for Congressional Votes: Is Timing of Contributions Everything?" *The Journal of Law & Economics* 41 (1): 85–114.

Stratmann, Thomas. 2002. "Can Special Interests Buy Congressional Votes? Evidence from Financial Services Legislation." *The Journal of Law and Economics* 45 (2): 345–73.

Stratmann, Thomas. 2005. "Some Talk: Money in Politics. A (Partial) Review of the Literature." *Public Choice* 124 (1/2): 135–56.

Strickland, James M. 2020. "The Declining Value of Revolving-Door Lobbyists: Evidence from the American States." *American Journal of Political Science* 64 (1): 67–81.

Thompson, Samuel B. 2011. "Simple Formulas for Standard Errors That Cluster by Both Firm and Time." *Journal of financial economics* 99 (1): 1–10.

Volden, Craig, Alan E. Wiseman, and Dana E. Wittmer. 2013. "When Are Women More Effective Lawmakers Than Men?" *American Journal of Political Science* 57 (2): 326–41.

Wawro, Gregory. 2001. "A Panel Probit Analysis of Campaign Contributions and Roll-Call Votes." *American Journal of Political Science* 45 (3): 563–79.

Weisman, Jonathan, and Jeremy W. Peters. 2013. "Government Shuts Down in Budget Impasse." *The New York Times*, September 13.

Wiener, Elizabeth. 2021. "Getting a High Heel in the Door: An Experiment on State Legislator Responsiveness to Women's Issue Lobbying." *Political Research Quarterly* 74 (3): 729–43.

Wilcox, Clyde. 1989. "Organizational Variables and Contribution Behavior of Large PACs: A Longitudinal Analysis." *Political Behavior* 11 (2): 157–73.

Wilensky, Gail R. 2006. "Developing a Center for Comparative Effectiveness Information." *Health Affairs* 25 (Suppl 1): W572–W585.

Wilkerson, John, David Smith, and Nicholas Stramp. 2015. "Tracing the Flow of Policy Ideas in Legislatures: A Text Reuse Approach." *American Journal of Political Science* 59 (4): 943–56.

Witko, Christopher. 2006. "PACs, Issue Context, and Congressional Decisionmaking." *Political Research Quarterly* 59 (2): 283–95.

Witko, Christopher. 2011. "Campaign Contributions, Access, and Government Contracting." *Journal of Public Administration Research and Theory: J-PART* 21 (4): 761–78.

Wright, John. 2004. "Campaign Contributions and Congressional Voting on Tobacco Policy, 1980–2000." *Business and Politics* 6 (3): 1–26.

Wright, John R. 1985. "PACs, Contributions and Roll Calls: An Organizational Perspective." *American Political Science Review* 79 (2): 400–14.

Wright, John R. 1989. "PAC Contributions, Lobbying, and Representation." *Journal of Politics* 51 (3): 713–29.

Wright, John R. 1990. "Contributions, Lobbying, and Committee Voting in the U.S. House of Representatives." *American Political Science Review* 84 (2): 417–38.

Yackee, Susan Webb, and Jason Webb Yackee. 2006. "A Bias Towards Business? Assessing Interest Group Influence on the U.S. Bureaucracy." *Journal of Politics* 68 (1): 128–39.

Zhang, Daowei, and Shaun Tanger. 2017. "Is There a Connection between Campaign Contributions and Legislative Commitment? An Empirical Analysis on the Cosponsorship Activity of the 2007 Tree Act." *Forest Policy and Economics* 85 (1): 85–94.

Index

For EU product safety concerns, contact us at Calle de José Abascal, 56–1°,
28003 Madrid, Spain or eugpsr@cambridge.org.

www.ingramcontent.com/pod-product-compliance
Ingram Content Group UK Ltd.
Pitfield, Milton Keynes, MK11 3LW, UK
UKHW010250140625
459647UK00013BA/1783